HAYNES
HOME
SECURITY
MANUAL

The step-by-step guide to a safe and secure home and family

SONIA AARONS AND DONNA GILBERT

First published in 1994

Published by:
Haynes Publishing
Sparkford, Nr Yeovil, Somerset BA22 7JJ

British Library Cataloguing-in-Publication Data:

A catalogue record for this book is available from the British Library.

ISBN 1 85010 930 3

Printed in Great Britain by J. H. Haynes & Co. Ltd.

Contents

Acknowledgements

The authors would like to express their thanks to the following for their help in compiling this book:

Advanced Design Electronics

Association of British Insurers

Benn Security of Northampton

BPT Systems

Chubb Security Group

Codalarm

David Darby (for his endless patience in photographing the fitting sequences).

Lynn East

ERA Security Products

Stuart Mundy of Hackney DIY

Hamber Safes

George Hodge

Dave Kennard

John Little Associates

Rachel Witts of The Laminated Glass Information Centre

Ken Marsden of Locksecure Services, Sevenoaks (for his assistance and advice in carrying out the lock fitting sequences)

John Gosling of Prolec Services (for his assistance and advice in carrying out our alarm fitting sequence)

Security Publications

Smiths Industries

Sgt Peter Hardy, Sussex Police

Martyn Williams (for his assistance and advice in carrying out the car alarm fitting sequence)

Foreword

Fighting crime is something we can all do, and is something we must all do. As Director of Community Action Trust which set up the Crimestoppers initiative in 1988 I heartily welcome a book which helps us all make life more difficult for the criminal.

Practical crime prevention measures such as those described in this book are essential. It is equally important that those who commit crimes are detected and brought to justice and Crimestoppers, now a nationwide scheme, has been extremely successful in encouraging us all to report information and suspicious activity which may eventually lead to an arrest and a conviction.

This initiative has also contributed to an increase in crimes that have been cleared up and has helped to recover millions of pounds worth of property.

Crime is a widespread problem, affecting everybody, young and old, working and retired, and requires a concerted effort by society to tackle it. While levels of home security protection have increased since 1988, it is alarming that in a fifth of incidents with entry doors or windows have been left open or unlocked.

It is vital we take a stand and in order to fight crime, fight apathy too. "If it doesn't affect me, it doesn't concern me" is too often the state of mind. Yet one day it may. If you see what you believe to be a crime taking place, report it to the police. If a Crimestoppers poster or campaign jogs your memory, all you need to do is pick up the phone and dial 0800 555111. You don't even need to give your name. And if your call leads to an arrest and charge you may receive a cash reward.

The *Haynes Home Security Manual* is playing its part in helping to improve awareness of what can be done, very often quite simply and cheaply, to increase our effectiveness in preventing crime and making it an easier task for our hard-pressed police to catch the criminal.

Initiatives such as Crimestoppers are just one way you can help the police. Reading the *Haynes Home Security Manual* and making practical use of its wide range of useful advice, is another.

Digby Carter
Director
Community Action Trust

CRIMESTOPPERS
0800 555 111

CAT

Introduction

We have all read disturbing reports of escalating crime across the country, and have felt sympathy for the people who have had their homes or cars broken into and their possessions stolen. Sadly, it is usually *after* it has happened to us that we decide to do something to prevent crime affecting us again. Yet the startling statistics on burglary and car crime should make us realise that any one of us is a potential victim, and that we should take some practical action now to guard against our becoming an actual victim.

The statistics – and don't forget these are only crimes reported by the police – speak for themselves. A staggering 94 per cent of all crime relates to property, and over half are burglaries or vehicle crime. Over 750,000 homes are burgled every year. The figures for car crime are even greater, with over half a million vehicles stolen each year,

and there are almost a million thefts from vehicles, including car radios, mobile phones, briefcases and other valuables.

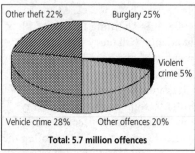

Notifiable offences for the year to June 1993 recorded by the police (Source: Home Office)

The most recent British Crime Survey, which is an independent report asking about crimes experienced in the last year, including those that go unreported to the police, estimates the figures to be much higher, with over 15 million crimes committed (three times the annual levels recorded for

equivalent police figures) and domestic burglary including attempts, at twice the figure reported.

From these figures, and from reports in newspapers and on television, it is sometimes hard to believe that anyone in the country is doing anything at all about fighting crime. Unfortunately, it is often only the bad news that makes the headlines, and much is actually being done, and many measures that are common-sense and cost little are proving successful.

The success of Neighbourhood Watch, with 120,000 schemes across the country, shows how local community spirit can work together with councils, police and other bodies not only to react to rising crime but also, and more important, to prevent it happening. Recent research carried out by West Midlands police, which has many thousands of schemes on its patch and which has an on-going crime pattern analysis system, showed that

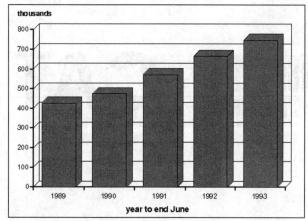

How the incidence of domestic burglary has risen

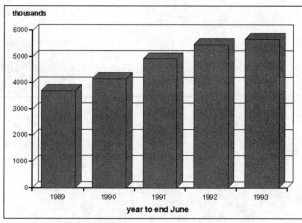

How the incidence of all types of crime has risen

Have you joined your local Neighbourhood Watch scheme? Start one, if there isn't one.

a house not involved in a Neighbourhood Watch scheme was twice as likely to be broken into as one which belonged to the scheme.

Styles of building, both houses themselves and the layout of entire estates are being influenced by schemes such as Secured by Design, a nationwide initiative that operates in conjunction with builders, and whose plans are assessed by police architectural liaison officers. This scheme was set up in 1988 and includes consideration of landscaping, door and window design and locking, security lighting, alarms and smoke detectors. The National House Building Council's requirements have since 1986 incorporated specific details of security measures to be taken if the house is to receive its 10 year guarantee, and some of these have been mandatory since 1989. All of these contribute to making the homes we live in today and in the future that bit more secure. But there is still much that needs to be done to homes as recently built as the eighties – and those designed centuries ago when doors were comfortably left ajar.

Initiatives by the Home Office, such as the Crack Crime campaign and the hyena of Car Crime Prevention Year are helping to make inroads into our thinking, but perhaps the greatest impact will

come from the insurance companies as they continue to mark up their premiums each year for our car and home contents insurance to match the increasing claims.

Insurers are already having a good deal of influence on car security – not surprisingly as they pay out more than £600 million in theft related claims every year. Thatcham, the motor insurance repair research centre, has set out a detailed document outlining criteria for testing the performance of security products and the cars to which they are fitted, certainly a step in the right direction. Meanwhile, the PACT scheme (Partnership Against Car Theft) is aimed at improving the security of cars already on the road via automotive retail outlets who recommend and advise on the installation of products. PACT, which started in Northumbria and is to be adopted nationwide, also plans to set up a grading system for products.

But it is not just being stung by the insurers that should influence us. The fear of crime has proved to be far greater than crime itself. Reports of violent crime – which actually account for less than 300,000 offences per year, of which just one tenth were said to be life threatening – tend to be widely reported in the media. While it is highly distressing

The Home Office used hyenas in their car crime prevention campaign. Did you get the message?

to see 90-year-old ladies as victims, the truth is that such incidents are few and far between. Far more damaging are the effects of such reports, emblazoned in screaming headlines. We can all protect our elderly and infirm relatives with a little care, attention – and DIY – and, in doing so, reduce their fear. Making sure they don't open the door to strangers, that they look through the door viewer first and that neighbours or friends call in regularly to see them are simple precautions to protect and give peace of mind.

> ## '...fear of crime has proved to be far greater than crime itself...'

Fire prevention and detection is another area which has been addressed by legislation and changing attitudes. The Smoke Detector Bill, introduced in April 1992, makes it mandatory for one or more smoke detectors to be fitted in new homes, and this is echoed in the Building Regulations.

While smoke detectors have to be fitted, by law, in homes in parts of the United States and in Scandinavia, in 1987 only 4 per cent of households in the UK owned a smoke alarm. Now, more than half UK homes have them fitted. But, of course, it is important not only to fit such devices but to maintain and use them properly.

This book will show you what security measures to fit and where, but it can do no more than emphasize the importance of you and your family regularly making use of the security you have installed. We can provide the knowledge, but only you can make sure you don't become one of next year's statistics.

CHAPTER 1

Understanding the nature of crime

Peak age for offenders is 15 – and he's likely to be based locally.

Every year more than 750,000 homes in England and Wales are burgled. This means that there is a house being burgled about every 50 seconds, and one home in 20 is burgled every year.

The statistics are frightening, and yet we remain complacent when it comes to securing our homes. What we tend to forget in the light of these figures is that many, if not most, of these break-ins could have been avoided and not necessarily by employing expensive, highly sophisticated security measures.

When you take into account the fact that, in three out of ten burglaries, a door or window had been left open, you will begin to see how even simple common-sense precautions can play a part in preventing crime. There is a great deal we can do to help ourselves, no matter what budget we have allocated for the purpose of securing our home.

The burglar

There are many misconceptions about burglars which can lead to an increased fear of crime. Very few burglaries are carried out by professionals – estimates put it at only one in five. The professional burglar has the experience and skill to overcome a reasonable security system, and will travel to commit his crime. He is probably part of a network, selling items on to a 'fence' (a receiver of stolen goods), and will take electrical items, jewellery, cash, credit cards and cheque books. The top grade professional will steal expensive items, such as antiques, and is likely to travel further afield to detached homes in rural areas. He may tour an area looking for a suitable house; then spend time watching the comings and goings of the occupants to gauge when they are most likely to be out.

Most break-ins, however, (around 80 per cent) are committed by opportunists – those on the look out for an easy target, and probably acting on impulse. The peak age for offenders is just 15 – some are even younger – and it's more than likely that the burglar is based locally, possibly even living on the same housing estate. A 15-year-old tends to be less mobile, so is more likely to rely on local crime for his income. He knows the area well – which areas he is most likely to be spotted in, which houses are likely to be unoccupied during the day, who owns a dog, etc. – and is most likely to steal cash and items for his own use, or which he can pass on to his mates.

The break-in

Two-thirds of burglaries take place during the week, when there is a greater likelihood of the home being unoccupied. The opportunist will firstly look for a house which appears to be unoccupied, and where security is lax – perhaps a window has been left open, or the key has been left in the back door. He may ring the door bell to see whether a dog barks, or if his call is answered. If it is, he can easily make his excuses and move on to a more likely target. If he can break in unseen, so much the better – 64 per cent of burglars gain access at the back or side of properties where there is less chance of being spotted by neighbours or passers-by. Once inside, the burglar will probably bolt the front door – to warn him if you return home. Then he will look for a quick exit – keys left in or near the front or back door, or patio doors which can be released from inside. If it is easy to get out, it means that larger objects such as electrical items can be carried away without difficulty, and he can leave quickly should anyone return home.

To reduce the likelihood of being trapped in a house, a burglar will often start upstairs in the main bedroom, pocketing cash, credit cards and jewellery; checking cupboards, drawers and the pockets of clothing where money may be kept. Once downstairs he will check the lounge and dining room, emptying drawers and shelves and pocketing small items of value.

'…64% of burglars gain access at the back or side…'

If he has an easy exit and transport available, larger items such as hi-fi systems and videos may also be removed. Finally, he may head for the kitchen to search for cash set aside to pay the milkman or window cleaner. He may also check the garage and shed, stealing tools to sell on to friends, or dispose of at a car boot sale. And all this can be achieved in a matter of minutes.

Most burglars believe they should have moved on to more sophisticated crime by the time they are 30. Most steal to gain money, either for their own leisure, or to pay bills and buy food. Many also claim that they experience a 'thrill' when they break into houses.

The majority of car thieves are also young people. According to a study by the Home Office Research and Planning Unit and the University of the West of England, entitled *Car Theft: the Offender's Perspective*, most begin in their early to mid-teens, with the help of more experienced offenders. Reasons given for their getting involved included the influence of friends, the excitement of stealing cars, and boredom. Eventually the ability to make money from car theft seems to take over, and over a third of the sample of 100 car thieves progressed to 'professional' car theft, involving stealing cars to order for financial gain.

According to latest official figures for the UK, there are 1.5 million thefts of and from vehicles, though an independent report puts this figure much higher, claiming that 4 million drivers in Britain claim to have had a car broken into and items stolen over the previous two years.

Despite the inevitable

Returning home to find you have been burgled can be a devastating experience.

inconvenience of a burglary, and the cost of repairing doors and windows, the value of the property lost may be very small. Statistics show that in 25 per cent of burglaries the value of property stolen is nil; in 23 per cent it amounts to under £100 and in 52 per cent of cases it is over £100.

Inevitably, with the ever-increasing incidence of crime, combined with poor clear-up rates and lack of police time, it is up to you to take responsibility for your own security. Should your home be broken into, and items stolen, there is only a 5 per cent chance that everything will be recovered. About 86 per cent have nothing returned.

Official figures reveal that only one in ten thieves are caught stealing from individuals and taking bicycles, and the detection rate for robberies stands at only 22 per cent. Undoubtedly, prevention is better than cure, and people need to work in partnership to fight crime in their communities.

Coping with the event

Many people live in fear of returning home to find a burglar in the house, or worse, waking up to find that there is an intruder. But in the majority of cases a burglar will try to avoid confrontation. If you do return home and think that someone is inside, do not enter. Go to a neighbour, or the nearest phone box, and call the police immediately. If you wake in the night and hear an intruder, the police do not recommend that you confront him, or pretend to be asleep. Instead, switch the lights on and make a lot of noise. If you are on your own, pretend there is someone with you and call out to them. Most burglars will leave as soon as they realise they have been heard. Phone the

police as soon as it is safe to do so.

While you are waiting for the police to arrive, do not touch anything, as you could destroy vital evidence. You will be asked whether you are immediately aware of any missing items; electrical goods will be the most apparent, and the police officer will need an immediate list to circulate in the hope they can stop someone. Other items may not come to mind until a month or so later.

Clues

If the door has been forced, or glass broken, or if there are jemmy marks, the house may be worth fingerprinting. If the Scenes of Crime Officer is called, you will be told to try to preserve the scene. Don't move anything that might be of assistance, and look out for

If the door has been forced it may be worth fingerprinting.

things that will be needed for fingerprinting. Any footprints outside should be covered with something that won't spoil the mark. The police will advise you on what should be preserved; you will probably be allowed to tidy up everywhere else.

If you need to carry out emergency repairs, make sure the firm you contact quotes a reasonable price; some take advantage of such situations. Keep receipts for your insurance claim. If cheque books or credit cards have been stolen, inform the issuing company immediately.

'...Try to preserve the scene. Don't move anything...'

It is only after you have dealt with the immediate tasks that you will have time to reflect. You will probably want to improve your security to prevent the same thing happening again, so ask your Crime Prevention Officer to call and advise you on which locks to fit and which other precautions he would recommend.

It's always difficult to forget a burglary; you may want to scrub the house clean from top to bottom, redecorate, even move away. But it's important to try to forget it and get life back to normal. Friends and family can help, as well as volunteers from the local Victim Support Scheme. These volunteers can provide practical advice as well as a shoulder to cry on, reassuring victims that their reaction is perfectly normal. The volunteer may also help you to improve security, carry out repairs, and help out with insurance claims and form filling. Your local police station will be able to put you in touch with your local Victim Support Scheme.

CHAPTER 2

Does crime prevention work?

The noise and time it takes to break through laminated glass will deter most intruders.

Crime has been increasing all over the western world for most of the past 30 years, with the majority of recorded crime – a staggering 94 per cent – against property.

There are several reasons why statistics for domestic burglary are so high. For a start, more crime is being reported to the police but, most important, there is an increase in opportunity. Rising affluence has led to more and more people owning cars and a greater range of portable electrical goods. Add to this the fact that very few people have installed what could be regarded as an adequate level of security, and it's not surprising that there are so many opportunists earning their living through burglary.

According to a research project carried out for ERA Security Products, out of a nationwide sample of 1,300 homes only 33 per cent had door locks approved to BS3621 – the standard recommended by most British insurers. The same survey found that 29 per cent of householders only had a night latch on the front door (a lock which, on its own, offers very little security), fewer than 25 per cent of homes had more than a basic mortice lock fitted to the front door, and only three in ten homes have bolts on the back door – in spite of the fact that 62 per cent of break-ins occur through the back or side. Furthermore, less than one-tenth of householders bother changing the locks when they move house, meaning that 90 per cent of British householders have no idea who has a key to their home.

Similarly, in a survey carried out by Mass Observation Ltd, commissioned by the Home Office, it was found that half those questioned (1,400 people) had no locks on their windows, one in four were without mortice deadlocks on their front door and 38 per cent were without a deadlock on the back door.

The most effective way to fight crime is to deny offenders easy opportunities. Crime prevention measures can and do work. For example, by studying the methods of the most common type of thief – the opportunist – it has been found

 11

Neighbourhood Watch schemes have been shown to reduce burglary.

police, probation services, the gas and electricity boards and a team of university researchers, the burglary level was dramatically reduced.

The problems were overcome by adopting numerous schemes. Probation officers interviewed 76 recently-convicted burglars to find out what sort of houses they targeted and what might have deterred them. It was found that Rochdale's burglars were not prepared to travel far from home and that signs that a house was unoccupied were of primary importance when choosing a target. The police provided a full-time local project co-ordinator, and by interviewing all burglary victims and their neighbours, found that 70 per cent of entry points used by burglars were visible from a neighbour's house. Consequently, neighbours were encouraged to participate in the scheme, keeping an eye out and maintaining signs of occupancy when neighbours were away. This led to the setting up of numerous Home Watch schemes and a 50 per cent reduction in the burglary rate in the first seven months of the project.

'...neighbours were encouraged to participate...'

This partnership approach led to the government's Five Towns Initiative and then the Safer Cities scheme which aims to cut crime and lessen the fear of crime in inner city and urban areas, by reducing opportunities for crime with better security. The initiative has concentrated on areas with high crime rates and socio/economic problems, and aims to involve local people in running local multi-agency projects to improve community safety.

Schemes have reported numerous

that he will nearly always opt for the house that is easiest to break into. Homes with security measures are less likely targets. A review of data from the latest British Crime Survey illustrated that in over half of all attempted burglaries where the burglar failed to gain entry, at least three or more security measures had been implemented. The setting up of Neighbourhood Watch schemes has also, in some cases, been shown to reduce burglary and car theft within the immediate neighbourhood.

In partnership

Over recent years a number of initiatives have been set up to fight crime, adopting a partnership approach. The Kirkholt project in Lancashire is one such example. The estate has over 2,000 semi-detached houses, and when the project started in 1986 it had a burglary rate of one in four households broken into every year. By bringing together local agencies, such as the housing department,

12

Physical security should be given priority.

successes: including a housing estate in Keighley where domestic burglaries were reduced initially by 85 per cent as a result of fitting improved window and door locks; a housing estate in Wolverhampton where burglaries were reduced by 40 per cent over three years through a range of target-hardening and social crime prevention measures; the Deptford High Street Business Security scheme which led to a 25 per cent reduction in crime; and a reduction in fear of crime in Sunderland where 97% of the 3,300 elderly people who had security lights and locks fitted to their homes reported feeling much safer as a result.

The 'Secured by Design' initiative reports remarkable achievements. The scheme began in 1988 as a police initiative in the south-east of England to encourage the house building industry to adopt recommended crime prevention measures in the building of new homes. It covers four main areas – estate design, to create an environment to deter unwelcome intruders by landscaping and natural surveillance; physical security, including the design of and security requirements for doors and windows; security lighting and smoke detectors; and the installation of integral basic wiring

for intruder alarms.

House builders who conform to the 'Secured by Design' minimum security recommendations can display a unique logo which shows purchasers which houses and developments meet police security recommendations. In Sussex, 2,847 homes have been 'Secured by Design', incorporating 65 housing estates, and remarkably, according to Sgt Peter Hardy of Sussex Crime Prevention Department Design Advisory Service, not one burglary has been reported since the schemes were initiated.

Government crime prevention publicity campaigns have also gone some way in deterring crime. In the first three months of its Car Crime Prevention Year, the Home Office reported a fall of over 2.5 per cent in car crime.

Where to start and what it costs

Accepting that you need to improve the security of your home is one thing. Knowing where to start is quite another. Basically, prevention measures can be split into three main categories:

1 Common-sense precautions

2 Physical security

3 Electronic security

Physical security encompasses locking devices such as door and window locks and padlocks, door chains and viewers, security marking, security doors, grilles and shutters and safes. Electronic security incorporates intruder alarm systems, security lighting, audio and video door entry systems, and closed circuit television monitoring.

When protecting your home, physical security should always be given priority, with good locks fitted to all entry and exit doors and easily accessible windows. This is the first step in any home security campaign.

'...your initial budget...must be spent wisely...'

Obviously the level of security installed will depend on your initial budget, and this must be spent wisely. Concentrate on the fundamentals; it's no good spending £150 on a safe if you haven't provided any deterrents to prevent a thief gaining access to your home in the first place. About 50 per cent of burglars break in through windows and 48 per cent through front, rear or side doors, so it's sensible to concentrate your efforts on these areas.

If you are willing to fit the locks yourself, you can achieve a good level of physical security for under £100 for an average semi-detached property. This figure is based on 5-lever mortice deadlocks fitted to the front and rear doors, a door chain, door viewer and locks fitted to eight windows. If you can set aside a larger sum you would be wise to consider securing outbuildings with locks or padlocks and installing security lighting devices. If you have a lot of valuables to protect, or live in a high risk area, consider fitting an intruder alarm system. A professionally installed system may set you back around £400 or more, but a DIY system will only be around £150. Although the initial outlay may seem expensive, it's a small price to pay for the security of your home and family. And check with your insurance company, too. By fitting the right products you may qualify for discounts on your home contents insurance.

CHAPTER 3

Getting advice

Being sure of your facts before you decide on how best to improve your security is a bit like reading the instructions before you tackle any DIY job. Lots of people don't bother, and then find they've gone about it in completely the wrong way.

There are numerous sources of information to help you choose devices best suited to your particular home as well as organisations which will help sort out any problems or deal with complaints.

One of the best starting points is the local police station, or Neighbourhood Watch scheme (see Chapter 5). What used to be known as the Crime Prevention Department is now often re-labelled Community Liaison and covers a vast range of crime prevention issues, including home security, car crime and even issues such as looking after stables, schools, safety of children as well as many other areas of concern.

'...One of the best starting points is the local police station...'

The Community Liaison Department usually includes a Crime Prevention Officer and a Community Liaison Officer who will co-ordinate the work of local beat officers and, in some areas, officers allocated especially to Neighbourhood Watch schemes. They are very approachable and usually willing to provide information in the form of advisory leaflets and product guidance, although they will not officially recommend specific companies or devices. The Crime Prevention Officer or a specially trained officer will also be able to carry out a free survey of your home and point out the vulnerable areas which need greater protection, and suggest the type of product to be fitted which would improve security. They will also be able to supply you with a list of local alarm installers and security stockists.

For more detailed information on products it is best to shop around. The problem with visiting a large superstore is that staff have an extensive range of products to advise on and, although many carry a good cross section of locks, lighting and even DIY alarm systems, they will not always be able to advise you specifically on the security problems of your own home. Better perhaps to visit a specialist security centre or alarm installer and ask them to talk you through the products of interest on show, in line with the type suggested by the police or Neighbourhood Watch adviser.

The local Crime Prevention or Beat Officer based at the police station will be happy to carry out a free survey for you, and suggest ways of improving your security.

A good security centre should be able to offer you a range of door and window locks, safes, security lighting, alarm equipment, access control products, personal alarms, car security, grilles and the fixtures and fittings necessary to complete the job. They should also have the technical ability to advise you on the right product to protect your particular windows, doors and valuables, given the right information (you may need to measure the thickness of the door and know what your windows are made of – wood or metal, for example).

Fitting instructions have greatly improved, so make sure they are included in the pack or, if there aren't any, that the retailer has suggested the best way of carrying out the installation. We have covered many of the most popular products in this book but naturally every product is different as will be the location for which it is intended in each home.

There are also a number of trade associations to which alarm installers and locksmiths may belong who are also prepared to give advice to the public. Professional associations help give you peace of mind in the knowledge that their members work to certain British Standards, will have certain qualifications and that their work is inspected on a regular basis. Associations may also give you some recourse if things go wrong (see our list of useful contacts at the back of this book).

The main association for locksmiths is the Master Locksmiths Association who will put you in touch with your nearest MLA members and offer an advisory leaflet *Guide to Home Protection*. You can write to them for this, or a phone call to their helpline will enable you to quickly locate a reputable locksmith in your area. The MLA runs its own examinations and includes locksmiths and manufacturers as members.

There are rather more associations co-ordinating the activities of alarm installers. NACOSS (the National Approval Council for Security Systems) is a regulatory body with over 500 listed companies. NACOSS recognised firms have to supply accounts for two years of trading, and their premises and installations are regularly inspected. As well as installing to BS4737, a recent additional requirement is to have achieved the quality assurance standard BS5750 within two years of gaining NACOSS recognition. NACOSS will send you a list of their approved installers, which includes information on the association itself, and if you use one of their installers the company should leave you a user's handbook. NACOSS will inspect your alarm system without charge if you have cause for complaint.

SSA (Security Services Association) has about 190 members and will always advise that you look carefully at the qualifications of anyone installing an alarm system for you. They

Good advice is available from a specialist security centre.

the complaint for you. The SSA is limited in that it does not have the same clout with insurance companies as NACOSS, but there are a growing number of insurers who will accept its members' work and offer insurance accordingly.

The BSIA (British Security Industry Association) includes many of the larger security companies as its members. It has available a free booklet (The Security Directory) which provides information on each member, as well as describing products offered by the companies, who are often also NACOSS recognised firms.

'...Professional associations help give you peace of mind...'

should ideally have at least the National Vocation Qualification (NVQ) or relevant City & Guilds qualifications, and SSA members should supply you with a leaflet explaining the benefits of having an alarm installed by an SSA member, as well as how to complain or ask

for help relating to an alarm system. The association charges a £75 plus VAT inspection fee if there is a problem with a member's alarm system which they are asked to investigate, or they will suggest talking to the local Trading Standards Officer who may take up

Many electricians now offer security systems. Some may belong to the Electrical Contractors' Association's security division, which requires members to have traded for a minimum of three years, to provide fully audited accounts and be inspected on a regular basis. The ECA also offers a list of members, will suggest various useful contacts and has a leaflet on how to choose a security installer.

Crime Concern is very much involved with helping Neighbourhood Watch schemes and has produced a booklet on how to set up a successful scheme. It gives advice on Neighbourhood Watch and suggests suitable contacts for those requiring more information on security matters in general.

Finally, the Association of British Insurers (ABI) produces a wealth of free advisory material on home security and other related subjects, including insurance, safety and vehicle security. To receive any of these please send them a s.a.e. (see the list at the back of this book for their address).

Check Yellow Pages for security installers.

Is this you?

Take two houses at night; one is in complete darkness, the other has lights shining from the windows and the sound of a radio or hi-fi can faintly be heard. Or look at the same two houses during the day; one has windows open, a dog in the garden and a radio playing indoors. The other appears to be completely shut up. The windows are closed, except for a small fanlight left open round the side, the house is in silence and milk has been left on the front step. If a burglar was in the area looking for a likely target, it's not difficult to guess which home he would be more likely to break into in each instance.

The scenario illustrates how important it is not only to make your house secure, but also to make it look occupied. Eight out of ten burglaries occur when the house is empty, and often they occur because

the owners have failed to take adequate security measures.

If you ever go out at night, leaving the house in complete darkness, or if you go out during the day, leaving the milk on the step, a note on the door for a delivery man, or even the smallest window inadequately secured, just like the owner of the house in our illustration, you are inviting the burglar into your home.

Notes left on the door inform unwelcome passers-by of your absence.

Once a burglar has ascertained that the home is unoccupied, the next thing he will do is study the security measures that you have implemented. Even if you have fitted locks to windows and doors do you remember to use them every time you leave the house, even if you're only popping down the road for a few seconds?

In three burglaries out of ten, an intruder gains access through a door or window that has been carelessly left open. Seventy per cent of burglaries involve forced entry, but this may mean no more than lifting poorly-secured patio doors from their tracks, levering a back door with a jemmy, or forcing a window secured with no more than a traditional fastener.

You may decide to improve the security of your home for a number of reasons. Perhaps there have been a number of break-ins in the area which have left you feeling vulnerable; or possibly you have been a victim yourself because of inadequate precautions. Or you may have recently joined a Neighbourhood Watch scheme and been made more aware of the importance of securing your home. You may just have moved into a new house, or you want to qualify for a home contents insurance discount.

4

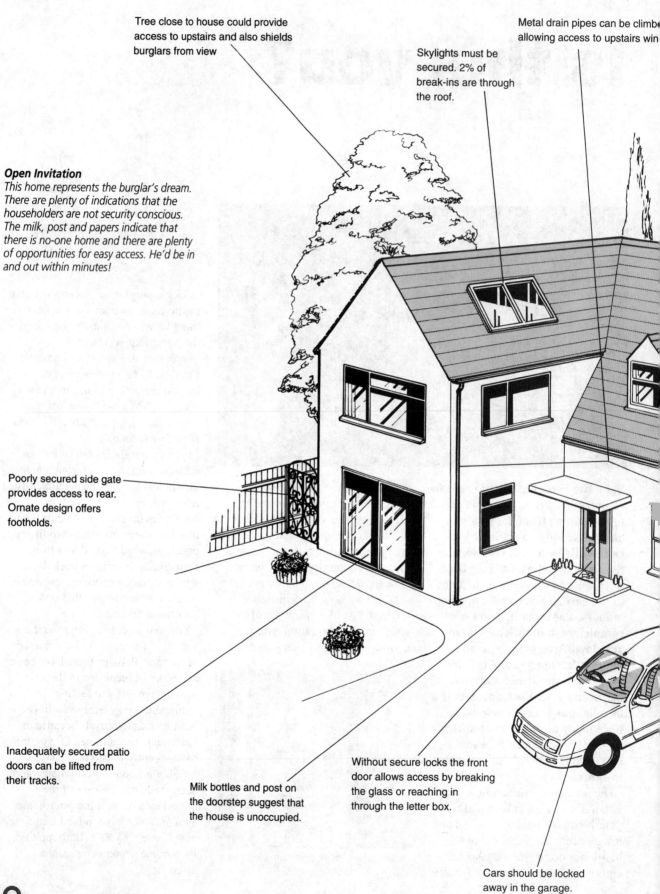

Tree close to house could provide access to upstairs and also shields burglars from view

Skylights must be secured. 2% of break-ins are through the roof.

Metal drain pipes can be climb allowing access to upstairs win

Open Invitation
This home represents the burglar's dream. There are plenty of indications that the householders are not security conscious. The milk, post and papers indicate that there is no-one home and there are plenty of opportunities for easy access. He'd be in and out within minutes!

Poorly secured side gate provides access to rear. Ornate design offers footholds.

Inadequately secured patio doors can be lifted from their tracks.

Milk bottles and post on the doorstep suggest that the house is unoccupied.

Without secure locks the front door allows access by breaking the glass or reaching in through the letter box.

Cars should be locked away in the garage.

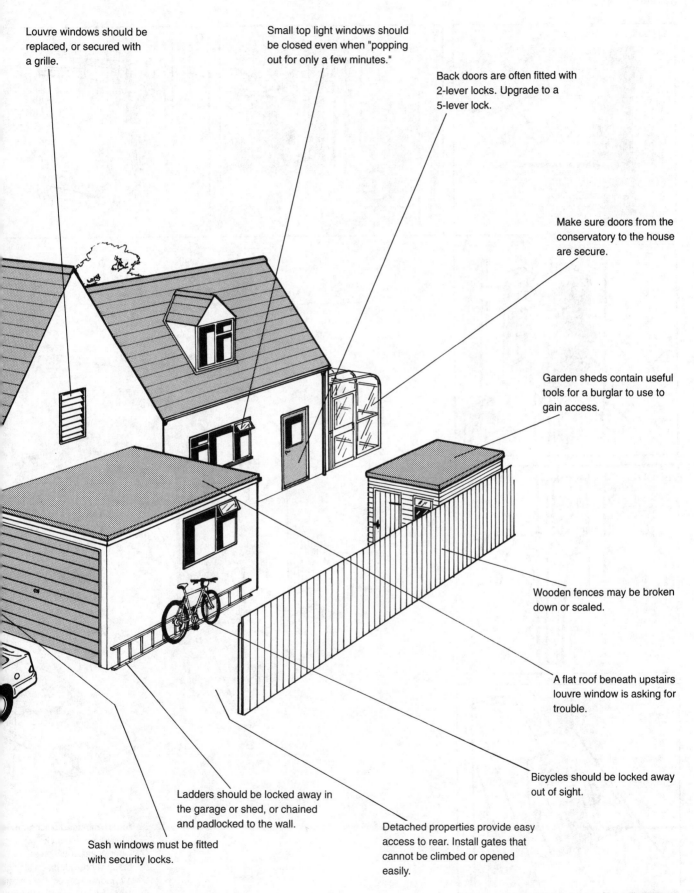

Louvre windows should be replaced, or secured with a grille.

Small top light windows should be closed even when "popping out for only a few minutes."

Back doors are often fitted with 2-lever locks. Upgrade to a 5-lever lock.

Make sure doors from the conservatory to the house are secure.

Garden sheds contain useful tools for a burglar to use to gain access.

Wooden fences may be broken down or scaled.

A flat roof beneath upstairs louvre window is asking for trouble.

Bicycles should be locked away out of sight.

Ladders should be locked away in the garage or shed, or chained and padlocked to the wall.

Sash windows must be fitted with security locks.

Detached properties provide easy access to rear. Install gates that cannot be climbed or opened easily.

4

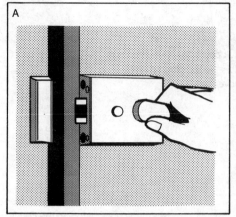

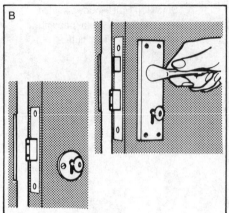

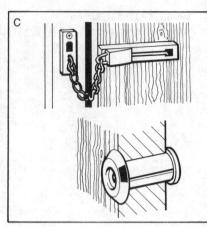

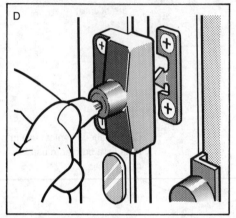

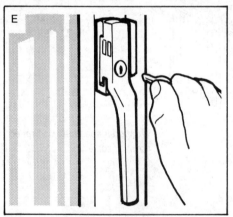

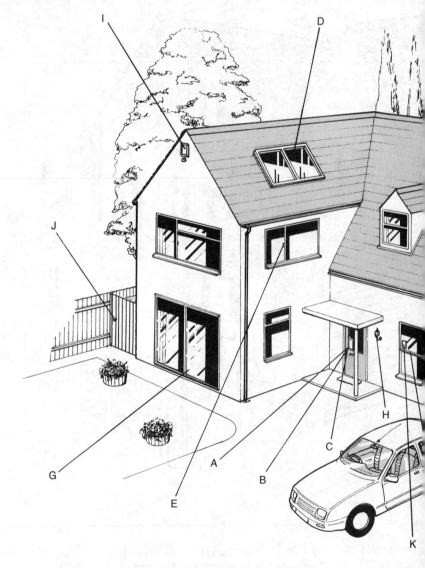

A Automatic deadlocking rim lo

B 5 lever mortice lock

C Door chain and viewer

D Metal window lock on skyligh

E Window lock (locking handle

F Window lock (sash window)

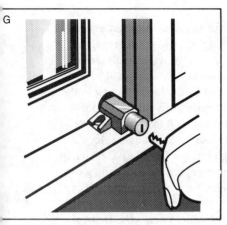

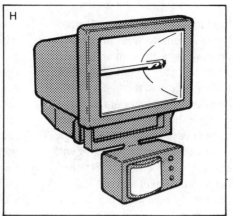

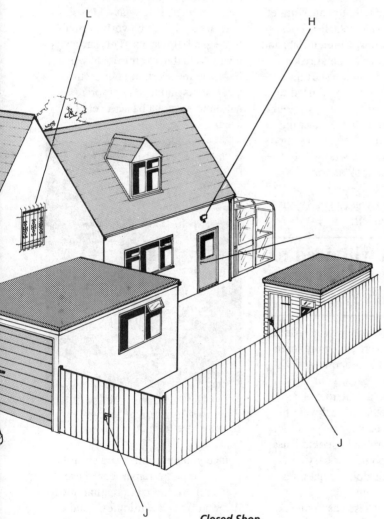

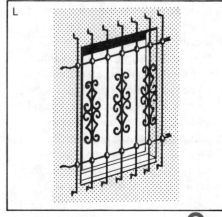

Closed Shop

The same house with security products in place and common-sense measures implemented. Few burglars would attempt to get in here – there are plenty of more vulnerable homes to choose from.

G Patio door lock
H Security lighting
I Alarm/strobe
J Padlock
K Neighbourhood watch sticker
L Grille on window

64 per cent of burglars break in through the rear of a property.

It helps first of all to know which are the most vulnerable areas of your home. Statistics show that 64 per cent of burglars break in through the rear of a property; 28 per cent through the front; 6 per cent through the side and 2 per cent through the roof. So, if you are working on a tight budget it pays to prioritize and secure areas according to their vulnerability.

The type of home you live in also needs to be considered. A terraced house may back on to neighbouring properties, granting limited access to the rear, so the front will be more vulnerable. An upper-storey flat may only provide access via the front door, so your efforts should be concentrated on this area. Detached houses offer most opportunities as there is often easy access to the side and rear, so all vulnerable entry points will have to be properly secured. Bungalows may offer access via all windows and possibly skylights, so all these areas will

have to receive attention. People living in remote areas may have to improve security with an intruder alarm linked to a central monitoring station. Because the house may not be visible to neighbours or passers-by a burglar will have more time to overcome physical security devices. A remotely-monitored alarm will ensure that his entrance to your home is detected, and the emergency services alerted immediately.

Contrary to popular belief, burglars do not tend to concentrate only on expensive detached houses or suburban semis. Council flats and houses are just as much at risk.

To make sure you are starting out on the right foot, you will need to carry out a security survey of your home. You can either contact the Crime Prevention Officer at your local police station, who will be happy to take a look at your property and advise you accordingly, or you can carry out the survey yourself.

'...You will need to carry out a security survey...'

Secure your home, as you would do when you were going out, then stand outside the property and pretend you have lost your keys. How easy would it be to gain access? Obviously you'll want to cause as little damage as possible, but you will probably spot at least three or four points for easy entry, and you will be doing what thieves do during their pre-call investigation. These easy points of entry normally include the back door, front door and ground floor windows, all of which may possibly grant easy access by breaking a small area of glass, or using brute force. Heaven forbid that you can get in by reaching through the letter

box for the front door key you left hanging on a string! Alternatively you may have left a small fanlight open upstairs which could be reached by the ladder laying in the back garden. If your back door is still fitted with the traditional 2-lever lock – the 'builders' lock' – a burglar may have a key that fits, or be able to pick the lock with a piece of wire.

When you carry out your survey, ask a friend to help you. He or she may well spot possible entry points that you miss. If it's easy for you to gain access it will be very difficult to keep a burglar out. This survey is a very valuable exercise that will help you to ascertain your security weak spots and take appropriate action to ensure a basic level of security.

Never leave keys in 'secret' places – a burglar knows them all!

Once you have improved security it's important to remember to use it – even if you're only popping down the road for a few minutes – and combine it with common-sense measures to avoid letting your home look unoccupied. Once you've taken steps to secure your home, check your security rating using our simple checklist. You may find there's still room for improvement.

Check your security rating

Convinced your home is secure? Get together with your family and spend a few minutes answering each question – honestly – to find out whether your security is really up to scratch.

Just tick the appropriate letter next to each question, then see what your final score reveals.

YOUR HOME AND ITS CONTENTS

	Always or Yes	Usually	Sometimes	Never or No
1 If you were uncertain about the security of your home, would you seek advice from the police, a locksmith, or other security expert?	A	B	C	D
2 Are all your exterior doors fitted with security deadlocks?	A	B	C	D
3 Is the back door also secured with mortice bolts and/or hinge bolts (or, if it is UPVC, a multi-point locking system)?	A	B	C	D
4 If you have a patio door, is it fitted with locks, top and bottom?	A	B	C	D
5 Are all easily accessible windows fitted with security locks?	A	B	C	D
6 Do you always lock doors and close and lock windows when you are going out?	A	B	C	D
7 Do you always keep your door keys in a safe place (i.e., not attached to a piece of string that can be pulled through the letter box, or under the door mat)?	A	B	C	D
8 Do you keep exterior doors locked when there is nobody in the house and you are out in the garden or garage?	A	B	C	D
9 Do you own either a dog that barks or an intruder alarm system?	A	B	C	D
10 Have you installed a smoke detector in your home?	A	B	C	D
11 Is your front door fitted with a door chain or limiter?	A	B	C	D
12 Is your front door fitted with a spy hole, video door entry system, or glass nearby which enables you to view callers?	A	B	C	D
13 Do you always put the door chain on before opening the door?	A	B	C	D
14 Do you thoroughly check the identity of strangers at the door before letting them in?	A	B	C	D
15 If you were suspicious about any travelling salesmen or callers, would you report it to the police or a Neighbourhood Watch co-ordinator?	A	B	C	D
16 Do you belong to a Neighbourhood Watch scheme?	A	B	C	D
17 Do you have a Neighbourhood Watch sticker displayed in your window?	A	B	C	D
18 Do you keep video recorders and other valuables out of sight of passers-by?	A	B	C	D
19 Have you postcoded or security-coded your property?	A	B	C	D
20 Have you displayed a sticker in your window informing passers-by that property is security marked?	A	B	C	D
21 Have you photographed smaller items of value which cannot be postcoded?	A	B	C	D
22 Have you made a list of your property, including serial numbers and distinguishing features?	A	B	C	D
23 Do you avoid keeping large sums of money in the house?	A	B	C	D

	Always or Yes	Usually	Sometimes	Never or No
	A	B	C	D
24 Are you adequately insured?	A	B	C	D
25 Can you say that you have never left a note taped to the door for delivery men, stating that you are out?	A	B	C	D
26 Do you always collect your milk from the doorstep and your post from the letter box promptly?	A	B	C	D
27 Do you avoid leaving the curtains drawn by day?	A	B	C	D
28 When you go out, do you ever leave a radio playing?	A	B	C	D
29 Do you leave lights on when you go out, or when you know you will be out after dark?	A	B	C	D
30 Are any of your lights fitted to timeswitches?	A	B	C	D
31 When you go on holiday, do you inform neighbours or the police?	A	B	C	D
32 Do you ask a neighbour or friend to pop in and collect the post and generally keep an eye on the place?	A	B	C	D
33 When you are going away, do you always remember to cancel the milk and papers?	A	B	C	D

AROUND AND ABOUT

	Always or Yes	Usually	Sometimes	Never or No
34 Is your front door visible to passers-by?	A	B	C	D
35 Is your home overlooked?	A	B	C	D
36 Are ladders locked away, or secured firmly to a wall?	A	B	C	D
37 Do you make sure that bricks and rubble are not left lying around in the garden?	A	B	C	D
38 Do you always lock garden tools away?	A	B	C	D
39 Is it difficult to gain access to the side or rear of your property?	A	B	C	D
40 Are side passages or back gates secure?	A	B	C	D
41 Do you close and lock the garage when you go out?	A	B	C	D
42 Do you lock the garage at night?	A	B	C	D
43 Is your garden shed secured with a padlock or other locking device?	A	B	C	D
44 If yes, do you always remember to use it?	A	B	C	D
45 Have you installed lights around your home?	A	B	C	D
46 Is the streetlighting in your area adequate, and in working order?	A	B	C	D
47 If you didn't feel that streetlighting was adequate, would you mention it to the police or local authority?	A	B	C	D

	Always or Yes	Usually	Sometimes	Never or No
48 If you saw a stranger loitering in your area, and acting suspiciously, would you report it to the police?	A	B	C	D
49 Do you have the telephone number of your local police station to hand?	A	B	C	D
50 Are you confident that you have taken all reasonable steps to beat the burglar?	A	B	C	D

Now add up your score

Add up the total number of As, Bs, Cs and Ds and write the total of each in the table below. Then award yourselves:

6 marks for every A scored;
4 marks for every B;
2 marks for every C and
0 marks for every D,
and enter this in the table.

	No.	
A	_____	x 6 =
B	_____	x 4 =
C	_____	x 2 =
D	_____	x 0 =

FINAL SCORE =

If you scored:
225-300: Congratulations. You've obviously given a great deal of thought to the security of your home. Your score indicates that your physical security is up to scratch and you remember to take common-sense precautions to beat the burglar. Be careful to remain vigilant and not become complacent.

150-224: You've obviously thought about the security of your home, but there's still room for improvement. Take another look at your physical security to see if it can be improved, and remember to put all these common-sense measures into practice when you leave home, or answer the door to strangers.

75-149: Definitely room for improvement here. There are plenty more steps you can take to improve security. Put some of the suggestions included in our checklist into action, and if you are concerned about the security of your home contact the Crime Prevention Officer at your local police station for some free advice.

0-74: It's all too easy to think 'it won't happen to me', but with statistics for burglary and theft continuing to rise you cannot afford to be complacent. Take advice NOW to improve security and check your security rating again in a few months' time.

Principal points of entry

Front door	25%
Rear/side door	23%
Rear/side window	43%
Front window	3%
Upper window	3%

Main methods of entry

Forced door or window	40%
Insecure door or window	22%
Break glass	21%
Use a key	3%
Other	3%

Burglaries: the facts

1 One dwelling is burgled every 50 seconds.

2 Eight out of ten burglaries occur when the house is empty.

3 70 per cent of burglaries involve forced entry.

4 In three burglaries out of ten, a door or window has been left open.

5 Two-thirds of burglaries are carried out during the week.

6 The peak age for offenders is 15.

7 Most burglaries are opportunist and 80 per cent of burglaries are not committed by professionals.

8 Only one in eight homes has adequate security locks.

CHAPTER 5

Good neighbours

Working together to fight crime.

Since the launch of the first scheme back in the 1980s, Neighbourhood Watch has played a vital role in the fight against crime, acting as the eyes and ears of the police.

Neighbourhood Watch is a very low cost security measure, yet it can have a phenomenal impact on local crime. A scheme in Bristol, for instance, reported a 90 per cent decrease in crime in the three years since their Watch was launched, and others in Wythenshawe – reputedly the largest council estate in Europe – reported a fall in house burglaries of almost 21 per cent in only one year.

Cynics, however, would say that such schemes are the exception rather than the rule, and it is true that many of the thousands of schemes set up today seem to exist in little other than name only, having little effect on crime. But the success stories prove that Neighbourhood Watch can work – and very effectively. So what exactly is Neighbourhood Watch and how can you ensure that, should you set up a scheme, it will be effective in fighting crime?

Getting to the roots

Neighbourhood Watch originates from the United States. Citizens of San Francisco were so desperate to reduce high crime rates that they decided to take action. The idea proved so successful that it spread to other American cities suffering from rising crime and violence.

The idea of neighbours banding together to beat crime captured the imagination of the UK population, though inevitably there were reservations. Some people felt that a successful Watch would simply divert burglary to a nearby neighbourhood that had not yet taken steps to protect itself. Others feared it would mean 'vigilante-style' gangs roaming the streets, and innocent people having their privacy invaded by well-meaning, if over-enthusiastic, neighbours. This, however, is not what Neighbourhood Watch, or Home Watch, as it is also called, is about. It's merely about neighbours keeping their eyes and ears open as they go about their daily business, and reporting anything suspicious to the police. Members work together with the assistance of a trained police officer. Under no circumstances are Watch members

Neighbourhood Watch or Home Watch street signs indicate that you are security conscious and watching out for suspicious activity.

A Neighbourhood Watch scheme is not a vigilante force. Members are simply asked to be alert, and to note discreetly any suspicious activity. A scheme should also teach members to be more security-conscious. The crime prevention officer may give a talk, show videos, or carry out home surveys to teach members how to improve their own home security. He, or the local beat officer, may also loan security marking kits to the scheme to enable members to mark their valuables, and will also provide literature which explains Neighbourhood Watch, incident report cards and Neighbourhood Watch stickers which members display in their windows to indicate that they are security-conscious.

Neighbourhood Watch areas are also identified by street signs displayed around the area which can be an effective deterrent. Again, the Crime Prevention Officer will be able to advise you on purchasing and erecting these signs.

encouraged to 'have a go', and put themselves at risk in a potentially dangerous situation.

Neighbourhood Watch was introduced to Great Britain in 1982, with the first scheme set up in the Cheshire stockbroker belt village of Mollington, following a spate of burglaries. Within just a few months the local burglary rate had dropped drastically, proving that Neighbourhood Watch could be a very effective tool in the fight against crime. As a result, with the support of police forces and the Home Office, Neighbourhood Watch schemes were set up all over the country, with numbers now totalling over 120,000.

Starting a scheme

Setting up a scheme sounds easy, and it is – providing your neighbours are keen on the idea as well. Before you take the matter further, it's best to have a word with some of them and find out whether

they are enthusiastic. If so, contact the Crime Prevention Officer at your local police station, who will advise you on setting up the Watch. One of the best ways to augment a scheme is to base it on an existing local community initiative such as a Residents' Association.

Organization

For a scheme to work effectively it needs some sort of organization; neighbours need to know who they

Some schemes organize activities to raise funds, improve the local area, and foster community spirit.

Watch has rekindled the old community spirit, bringing neighbours together as friends and encouraging them to look out for one another.

scheme area they are already involved – and you can look out for their property even if they don't want to play an active role.

When a Neighbourhood Watch scheme is first set up, enthusiasm amongst members is high, with everyone keen to play a role. Meetings will probably be held regularly and be well attended, literature will be distributed promptly, suspicious activity will be reported and, if crime falls in the immediate area, the scheme will be deemed a success. This is often when complacency sets in and crime figures start to creep back up. The secret of a successful Neighbourhood Watch scheme is maintaining this initial level of enthusiasm. This can depend largely on the personality of the co-ordinators. As such, the appointment of these people should not be treated lightly. An enthusiastic and active co-ordinator will ensure that a scheme remains active, and that members continue to take an interest in it.

> ## '…When complacency sets in…crime figures start to creep up…'

Schemes often fall by the wayside because members are not kept informed of what's happening. The publication of regular newsletters is vital, keeping members up-to-date with local crime trends and incorporating home security advice. For added impetus the newsletter can also contain community news, such as local events, births, marriages and anniversaries, fund-raising activities, quizzes, even a page for children. Meetings should be made interesting to encourage people to attend, with videos and guest speakers organized from the police, fire brigade, security

can contact for advice, and how and to whom to report suspicious incidents. The organization of a scheme depends largely upon the area in which it is situated. Generally, in residential areas schemes are divided up into small, manageable zones so that each scheme has a well-defined area of the neighbourhood to watch. One of the neighbours – preferably an enthusiastic, active one who is home all day – is then appointed area co-ordinator. He or she is responsible for regular contact with the police, recruiting and maintaining day-to-day contact with the street co-ordinators, and organizing Watch group meetings.

Each street or block of flats within the Watch should have a street co-ordinator who remains in regular contact with their members, and who can be contacted easily should any suspicious activity be noted. They in turn contact the police and

area co-ordinator. They should also hold regular meetings with their own Watch members, invite newcomers to join the scheme, and distribute newsletters and/or other literature.

In most neighbourhoods there will be some neighbours who don't want to get involved, usually because they are under the false impression that they will have to act as 'snoops', or patrol the streets at night, or that it will cost them money!

Because Neighbourhood Watch is community-based it's best to try to involve everyone. Make sure, therefore, that you know exactly what being a member of a scheme involves so that you can counter such ideas. You could organize a meeting with the Crime Prevention Officer as well to add some weight to your arguments. If people are adamant that they don't want to join, don't worry. By living in your

experts, Victim Support, or other relevant bodies.

A further incentive which will encourage people to maintain a Watch scheme is the fact that several major insurance companies offer discounts on home contents insurance to active Neighbourhood Watch schemes. Contact a local broker for more information.

Of course, meetings and newsletters have to be paid for, and schemes have implemented various methods of fund-raising. Some ask members to donate a small sum of money each year to scheme funds, others carry advertising in their newsletter from local businesses, some have secured sponsorship from local companies, and others use fund-raising as a way to further foster community spirit, with social events held throughout the year.

Some enthusiastic schemes have taken fund-raising a lot further, raising money for local charities, organizing outings for Watch members, even raising money to buy locks and alarms for elderly neighbours, or to buy their own photocopier, printing press or word processor for publication of their own community magazine or newsletter.

Neighbourhood Watch is not just about fighting crime. Community involvement has re-kindled the old community spirit, bringing neighbours together as friends and encouraging them to look out for one another. Contact is being established with those living alone, Childwatch schemes are ensuring that children are escorted safely to and from school, and, perhaps most important, Neighbourhood Watch schemes have reduced the fear of crime which restricts some people's lives.

Neighbourhood Watch activity list

Successful schemes tend to rely on fund-raising schemes and social activities involving Neighbourhood Watch members to maintain enthusiasm and raise funds for charities and/or scheme coffers. Here are a few ideas you might wish to implement.

- Approach local companies to ask if they would like to sponsor your scheme, helping out with photocopying, printing etc.

- Sell advertising in your local newsletter.

- Organize sponsored events, such as litter clean-ups, walks or runs.

- Hold a property marking day with the local police.

- Ask neighbours to donate items for a jumble or car boot sale.

- Organize coffee mornings.

- Involve local children – organize discos or games days or competitions for younger members.

- Ask an appropriate charity whether they would be willing to donate locks or door chains for the local elderly.

- Organize security displays and exhibitions.

- Ask members for a small annual donation.

- Hold dances or amateur theatre evenings.

- Organize outings to the seaside, famous gardens, popular shows etc.

- Hold a barbecue, or a safari supper.

- Ask local security firms for a group discount on products.

Above all, make fund raising fun!

WATCHPOINTS

1 Make sure you have the support of neighbours before attempting to set up a scheme.

2 Contact the Crime Prevention Officer at your local police station for advice.

3 Appoint enthusiastic, active neighbours as co-ordinators.

4 Display NW street signs and window stickers to deter thieves.

5 Keep members interested and informed with monthly meetings and newsletters.

6 Organize social events to maintain enthusiasm and neighbourliness.

7 Ask for feedback on successes from the police, and document local crime statistics.

8 Maintain regular contact with your local council, as well as voluntary organizations.

9 Contact insurance companies to find out whether they offer discounts to Watch members

CHAPTER 6

Security at the door

The front door is automatically the point at which most people begin to think about security. Indeed, the first thing most of us should do when we move house is change the front door lock. However, there are a number of things we should consider even before that.

Take a closer look at the door frame. Make sure it is secured firmly to the surrounding wall, that it isn't rotting or warped and that it is fixed at intervals no more than 600mm apart as well as, if possible, at the head of the door and the threshold.

Now look carefully at the door. It should be no less than 44mm thick and ideally of solid wood. The door stile, that is the amount of solid wood you have available to cut into from the edge of the door to the centre of the keyhole, should be a minimum of 119mm to allow room for a security mortice lock (see fitting sequence). If it is less than this but over 92mm you will need to fit a narrow-stile lock.

Unfortunately, many builders working under pressure to meet budgets, particularly in flats, fitted cheap, hollow egg-shell or plywood construction doors which easily give way with a hefty kick, let alone more forcible attack. You should replace such doors or anything that you think looks flimsy. Instead, fit

one that has a solid hardwood core or, even better, a wood laminate door (a sandwich of ply and other wood) with little or no glass and preferably without panels, particularly in the lower section, which are often made of plywood alone. Much thinner than the main door they could be easily kicked in.

Glass panels at one or both sides of the door inevitably reduce security (the safer side is on the hinge side where, even if the glass were broken, a hand could not reach the lock). Ideally, replace these and any window which is part of the door's design, with laminated glass which is much stronger and safer. (See Chapter 21).

The letter box in the door should be the minimum recommended by the Post Office (38mm x 250mm), so that a hand would not be able to reach in and attempt to open the lock from the inside.

A door viewer is an excellent precaution, along with a door chain, and these are covered in Chapter 7.

Three strong hinges should be fitted to the front door, and on outward opening doors it is advisable to fit hinge bolts positioned mid-way between the hinges. The bolts help prevent the door being levered off its hinges from outside if the hinge pins are successfully removed.

You should also look at any back or side doors, easily left inadequately secured (often with an inferior two or three-lever lock) and of weak construction while we concentrate on the front door. Being out of sight they are often an easy way in for the casual thief, and 62 per cent of all burglaries occur at the rear of property, and the rear or side door is the point of entry in 23 per cent of cases. Once again, fit hinge bolts to prevent the burglar removing the pins in the hinges, and fit key-operated surface mounted or mortice bolts to the top and bottom of the inside of the door. Don't rely on the sliding bolts so often fitted.

'...You should also look at any back or side doors...'

There are a number of ways of reinforcing both door, door frame and door lock. Frames can be reinforced with steel sections, and doors themselves can be given additional protection with vandal and attack resistant facings – either steel, laminates of wood or plywood and glass reinforced plastic (grp), a particularly tough material. These are sometimes incorporated as a layer beneath a wood veneer so that, on the face of it, the door looks perfectly normal.

A London bar is a steel strip which fits the entire length of the door, protecting the rim lock on one side and reinforcing the frame on the hinge side. It is designed to spread the force of an attack – something a multi-point locking system, a series of three or more locks operated simultaneously from one point, will also do.

Some multi-point systems can be morticed into a new or existing suitable door by a specially trained locksmith, and there is a surface-mounted kit, Multi-bolt, on the

Reinforcing kits protect against attacks on the lock, and levering.

market from Chubb which locks in three points and incorporates a door chain. It needs a door stile of at least 100mm and a visible door frame of at least 35mm width.

There are also reinforcement kits which are designed to fit around the lock area and protect it from attack, and you can find anti-tamper and lockable letter boxes, some of which are designed to resist arson attacks. The lock itself can be protected with special reinforcement kits – Chubb and Barrs Security both do one.

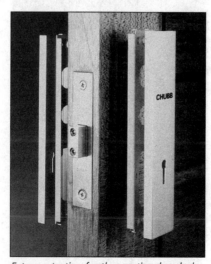

Extra protection for the mortice door lock from Chubb against forceful attacks.

Locking up

There is a wide variety of door locks available but the two main types are rim (which are surface-mounted) and mortice (which involves chiselling out a section of the door to insert the lock). An ordinary rim night latch which incorporates a standard cylinder offers little security alone. It can easily be opened by an intruder if the inside knob can be reached and is also vulnerable to manipulation – a credit card slid between the door and frame could easily force back the bolt.

Surface-mounted, an automatic deadlocking rim lock is relatively easy to fit yourself. This is Chubb's 4L74.

A deadlocking rim lock (night latch) is automatically deadlocked when the door is closed and the knob inside can be locked from inside or outside. The knob is then released by turning the key from the outside. Such locks have hardened steel bolts which are resistant to hacksaw attacks and the lock case and cylinder are, in high security models, protected from drilling, wrenching and other forceful attacks. An insecure rim lock can usually be replaced by a security version on wooden doors without too much additional woodwork and, being surface mounted, is relatively easy to fit. Look for a model with a box strike, which prevents the bolt being jemmied back into the lock case, and with concealed fixing screws. There are models for standard and narrow stile (approximately 40mm from edge of door to centre of keyhole) and suitable for varying thicknesses of door. Measure the stile and thickness of your door before choosing the lock.

Yale's PBS1 automatic deadlocking rim lock which has the BS3621 kitemark.

A rim lock with a built-in door restraint, which engages automatically every time the door is opened, is ideal for people on their own, or the elderly. This is Yale's 93 'Checklock'.

The other type of lock, the mortice, is concealed within the door and the best carry a kite-mark, to show they meet with BS3621, in particular for insurance company requirements. The British Standard specifies a minimum 1,000 key variations, at least five levers with measures incorporated to prevent picking, deadlocking which prevents handles and knobs from operating, a bolt which projects at least 14mm when it is locked and anti-drill plates fitted to protect the lock body. Fixing screws which are open to attack must be concealed or inoperable when the door is locked.

Chubb's 3G115 five-lever mortice deadlock is suitable if you are also fitting an automatic deadlocking rim lock on the front door, and will cost less than the BS version.

Having said all that, new European standards are being drawn up which will have considerable influence on the types of lock we fit in the future, and discussion between the lock industry's organization, the Master Locksmiths Association, and the Association of British Insurers is likely to result in certain non-BS3621 locks being approved by insurance companies. There are many excellent locks on the market which, because of their mechanisms, do not fall into the categories of BS3621 but are more than adequate security, including those installed with double-glazing units.

A cylinder-operated mortice sash lock for doors where a handle is required for opening from the inside.

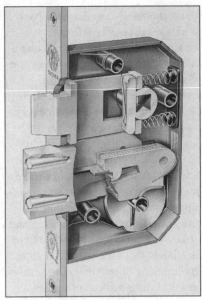

Inside a five lever mortice lock.

The mortice lock is either a deadlock with one hefty hardened steel bolt, usually fitted on a front door along with a rim night latch to reinforce security, or a mortice sashlock which, operated by a handle on one or both sides of the door, is ideal for back or side doors. This type of lock will have a latch bolt and a deadlock (see pictures). Once again various attack resistant features improve the security of these locks, and narrow stile versions are available for use with glazed doors which cannot accommodate the regular size. They are usually 2½ inch or 3 inch and should not be fitted to a door less than 42mm thick.

Since 1957, British manufacturers have made lever locks to the same overall size, with spindle and keyhole in the same place, so mortice locks are easy to replace.

High security cylinder locks

There is a quiet revolution going on in the lock industry, with the increasing use of cylinders. As usual, the British have had to be different. The traditional mortice

All types of cylinders are available to enable all the locks to be operated by a single key. A system can include padlocks and front door locks. If a key is lost, simply change the cylinder – not the entire lock.

lever lock, which has monopolized the market in Britain, is hardly used elsewhere. The cylinder lock is used throughout Europe and is beginning to be far more widely available here. In addition, it is cylinder locks that will be the basis of new European Standards. For those requiring a higher level of key security and the convenience of simply replacing a cylinder rather than the entire lock if a key is lost, it has many advantages. The cylinder also allows you to use the same key for the front and back door locks, and even for key-operated window locks.

High security cylinders, available for both mortice locks (look for the Euro-profile cylinder models) and rim locks, use registered keys, copies of which can only be obtained from the manufacturer or from a specially appointed locksmith on confirmation of the user's signature. There are many different types – Evva, Mul-T-Lock, GeGe, Chubb Biaxial, Abloy and ASSA are a few names to look for. With the assurance that if a key is lost, it cannot be easily duplicated in any keycutting kiosk and you can continue to use the existing lock case, the extra expense can perhaps be

justified. Often cylinders alone can be fitted to your existing locks, so check with your local locksmith first.

French doors and patio doors

These need special attention. The ideal type of lock for French doors is either a surface-mounted bolt or a mortice bolt with one fitted to the top and bottom of the door, shooting up into the head of the frame and down into the sill.

Particularly useful for wooden patio doors where you need more track clearance, ERA's multi-purpose bolt can be fitted to large windows, doors and even garage doors.

The aluminium framed patio door is particularly vulnerable and can easily be levered out of the frame. While some manufacturers are improving the security of double-glazed units, it is best to fit a purpose-made patio door lock. Some care is needed when fitting these – ideally install one top and bottom of the door – as the sliding mechanism and glass may be very close when drilling the holes for the lock. Our picture sequence shows how it's done. Look for a lock which has a push bolt and only needs a key to unlock it, and has concealed fixing screws.

Digital locks

If you want something a little more up market than a key, there is a growing choice in locks which operate using a digital code. Usually the code is four numbers, a PIN just like a credit card code, which you can change whenever you like. Some digital products are purely mechanical, operating a deadbolt, while others combine mechanical and electric operation. Alternatively there are access control systems which depend entirely on electronic operation. Any system that uses electronics will need an electric strike which incorporates the release mechanism, in general supplied for use with a 12v supply but this will usually need to be wired separately. Sometimes a transformer is included in the kit so that the digital unit can be plugged into the mains, or you will need to wire it direct into the power supply. Increasingly there are systems available which are battery-operated, which enables the lock unit to remember codes and any other programming facilities it offers. For example, the Touchlock range from Paxton Automation includes a battery-operated and a mains-operated keypad access control system.

Perhaps the simplest system on the market is the mains-operated

A digital lock which operates mechanically using a four digit code.

version – Touchlock compact only requires three cables for connection. It is packaged as a kit with a transformer, rim electric release and mortice plate (allowing you to adapt your existing lock to an electric one) plus a slimline keypad which incorporates a microprocessor which handles all the programming necessary. The keypad can also be linked to a new or existing doorbell.

Combining electronic and physical security gives you far more options – for example, you could have a different code for a cleaner or visitors which you could block when no longer needed. Ordinary five-lever mortice locks and electronic access control systems can be linked to an alarm system, or even security lighting, using a microswitch fitted in the strike. If you want to do this, ask your locksmith to advise you on the right lock to buy. You'd be surprised how a simple door lock can be adapted.

An easy to install and simple to operate electronic digital lock, the Touchlock kit comprises everything you need to transform your existing front door lock. Shown is an electric strike, for either mortice or rim lock, a transformer and power supply. The keypad is self-contained and allows you to program your own code and link it to your door bell.

▼ Fitting a mortice door lock

1 *We fitted Ingersoll's M50 British Standard five-lever mortice lock in place of a three-lever lock. It has a hardened deadlocking bolt, 1,500 key combinations and a solid steel box locking plate.*

2 *First step is to remove the old mortice lock. But don't try to lever it out. Unscrew the face plate. Then, by turning the key in the lock put it in the locked position with the door open. Holding the bolt firmly with a pair of pincers or pliers, pull the lock out, taking care not to damage the wood.*

3 *Make sure when you are replacing an existing lock that the backset (the dimension from the face plate to the centre of the keyhole) is the same, or you'll make yourself a lot of extra work. Ideally, the new fore-end (the vertical flat bit) should cover the old area easily.*

WATCH POINTS

1 If you move house, change the locks immediately. You never know who may still have keys that fit.

2 Ladies – don't keep your house keys in a handbag when you are out. Put them in a separate jacket pocket or purse.

3 If you are always losing your keys and having to change the locks, think about fitting a high security cylinder lock. Then you can just have the cylinder changed.

4 Have keys cut by a good locksmith. Some, but not all, keycutting outlets use inferior blanks which may break. A locksmith uses the correct equipment and will produce a good quality, well-finished key that will work.

5 Never leave spare keys under a doormat or flowerpot – that's where the thief will look first. And never hang a key inside the letterbox.

6 Never mark your keys with your name and address.

4 Mark the top and bottom of the fore-end with a chisel (it may well be slightly taller than the original lock) ...

7 Mark with the edge of the chisel (which is sharper than a pencil) around the front of the new lock, then with as wide a chisel as possible, gently tap around it, using a soft hammer, to make a dent in the wood or paintwork. Chisel out to accommodate the thickness of the fore-end so it fits nice and flush to the wood.

10 Use a file (⅜in should do) to increase the size of the hole, clearing out any bits of sawdust from the mortice afterwards.

5 ... and chisel out as necessary.

8 You can now see how the keyhole and the new lock are going to line up. If necessary you can fill any odd holes, which could prevent screws going in correctly, with a small wedge of glued wood.

11 Drill pilot holes using a 3mm drill. Harder wood doors (such as oak and mahogany) may require a larger pilot hole. Screw the lock into position using the screws provided.

6 With new lock in locked position (the bolt out) slide it into the mortice and peer through the keyhole to make sure the alignment is correct.

9 Mark with a pencil if you need to adjust the hole in the door to ensure it is wide enough; if it isn't the key may bind.

12 In theory, the keyhole flaps should go on the outside, but as most front doors open inwards it is possible for the flap to be trapped in the door stop. So there is a case for fitting it on the inside. With key in the lock, mark the position of the escutcheon with a bradawl and screw it into position.

6

SECURITY AT THE DOOR

13 The key flap fitted.

14 A better quality strike is usually larger than the original lock. It is very important to fit it accurately or the door will be a loose fit. With the lock in the locked position, first gently close the door so that the plate hits the side of the door jamb. Mark the height on the jamb where the strike is going to be.

15 This may not always give you the most central position, so holding the striker over the mortice lock bolt, measure from the edge of the striker to the outside of the door (in millimetres). Making sure the door shuts (you may need to adjust the measurement by a couple of millimetres) this measurement will give you the outer position of the striker (while the inner sorts itself out). Keep checking that the door shuts fully.

16 Mark the recess out and chisel, just as you did for the fore-end, allowing for the thickness of the striker plate. But bear in mind, once you have cut it out, if you have made a hash of it, it can be difficult to recover!

17 Don't rush to make the screw holes. If it's not right and the door doesn't close correctly you will have to fill them. Close the door with the strike in position and make any adjustments at this point. Then drill the pilot holes ...

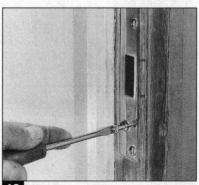

18 ... and insert the screws to hold the face plate in position.

▼ Fitting a rim lock

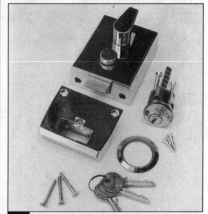

1 As we had fitted a good quality mortice lock, we chose a middle price range Union Night Latch to complement it. More expensive automatic deadlocking locks are also available.

2 This is the sorry specimen we had to remove first which offered virtually no security by itself.

3 Unscrew the back plate of the old lock and remove. Our particular door was fitted with a Trinity set (which has a hole for a cylinder, a door knocker and a letter box all in one unit). If possible avoid fitting one of these as they weaken the door because of the number of holes cut in one area. Remove the old cylinder from the outside of the door.

4   *Check that the new cylinder will fit comfortably in the old cylinder hole.*

5   *Holding the cylinder in position, screw the back plate into position. The lock should fit flush to the door.*

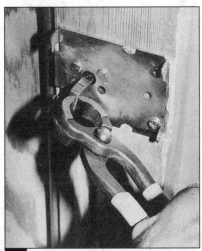

6   *The tail of the cylinder will protrude from the front through the back plate. You may have to cut the tail to the right length. As the tail is in sections you can snap them off with a pair of pliers, as seen here. It will need to protrude about 15mm.*

7   *Check that the back plate is square, and knock it gently into position with a soft hammer or your hands.*

8   *Offer up the lock body. (If there is a lip which fits round the door you will have to chisel a little so it sits flush). It is also important that the round part (the follower) is in the right position, or the lock will not double deadlock. Check the manufacturers' instructions and turn it using a screwdriver so it is in the right position.*

9   *Dab a little drop of Loctite or paint on the thread of the screws to prevent them shaking loose as time goes by and screw the lock case into position.*

10   *Before positioning the lock's box strike, make sure the door shuts flush.*

11   *Offer the striker up to the jamb and mark for the recess (it has a lip which will need to be accommodated).*

12   *With a soft hammer, knock the striker into the recess you have chiselled out.*

13 *Before drilling the screw holes, ensure the door will shut snugly, but adjusting if it is too tight.*

14 *An additional angled screw provides greater security and helps pull the box strike square.*

15 *Seen from the outside, the rim lock cylinder and box strike.*

▼ Fitting hinge bolts

1 *We fitted Chubb's WS14 Hinge Bolts to our front door. They are designed to resist forceful attacks and to secure the hinged side of the door. Fit two.*

2 *Position the bolts approximately 15mm down from the hinges. You will be drilling into the door itself first and making a 10mm hole (so you may wish to use a power drill) to a depth of approximately 38mm. Sometimes the manufacturer's instructions may say a smaller hole, but this may result in too tight a fit.*

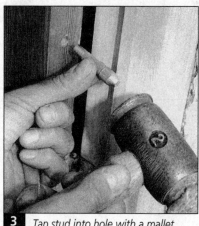

3 *Tap stud into hole with a mallet.*

4 *To find the right position for the hole in the door jamb, gently push the door to with the stud in position. This will leave a small mark on the door jamb and give you your drilling point. Drill a 16mm hole to a depth of approximately 18mm.*

5 *Position the face plate centrally over the hole and mark it with a chisel.*

6 *Pare the wood away around the hole to recess the face plate neatly.*

7 Drill the two screw holes ...

8 ... and screw the face plate into position. Make sure the door shuts with no resistance, and fit the second hinge bolt.

▼ Fitting a mortice bolt

1 We fitted Chubb's 8002 door mortice bolt. Ideally fit two.

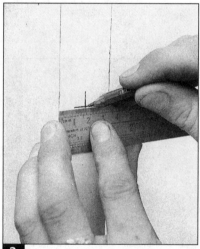

2 Mark the central position of the bolt on the door, approximately six inches down from the top in this case.

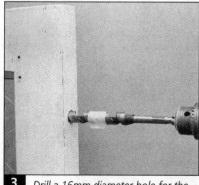

3 Drill a 16mm diameter hole for the bolt. Marking the drill bit with a piece of masking tape or similar will prevent you drilling in too far as this type of drill bit used with a power drill tends to draw itself in before you know where you are!

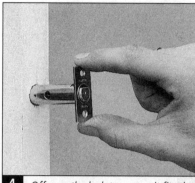

4 Offer up the lock to ensure it fits the hole correctly, and to position face plate

5 Mark position of face plate top and bottom.

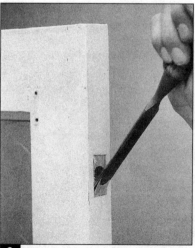

6 Chisel out recess so that the plate fits flush in the wood.

7 To find correct place to drill for keyhole, hold bolt flush with the face of the door, insert key and give it a tap with a hammer. Make sure it is positioned on the inside of the door (not the outside!).

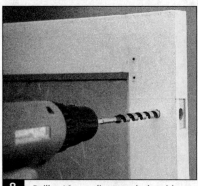

8 Drill a 10mm diameter hole with a 10mm drill bit (also known as an auger drill). Just drill through until you meet the horizontal hole (you won't need to drill very hard).

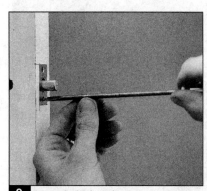

9 Knock the bolt firmly into position in the mortice with a hammer and, using a bradawl, mark the pilot holes for the face plate. Screw it into place with a ratchet screwdriver.

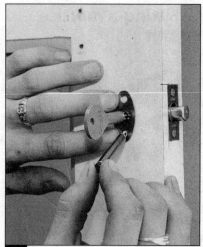

10 To fit the escutcheon on the inside of the door, line it up with the 10mm hole with the key in position. Then mark screw holes with a pencil or bradawl.

11 Drill the holes for the escutcheon's screws rather than simply screwing them in. Just screwing them in may result in them going off-line and may cause problems with the operation of the lock itself.

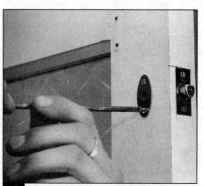

12 Screw the escutcheon plate into place. Then, having checked that the lock works correctly, shoot the bolt with the door closed so that it marks the door jamb.

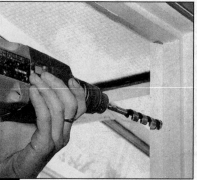

13 Drill the door jamb, using a 16mm drill bit, for the bolt engagement hole.

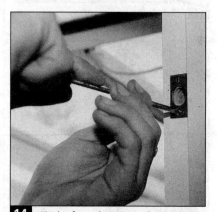

14 Fit the face plate, recessing it as described above.

15 The mortice bolt fitted and in the locked position, ready for the key to be placed somewhere safe!

▼ Fitting a patio door lock to an aluminium door

1　We fitted Chubb's 8K119 patio door lock. Fit one top and bottom. It uses a convenient push-to-lock mechanism and a key to unlock.

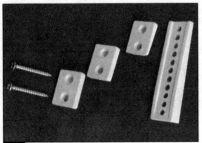

2　An anti-lift device is also available, but check that the width of your door rail is suitable.

3　Holding the lock snugly against the central vertical frame where the two doors meet, turn the key clockwise to release the bolt and tap the end of the bolt so it leaves a slight indent on the frame.

4　To make a more distinct mark, if necessary, use a centre punch.

5　Start to drill the hole for the bolt with a small bit. This is because drilling so close to the sliding mechanism can be a bit hit and miss! It may mean you will have to re-position the lock sideways to avoid drilling through the wheels or another section of the rolling gear. The glass may also be closer to the runners than you may have thought. So work carefully.

6　Build up to the larger 10mm drill required to make the final hole, and clean out the metal swarf afterwards.

7　In the same way as described above mark, punch and drill the holes for the fixing screws in the side of the door. Use a 3.4m drill to drill the holes for the fixing screws, making sure you don't overshoot and touch the glass. Just one touch on the corner could break the glass.

8　Re-position the lock with the bolt out and the door open (so you have room to manoeuvre the screwdriver) and screw firmly into place. A little drop of lubricant or grease on the self-tapping screws will help them locate more securely.

9　To lock, push the bolt home. A key is required to release the bolt.

CHAPTER 7

Who's at the door?

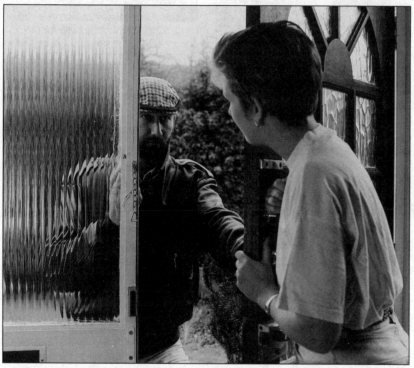

Is it always wise to open your door without checking it's someone you want to see and talk to?

Tales are frequently heard of unscrupulous conmen tricking their way into people's homes and stealing possessions, or convincing occupiers to have unnecessary repairs carried out. Of course, most callers are genuine but, sadly, with an increasing army of tricksters preying on the vulnerable, no-one can afford to be too trusting.

Beating the doorstep conman costs very little in monetary terms, but commonsense precautions are needed to ensure that a caller is genuine, and to avoid being pressurized into buying goods or services that you do not really want or need.

Security devices

The most important point is to ensure that you can see and talk to the caller before opening the door and putting yourself at risk. If the front door or nearby windows do not provide a good view of the caller, you should install a door viewer. Simple to fit and unobtrusive once in place, it comprises a wide-angle lens which normally provides a viewing angle of between 160° and 190°, enabling you to see the caller clearly, even if he or she is standing to one side. The installation of a porch light which comes on automatically or

can be switched on from indoors, will ensure that callers are clearly visible after dark, or in shadow.

The front door should also be fitted with a door chain or limiter. This prevents entry by ensuring that the door can only be opened a fraction – just enough for you to talk to the caller and check credentials, or sign for a package or letter without allowing him in. To be of real use, however, the chain must be strong and should be secured with screws that are at least 30mm long. A door limiter is often of more solid construction, utilizing a steel bar rather than a chain, and therefore offers a greater degree of resistance should someone try to force their way in.

An alternative device is screwed to the bottom of the door and activated by pressing your foot against a mechanical lever. This lever allows the householder to quickly secure the door in a partially open position, and the locking device enables the door to be pushed closed, but stops any attempt to force the door further open.

'…ensure callers are clearly visible…'

Some personal attack alarms – which can be triggered in the event of an attack to sound an ear-piercing

Fitting a door viewer ...

... and a door chain are both simple, inexpensive precautions, and they will make you feel safer.

screech – are sold with wall mounting brackets and can be kept conveniently near the front door. In the event of someone trying to force their way in, the alarm can easily be triggered to alert neighbours or passers-by.

'...Conmen are crafty...'

Once the door viewer and door limiter are in place, don't forget to use them. Conmen are crafty and will use numerous tricks to try to force their way into your home. Don't assume, for example, that it is only male callers you must be wary of. Many people have also fallen victim to female and child confidence tricksters.

Communal entrances

Many blocks of flats these days utilize 'entry-phone' systems to ensure a greater degree of security (more of these later). If you admit a person to your flat you cannot be sure that he actually exits the building after leaving you. If a criminal should gain entry to the block, he can easily go from flat to flat unchallenged until he finds one to break into.

'...never hold the door open for a stranger...'

If the caller is a stranger, it is best to play safe and either refuse admittance, or at the very least, personally escort him off the premises. For the same reasons, never hold the door open for a stranger who arrives when you are entering or leaving the building. For additional security, fit a door viewer and door limiter to your flat door so you can still refuse admittance when necessary.

Dealing with callers

Anyone who calls on you uninvited has no right to assume that you want to talk to them, let alone invite them into your house. Keep the back door locked at all times as well. Many tricksters work in pairs and one may keep you talking while the other slips round the back! Don't feel guilty about leaving them on the doorstep while you check their identity. Genuine callers will not object to you taking sensible precautions.

Common confidence tricks include the bogus official who claims to be from the water, gas or electricity company, needing to gain admittance to your home; the doorstep salesman who may try to pressure you into buying expensive products, or persuade you to order some goods and pay a deposit with your order; the workman who claims that there are slates missing from your roof; even the social worker who wants to check on your child.

The official

Once you have checked the identity of the caller through the door viewer, secure the chain or limiter before opening the door. Then ask the caller for some identification and examine it carefully; do not rely on the sight of an official-looking uniform. All officials should carry an identification card so make sure they show it to you. If you are still in doubt, ask the caller to wait outside and close the door while you telephone the relevant authority. If you are still not satisfied, trust your instincts and ask the caller to come back so that you can arrange for a friend, relative or neighbour to be with you. Phone the local police and let them know what has happened. They may know of tricksters operating in the area, and will certainly look into the matter if they feel your suspicions are justified.

Doorstep salesmen

Many unsolicited callers will be trying to sell goods or a service. People selling expensive home improvement products can make a great deal of commission on sales and may therefore be very keen to persuade you to part with your money, often offering what appear to be very attractive discounts or special terms.

The salesman may offer a large discount if you sign on the spot, or may try to pressure you by saying that prices are about to rise. No matter how persuasive the salesman is, do not be tempted to make a decision there and then. Ask for time to think about the offer. You will often find that the same discount is available if you phone back a few days later.

Also be wary of promises that you can always cancel the deal if you change your mind. You may have cancellation rights, but salesmen know that once they have a signed piece of paper, the chances are that you will go ahead with the purchase. Similarly, do not be swayed by the offer of a generous guarantee.

Do not give the doorstep salesman a deposit for orders placed, or goods promised. It is always possible they will not come back with the goods.

The workman

It is easy to be taken in by workmen coming to your door and claiming that there are tiles missing from your roof, or that the guttering is leaking and needs replacing. These tricksters may try to panic you into having the work carried out immediately by telling you that serious damage could occur. You could find yourself paying an extortionate fee for what may be an unnecessary job, or you may have to pay twice for a professional builder to rectify their shoddy workmanship.

Do not accept their claims that work needs doing. If in doubt, get a second opinion from a reputable workman – one who is personally recommended or who belongs to a trade association such as the Federation of Master Builders, or the Guild of Master Craftsmen. And certainly get two or three estimates before you agree to have any work carried out.

What the law says

When you buy from a trader who has called at your home without an appointment, you have seven days in which to cancel the contract and reclaim the money you might have paid. This applies to goods you buy and to work you have arranged to have done, provided the sum involved is over £35. This law covers home improvements such as replacement kitchens or double glazing, but not new building work such as home extensions. If in doubt, contact the local Citizens Advice Bureau.

Audio and video entry systems

There are other more sophisticated ways of identifying who is at the door. With an audio or video entry system, you can hear and, with the latter, see your visitors from the safety of your lounge, and even let them in and switch on the hall light – particularly useful if you live in an upstairs apartment or large block of flats, or even a large house.

Audio and video entry systems have become more competitive in price, easier to install and are growing in popularity. They offer convenience, safety and security with the benefit of being able to control who comes in at the touch of a button. There is also, of course, the advantage of being able to have a chat with the milkman and the postman without having to run down the stairs in your bathrobe!

How simple is it?

Entry systems can be installed in single homes or, using modular components, can be designed to serve as few as two or as many as several hundred residents in blocks of flats or

A simple intercom system, such as Friedland's Password Doorphone, will help you identify the caller and allow you to talk to them without having to open the door.

WATCHPOINTS

1 Fit a door viewer and limiter, and remember to use them.

2 Ask for identification. Check it carefully. If in doubt telephone.

3 Still suspicious? Ask the caller to come back. Notify the police.

4 Don't respond to pressure. Ask for time to consider. Obtain more quotes.

5 Don't give a deposit. He may not come back.

6 Know your legal rights. You can cancel a contract made with an unsolicited caller within seven days, and reclaim your money if it is over £35.

The audio only kit

Gone are the days of crackling voices when microphones used carbon granules, highly susceptible to the first signs of moisture. The use of the electret microphone has vastly improved, and ensured the reliability of two-way speech.

A typical audio-only system consists of an entrance panel with a push-button door bell, for a single home or several apartments, and speaker unit, linked to a telephone handset in the apartment. Normally a 12v electric release will also be part of the kit to convert the door lock to remote control.

apartments. While early systems were quite complex and used larger bulky outside cameras, simpler, more compact systems are now available. The most basic systems use existing bell wire to send both sound and picture from an entry panel incorporating a microphone and a miniature camera, installed at the main door, to a monitor and telephone hand-set indoors.

own to tackle the job. You are likely to be encountering higher voltages and a multitude of other control equipment, and only the building maintenance manager or a qualified electrician should carry out the work.

A smart audio-only door entry system with push-buttons for each flat.

What it costs

Cheaper systems may be limited in range, i.e. by the length of the cable over which the system is able to provide good visual and audio communication, but they may be quite adequate for the single home and they are affordable – around £500 complete for a video entry system. It is quite possible to use your own TV monitor, running coaxial cable from the outside camera unit via the household aerial and linking in to a spare channel on your set. Many large apartment blocks have a facility built in to do just that, but if you are a resident in a block, please don't go off on your

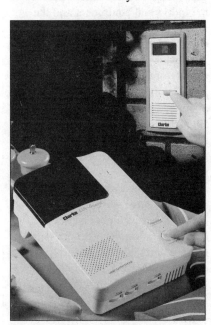

Some systems are now relatively inexpensive and can be DIY fitted using just two-wire cabling.

The video entry kit

Video entry systems have also been improved dramatically with better and smaller cameras. The video entry door panel incorporates a miniature camera with a lens which is able to adjust automatically to low light levels. So you should be able to see your caller clearly at night as well as during the day.

The monitor/hand set indoors will have a number of buttons which

allow audio and visual communication, and this is usually limited to between a few seconds and a few minutes duration. Just press the button again to restore communication. (Some systems will allow you to view the caller automatically when the door panel button is pushed, using a sensor at the point of entry.)

'...Video entry systems have been improved dramatically...'

The depth of the door entry panels available, even those incorporating cameras, has been markedly reduced, often less than one brick deep, which reduces the possibility of knocking a hole in your lounge wall, or they can be surface mounted. If recessed, the panel will be supplied with an embedding box. Panels are available in varying materials – anodized metal, aluminium, brass and stainless steel or, if they are likely to be vandalized, you can choose polycarbonate or impact-resistant ABS plastic housings. They can also be fitted with weather resistant hoods.

Monitors

Monitors can be table top or mounted on the wall (just as a telephone). Wall-mounted screens vary in size from as large as seven inches to 3.5 inch flat screen models and usually provide a black and white picture. They can also be flush or surface mounted. The unit is likely to have volume control, remote door release, brightness control and possibly an anti-tamper alarm (alerting the occupier if, for example, someone tries to prise off or damage the outside panel) and light switch (to provide lighting in a

Today's stylish monitors blend very easily with your decor. Most can be wall or table-top mounted.

hall or staircase). There is also a system from Aiphone allowing the camera to 'pan and tilt', which extends the vertical view from 20 inches to 36 inches, and the horizontal view from 26 inches to 72 inches. So no-one can lurk undetected.

Power and wiring

Power supplies vary considerably depending on the level required by the individual equipment and the range within which it should operate (the greater the range, the greater the power needed) but these are usually provided with each kit. Power will also be needed to operate the electric release which is fitted with the system and allows remote control of the door. This is usually converted from the supply provided.

Wiring also varies considerably on wire (bell wire) systems to four-core, six wire telephone cable (standard 0.5mm single core with twisted pairs is often specified) and coaxial cable for video connection. Most equipment is, however, sold in kits and should be supplied with appropriate connections and, of course, instructions. However, to give you an idea of how it should be done we have installed our own system.

▼ Fitting a video entry system

1   *In a flat it can be a great advantage not to have to go down perhaps several flights of stairs to open a door to a double-glazing salesman, and to be able to release the lock remotely to admit welcome visitors. We fitted our system to a home with living rooms on the first floor.*

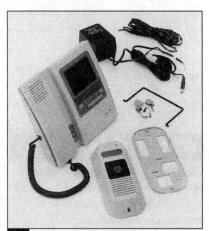

2   *The components of the Vision One video entry system, supplied by BPT, include the monitor (fitted indoors) and camera unit which replaces the normal bell push. In addition, there is a power supply unit, mounting plates and two-core wire (or you can use existing bell push wire if in the right place and in good condition). If you want to fit an electric lock release later you will need to use multi-core cable.*

entry hole (if cable is being fed in from behind) with a soft pencil. If cable is to be fed through the mounting plate, drill the hole. If not, there is a slot in the plate to accept a cable from below. The bell wire hole could be used for the wiring in this case.

If the mounting surface is not flat, mark the outline of the plate in order to remove protruding woodwork (as shown here).

3   After two false starts when a steel joist got in the way (these things happen!) the most direct route for the cable was through the landing window. Drilling the window frame is easy enough, but drill from the inside to avoid break-through splinters that can involve you in re-decoration later. This frame was very deep and required either a long bit or the hole to be drilled from each side. Drill from inside first and then measure and mark the same distances on the outside of the frame drilling where they meet. Then estimate the cable length needed outside the house and feed it through the hole you've drilled.

5   Work round the outline with a chisel, using a narrow one on the curved sections. Remove the wood to a suitable depth with a broad chisel.

7   If you want the cable to enter the unit from the back you will need to take the cable inside the house and again drill a hole in an inconspicuous place. If you decide to use the cable entry slot in the mounting plate this won't be necessary.

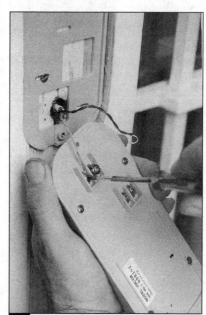

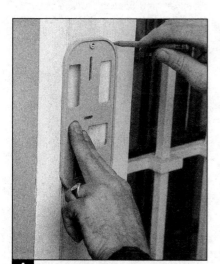

4   Mount the camera unit at around eye level (BPT recommend 140cm from the floor). This takes into account the angle of camera view and the average height of people. Avoid mounting it in a position where sun will shine on the camera from behind the visitors, as the automatic adjustment in the camera will mean bright light will make the visitors' faces dark.

Existing bell wire may limit the position, but here our porch was deep enough to avoid the problem.

Offer up the camera mounting plate and mark fixing screw positions and the cable

6   Screw the mounting plate to the surface.

8   Feed the cable through the hole and strip off the insulation about ½ inch to ¾ inch from the ends of the wire cores. It may be difficult to negotiate a right-angled hole with flexible cable; if so feed in a stiffer piece of wire from the outside and attach the cable to it with insulating tape or similar and pull it through. We used eight-core cable and doubled up two of the wires for each connection leaving the other two doubled up connections for a lock release.

To make secure connections to the unit, bend the wire end in the form of a cup hook and place it under the securing screw so that the screw rotates toward the open end. As the screw is tightened, it winds the wire firmly under it to close the loop. If you get it wrong, the loop opens and is forced from under the screw head.

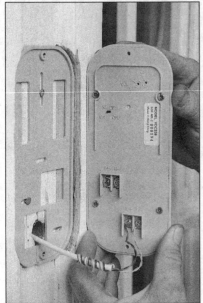

9 Adjustments to the chime and speech volume can be made on the back of the unit before mounting. A switch can be used to stop the internal chime, and if you want to fit a bell to provide a louder warning, connect it to the two extra terminals shown.

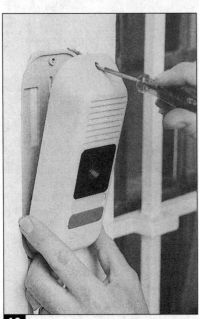

10 Having connected the wires, screw the camera unit to the mounting plate. As a weather seal is not provided it is wise to apply a smear of silicon grease to the mating surfaces to prevent moisture getting in.

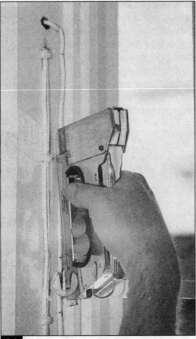

11 Clip the cable neatly into place back to the monitor unit, leaving an extra length of cable behind the camera unit for easy servicing. Hiat clips are generally used for cable clipping but a cabling gun makes fixing cable to wood very easy. If you are fixing around a window, check that the window opens without damaging the cable.

12 If you run cable over brickwork you need to use a hammer and fix the cable run with Hiat clips. If the mortar is hard, you must wear protective goggles.

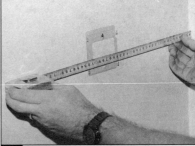

13 Choose the most convenient room for the monitor – the kitchen, living room or a central landing are all possibilities. Place it near a mains outlet which will provide power, and choose a good quality wall where it can be firmly fixed. This particular model could also be placed on a desk or hall table, and an angle bar to give a 25° viewing angle is provided.

Mark the wall for drilling the fixing holes and ensure the screen can be viewed comfortably by the smallest adult in the house.

Drill and plug the top hole, then screw the plate for a temporary fixing. Measure, as shown, from the edge of the plate to the wall to ensure a square mounting, and mark the lower screw position. Drill and plug it, and secure the mounting plate, checking it is square and flat. If it isn't you will have problems when you fit the monitor.

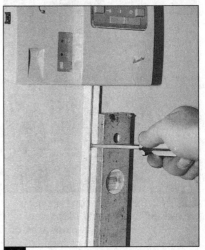

14 To make a neat job of running cables to the monitor, you can chase out the wall and plaster them in. But the simplest way is to use some trunking. Measure the length needed and cut it to size. Then cut the top edges at an angle to make the trunking fit the curve of the back of the monitor. Check the vertical with a spirit level, and drill, plug and screw the trunking to the wall.

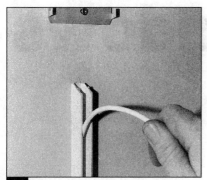

15 Lay the cable in the trunking, and measure for the correct length to the monitor terminals.

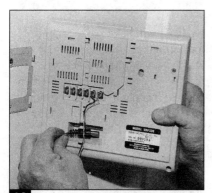

16 Looking at the rear of the monitor, strip the wires back for connection and attach to the two appropriate terminals. The other terminals are for a lock release and an additional speaker for the monitor. Plug the power supply output cable to the monitor and lay the wires in the moulded grooves to ensure flush fitting. Slide the monitor on to its mounting plate. If you have difficulty the plate may not be flat or square.

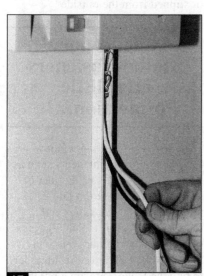

17 Thumb the cables into the trunking.

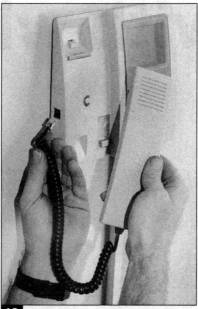

18 Cut the trunking cover to length, clip it into place and plug the handset into its socket on the monitor.

19 Wire a 13 amp plug to the power supply input cable and plug into the mains outlet. Clip the cable up to the socket and tidy surplus cable with ties, placing the power supply in an inconspicuous position. A metal or plastic strap to secure it to the skirting board or behind a piece of furniture would be a good idea.

20 Switch the power on and ask someone to call from the front door. Pressing the bar should result in a chime at the camera unit and the monitor.

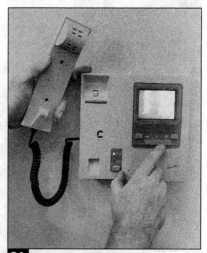

21 The screen powers up for 30 seconds and enables you to adjust the contrast with the slide bar to suit the light conditions at the camera. Pick up the handset and talk to the caller to ensure the audio quality of the system. If volume needs adjusting do this with the ear-shaped symbol control button mounted under the handset.

Press the button with an eye symbol and check the screen is powered for two minutes. This allows a longer conversation, or enables the occupant to watch the camera viewing area silently.

The face without handset symbol allows hands-free communication, useful if you have dirty hands or a person without full mobility wishes to use it.

Having tested the system and adjusted it as necessary, make good the various holes by filling with mastic.

CHAPTER 8

Ways with windows

In more than half of all reported break-ins, burglars have gained access through a downstairs window. And in a lot of instances they haven't even had to force their way in – access has been granted through an open window. Proof, if that were needed, that easily accessible windows, no matter how small, should never be left open when the home is unoccupied.

When securing your home, windows must be one of your first considerations. Although a really determined thief could probably defeat most window locks, the majority of break-ins are committed by the opportunist – and the last thing he wants is to spend a lot of time breaking into a house. He is more interested in a quick entry and exit to reduce the chances of being caught!

If you own a recently-built house it is quite likely that window locks have already been installed. Homes built to standards laid down by the National House-Building Council

(NHBC) will have key-operated locks fitted to all downstairs windows and others which are readily accessible. This requirement became mandatory at the beginning of 1989, but if you are uncertain about the locks fitted to your windows, a quick call to your Crime Prevention Officer at the local police station should put your mind at rest.

The traditional window fasteners fitted in older houses offer very little protection. Smash a small area of glass, slip a hand in, release the catch and all your possessions are there for the taking – conveniently carried out through the door. It's easier still if the catch can be forced or slipped from the outside.

'...Traditional window fasteners offer little protection...'

The purpose of fitting window locks is to prevent incidents such as these occurring. A vast number of locks are available from DIY multiples, hardware stores and security locksmiths to suit all types of windows, and all are relatively inexpensive. But before rushing out to buy the locks there are a number of points to take into consideration.

First, you'll need to take a look at what type of windows you have. Are they made from wood or metal (steel or aluminium)? How do they open – are they hinged or sliding? Also take a note of the width of the stile or rail where the lock will be fitted. Finally, take a good look at the frames. Window locks fitted to rotten wooden frames, or poorly fitting windows will provide little protection, and these areas will have to be attended to first, either by strengthening, repairing, or replacing windows and frames. Make sure that window putty is in good condition, too. Dried out putty is easily removed, allowing the glass to be lifted out.

You will then need to ascertain how many window locks are required. All downstairs windows should be secured (including basement windows) and any upstairs windows which could be reached by a flat roof, wall, drainpipe or anything that a burglar could climb. Casement windows which are one metre (3ft) high, or more, or sash windows one metre wide should be secured with two window locks. To keep costs down, windows which are not used frequently could be screwed shut. However, this is not recommended as a window may

The Chubb 8K100 for wood or metal framed windows.

need to be used as an emergency exit in the event of a fire.

With such a wide variety of window locks available, it is important that you choose carefully. Consider how often each window is used, whether it may need to be used as an exit in the case of a fire, and also who will operate the locks. An elderly person might need locks which are specially designed to be easy to operate. If there are children in the house you may prefer to install locks in their room which enable the windows to be opened slightly for ventilation, but not wide enough for a child to fall out.

The ERA Securistay allows windows to be opened slightly for ventilation, but not sufficiently wide for a child to fall through.

There are a surprising number of points to bear in mind, but if you are in any doubt, remember that advice is available from Crime Prevention Officers and security locksmiths who will be able to demonstrate a range of locks and recommend those to suit your particular requirements. Window locks may be slightly cheaper from a large DIY store, but do bear in mind that there may not be an expert on hand to advise you.

Casement windows

In most modern houses it is more than likely that casement windows have been installed. They may be hinged at the side or top, or pivot vertically or horizontally.

Most casements are secured with a cockspur handle. This is easily

replaced with a locking cockspur – readily available and quite secure providing the handle cannot be removed – but particularly on larger windows, a higher degree of security can be obtained when the window is actually locked to the frame. Locks that secure the window latch or catch could, in a determined attack, be levered apart.

Cockspur handles are easily replaced with locking versions like this one from ERA.

Although there are many variations, there are only two types of window lock – mortice and surface mounted. Mortice locks are neat and unobtrusive, but may be more fiddly to operate and are certainly more difficult to fit. Fitting requires the removal of wood and, on narrow frames, this could undermine the strength of the frame. All locks, whether mortice or surface-mounted, must be fitted accurately to be really secure, with holes drilled to the exact size.

Surface mounted locks are easier to fit by anyone with reasonable DIY skills, and they provide a much greater choice in terms of style, strength and price. However, surface-mounted locks do rely on their fixings for strength, and any fixing screws which are still visible when the lock is secured should be drilled out, or burred over, so they cannot be unscrewed. When installing window locks do take care not to insert screws too near to the glass which is recessed in the frame, otherwise the window may crack. Bear in mind, also, that striking plates may have to be morticed into the frame. The lock's packaging should provide detailed fitting instructions and dimensions. To cut down on cost, window locks are often sold in packs of four or six, and supplied with a key to operate all the locks. Additional keys are available.

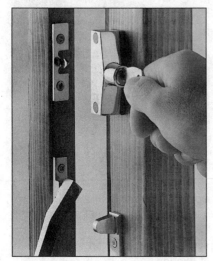

For convenience, the ERA Snaplock locks automatically when the window is closed.

Probably the simplest locks to operate are those which lock automatically every time the window is closed, or those which have a button which you push to lock, and use a key to unlock – so there's no excuse for not locking the windows every time you leave the house. Other surface-mounted locks have a special key which screws the lock shut and is used again to unscrew it.

Fanlights

Don't make the mistake of thinking that a fanlight is too small to provide access. It grants access for a thief to tamper with locks fitted to the larger window, and remember also that the opportunist burglar these days could be a small child!

Fanlights are kept closed with a stay which provides very little security. They can be secured with a casement stay stop or screw, but ideally you should fit a surface-mount casement-style lock which secures the window to the frame. There are also locks which enable a fanlight to be locked in a slightly open position to provide ventilation.

Sash windows

Sash windows, consisting of two windows which slide up and down, are commonly found in older properties and often provide easy access. The major manufacturers, such as Chubb and ERA, provide locks specifically for sash windows. Particularly useful is a locking stop which allows the window to be secured in a closed or slightly open position. Bolts and screw locks are also available. A cheap and effective method of further improving security on a sash window is to cut a broomstick to fit tightly in the sash channel. This could only be removed if the glass is broken.

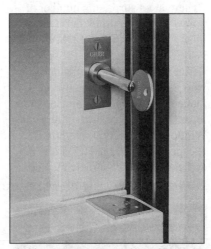

Chubb's WS1 secures a sash window in the fully closed position, or slightly open for ventilation.

Louvre windows

Louvre windows are particularly vulnerable as the individual glass

slats can be easily and quickly removed. Ideally they should be replaced with more conventional windows, but if cost prohibits this, glue each slat in place with a strong epoxy resin. A grille or shutter fitted over the window provides much greater protection.

Rooflights and skylights can also permit entry, particularly if they are accessible from a flat roof. If they cannot be secured easily with locks, consider installing window bars, or a grille.

Metal frames

The Chubb 8K106 is easily fitted to steel and most aluminium-framed hinged windows.

All the major manufacturers provide surface-mounted locks specifically for metal window frames, but installation is slightly more difficult than for wooden frames as it requires the drilling of holes in thin strips of metal, and special screws for aluminium. If in doubt about the installation of locks, call in a locksmith.

Locks for metal windows may secure the cockspur handle by stopping the handle being opened; they may fit on to the opening window and are secured by throwing a bolt against the fixed frame; they may operate on a 'swing lock' principle similar to a lock for a wooden window, and there are also locks available to secure metal sliding windows which work on a similar principle to a patio door lock.

Keys

Window locks are normally supplied with a universal key which fits all locks of the same type. This is helpful in some ways, enabling you to purchase as many keys as you want, but it also inevitably reduces the degree of security which window locks provide. Having said that, it's important to remember that most break-ins are committed by opportunists and the sight of window locks will probably send them scuttling off in search of an easier target. Also, with the wide range of locks available on the market, the burglar would have to carry a huge bunch of keys around with him to make sure that he had the right key to release your window.

If you live in a high risk area, however, some major manufacturers, including ERA and Chubb, do offer window locks with the option of high security keys which provide a number of key differs (i.e., the number of variations of keys for any one lock design). This does increase security considerably, but it also means you will have to go back to the manufacturer or specialist locksmith should you lose the keys!

Double glazing

Double glazing can in itself improve security. Well-fitted units prevent catches from being slipped, and leave the burglar with two panes of glass to break rather than just one. In particularly vulnerable areas laminated glass could be installed for greater security (see Chapter 21). UPVC units are normally supplied with security locks built in, and these often feature multi-point

WATCHPOINTS

1 Fit locks to all accessible windows, including fanlights.

2 Make sure you know exactly what you need before you buy.

3 Locks should secure the window to the actual frame.

4 Frames and windows must be in good condition.

5 Any doubts, ask a Crime Prevention Officer or security specialist.

6 Surface-mounted locks require slightly less DIY expertise.

7 Choose locks that are easy to operate, so you'll use them.

8 Louvre windows are vulnerable and should be replaced.

9 Locks with high security keys provide greater protection, particularly for high risk areas.

10 Check for optional/standard security features on double-glazed windows.

locking systems which shoot bolts into the frame all around the window to provide a high degree of security. However, if installing double glazing you do need to take care, and you should use a reputable firm. In UPVC and aluminium window units suitable fixings must be used to ensure that the glass cannot be removed externally unless it is actually broken. It is not unknown for external beading to be removed within a matter of seconds, allowing the entire pane of glass to be lifted out. External glazing beads should be 'security glazing beads' which cannot be removed without special tools. Alternatively the glass may be bonded to the frame or secured with glass retaining clips. Internal glazing beads should be designed to resist being dislodged

by external impact.

The last thing you want, of course, is to make your home look like a fortress. Window locks are, in most cases, unobtrusive and these days are available in a wide choice of finishes, including white, brass, chrome and brown, to suit all types of property.

'...choose locks that are easy to use...'

Appearance, obviously, will be a consideration, but far more important is to choose locks which are easy to use and which will offer you the degree of security you require. You may have to pay a bit more for attractive appearance, convenience and security, but at the end of the day it will be money well spent.

▼ Fitting a metal window lock.

1 *We fitted Chubb's 8K106 specially designed for metal windows and supplied with drill bit and self-tapping screws. The key supplied will also operate Chubb's 8K101 for wooden windows. You may need to chisel out some wood from the surrounding frame to fit this type of lock, particularly if the window doesn't shut flush. It's also a good idea to wear safety glasses when drilling metal.*

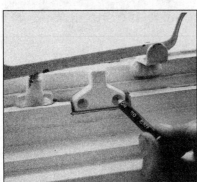

2 *With the window open, mark the position of the lock base unit's (the staple) screw holes, first with a pencil. Note that here the wood surround has been cut away to permit flush fit of the staple on metal frame.*

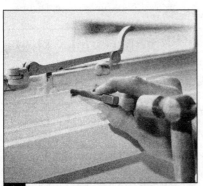

3 *Use a centre punch to make a clearer indentation. This method also gives the drill something to bite into and stops it going off.*

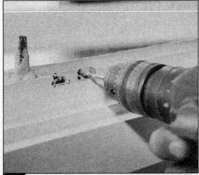

4 *Drill, using the drill bit supplied with the 8K106 lock and the black sleeve also supplied which indicates how far to drill safely without hitting the glass.*

5 *Position the staple and screw into place, using the self-tapping screws provided.*

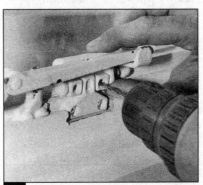

6 *With the window closed, sit the lock body on the staple and mark the fixing screw holes.*

7 *Using the drill plus sleeve, and watching out for the glass, drill the holes for the lock body.*

8 *Screw the lock body into position.*

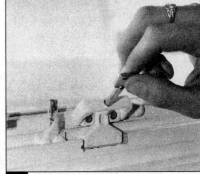

9 *The key locates in the lift up section of the lock body and ...*

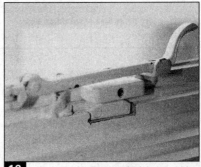

10 *.. is brought down to lock into position.*

▼ Fitting a sash window lock

1 We fitted Chubb's 8013 dual screws. You will need to fit two to a standard sash window. These may not be suitable for older style sash windows if there isn't enough overlap to line up, or they close imperfectly. If that's the case, choose another type of sash lock.

2 To begin, unscrew the removable pin which fits in the bush. The bush will be fixed to the bottom (inside) sash. Making sure the windows are tightly closed, drill two 10mm holes. To ensure you don't hit the glass with the drill, measure the depth of wood to the glass and mark the drill with a piece of masking tape or plastic insulation tape.

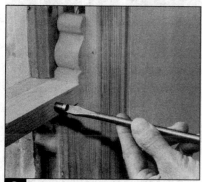

3 Using a large screwdriver, screw in the dual screw.

4 Reverse the windows completely so you can get to the bottom of the outer sash and offer up the face plate, finding the central position.

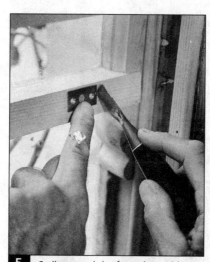

5 Scribe round the face plate with a chisel.

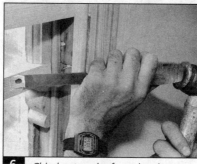

6 Chisel out so the face plate is recessed and flush. Work gently as putty may be loose.

7 Mark position of screws with a bradawl and screw the face plate into place. A ratchet screw driver is useful here.

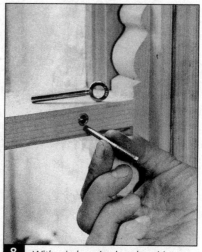

8 With windows in closed position, wind in pin with the key provided.

CHAPTER 9

Guarding with grilles

Secur + DIY grilles are clamped together with security rosettes. Just order the components you need for the size of window.

While a grille or shutter is an obvious visual deterrent to those on the outside, you don't want to feel you're imprisoned behind bars in your own home, and there is no reason at all why you should. There are many very attractive and effective grilles and shutters available, some of which are designed to be DIY fitted quite easily. What you must be sure of is that you are not permanently blocking a possible means of escape in a fire, although not every window need be considered a potential escape route.

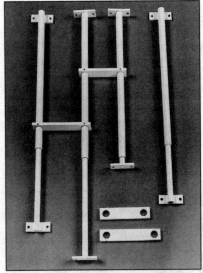

Adjustabars from Baddeley Rose allow you to protect a small or large window and even a glass door.

It may be that you have one or two windows that are just asking for a thief to break in, and window locks simply won't be enough.

A patio door, side window out of view, or a window looking out over a flat roof may all be candidates for the extra protection of a grille or shutter.

This expandable lattice grille can be slid to one side when not required.

It may not be necessary for a grille or shutter to be in the secure position all day and every day. One that slides to one side, concertina fashion may be the answer. Other kits, especially useful for protecting patio doors and French windows, are simply a series of adjustable bars ready for you to assemble and fit, and which can be left to hang down by the side of the door when you are at home. Alternatively, you can buy units which are designed for individual windows and are quickly removable; either they can be unlocked and lifted away or are collapsible.

Some grilles are secured with a padlock, but do ensure this is of good quality and offering key and physical security. Preferable is an integral lock usually with a clutch bolt which when it is in the secure position expands in size. This type of lock is far more likely to be used than having to fiddle with a padlock.

A fixed decorative grille would suit a small side window, but beware, if it is fitted outside, of giving a thief a convenient leg up to another less well protected window, drainpipe or roof.

'...a grille or shutter is an obvious deterrent...'

Many grilles on the market are perfectly suitable for DIY fitting and are produced as made-to-measure kits. They may be in lattice style or be more decorative, such as Adjustabars' Insta-Grills which combine a 'tablet' shaped steel unit with an adjustable steel bar, or the Secur + System which uses traditional wrought iron designs in solid steel, clamped together with specially designed rosettes.

Usually the manufacturer or supplier provides you with a grid to draw the size of the window and instructions on how to work out the components you will need. Alternatively, if you go to a good locksmith or a security centre, their staff may well be prepared to survey the site for you and supply the made up grille for you to fit.

Extra door defence

Often you can adapt such kits to create an outside grille for a complete door or to protect a window panel in the door or to one side, without losing the benefits of

Homeguard grilles can be lifted away from the window and can be fitted with an emergency release lock. Extension arms are telescopic for an accurate fit.

light. Alternatively, there are 'secondary' grille doors on the market which are fitted rather like a full-height gate outside the front door allowing you to open your front door and communicate with callers safely. These can also be used on back doors, to secure porches or alleyways.

A decorative grille could also be used to protect a doorway or patio door. Ensure it does not seal off a potential fire exit, though.

It is always important to ensure that quick exit in an emergency is possible, and the Moat door, for example, has been tested by the London Fire Brigade and is fitted with certain weak-weld points which would enable the fire brigade to release the door rapidly in an emergency. (This precaution is particularly welcome following the tragic cases in recent years of firemen being unable to reach people trapped behind steel security doors.)

The Moat door also has a quick-release locking mechanism which allows immediate exit, and a number of other security features which include a lockable letter box

and continuous hinge (see Chapter 6 for more door security measures). It will fit any existing door and frame set from 6ft 6in by 2ft 6in to 7ft by 3ft, and according to the suppliers it can be fitted in 30 minutes.

Similar doors may be fitted with either a key on both sides, or a key one side and a protected knob on the inside which would prevent the lock being hooked open from outside.

Fixtures and fittings

Materials used for bar-based grilles vary. Avoid hollow tubular bars which are usually easy to saw through. A solid, high grade steel or mild steel bar is ideal, and it is important that the surrounding wall is sound and that the fixings used are of good quality (Fischer and Lintite both produce security screws and nuts, and some kits have them supplied as standard).

If you are making the grille or having it made for you, make sure the joints are arc-welded, rather than MIG-welded which isn't nearly as strong. Check all the joints because they may simply be spot welded.

Bars and grilles should not be fixed to plastic window frames, even those reinforced with metal, mainly because they are too heavy, but also as drilling the frames would probably damage them beyond repair. You could, however, fix them between the window ledges and the window's lintel.

Fixing methods

To fit a grille or bars you must first decide on whether to fit them permanently on the outside, or whether they should be fitted inside and, if necessary, be removable. Inside will be more secure as it will be more difficult for the opportunist burglar to get at fixing points or attack the grille itself.

Instructions should be given with the kit on how to measure up and fix a grille or bars, but here is some guidance on what you will need to do.

Grilles can be face-fixed – that is fixed to the window frame or to the face of the inside wall itself – or reveal fitted – that is fitted to the vertical wall to the side of the window. These will require different fixings, so make sure you tell the manufacturer which you want.

If you are fixing the grille in the reveal you should have a minimum depth of 95mm to allow for the window to be opened if necessary, and you should also check whether the reveals are splayed at an angle and whether there are any likely obstructions causing an odd-shaped opening – like a fanlight or a sink. Sometimes the reveal may bulge in the middle so check the width and the height all the way along and make sure you take the smallest measurement. If it does vary too much you may need to use small packing pieces of hard wood (no more than ⅛th of an inch though).

> ### '...Protection is only as good as the weakest point...'

The most important thing to remember is that any protection is only as good as the weakest point. Often that's the wall or woodwork to which the grille is fixed, so you should make sure that this is sound before you begin. For example, brickwork can become friable and woodwork can rot. It is sometimes possible to use a two-part epoxy cement to hold the wall plug in a brick wall, but deteriorated woodwork should be replaced or some other fixing point found.

If you are fixing the grille to wood, use one-way wood screws – and drill a pilot hole first to ensure you can tighten it easily – it's virtually impossible to reverse them if you make a mistake. The best approach is to get the position right with ordinary screws first and then replace them one at a time with the one-way screws.

If you are attaching the grille to brick, then drill and plug the brickwork avoiding mortar joints, and attach using one-way wood screws. You can treat concrete blockwork in the same way, or you could use expansion studs. Make sure the studs are blocked with armour rings to stop them undoing. Don't use an expanding fastener on plaster board or similar hollow walls. It is best to fasten a hardwood batten to the ceiling or walls and fix the grille to that.

'...Don't use bars which are too long overall...'

Have as many fixing points as possible at regular intervals, which will help hold the grille rigid, and don't try to fix both ends of a rectangular grille while the long sides are free. If you are using bars, make sure they are no more than four inches apart. This recommendation is now incorporated in the Building Regulations for child safety, although the requirement for British Standard is five inches, and insurance specifications are often somewhere between the two.

Don't use bars which are too long overall or not 'tied' together by a horizontal or some other secure fixing. If they are too long they could be sprung or distorted using very little force.

Don't forget if you are fitting bars that you will need one less than the number of spaces and it is helpful to have an even number of spaces so that you can have a centre point fixing.

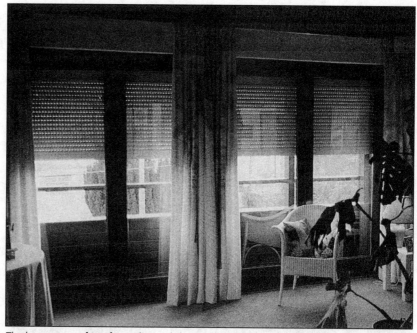
The latest types of 'perforated' metal shutter allow light to filter through to the inside and are available in a variety of colours.

Make sure that the grille or bars you buy are weather resistant – probably epoxy coated – and that any locking devices not only offer good security but are also quick-release if necessary.

The Continental look

Shutters are a completely different concept, not only offering security but also insulation, protection from sunlight damage and reduction in noise. Privacy, too, may be an important element for people living alone. If, for example, you have a holiday home, these can be particularly useful for protection while you are absent. Rather more complicated to install, they will usually be of aluminium, steel or PVC and require a box, the width of the window, to be fitted at the head of the window for the shutter to roll into.

While they can be fitted to bay windows, they are not suitable for bow windows or curved frames.

Shutter operation

Fitted outside, the shutter will be operated from inside, manually using a handle, or motorized using an electric motor which may be operated by remote control or by a switch. If operated electrically, it may also be possible to link them to an alarm system, or a timeswitch for operation at pre-set times. Usually shutters are sold made to order and fitted professionally, and it is also possible to have the shutters supplied complete with window.

Shutters are ideal for holiday homes, providing privacy and security. They can also protect furnishings from fading in the sunlight.

CHAPTER 10

Choosing an alarm system

Some security centres such as Benn Security in Northampton are prepared to put together an alarm kit to suit your home for you to fit. And they give you instructions too!

If you are thinking of fitting an alarm system it may be that you, or perhaps a near neighbour, have been burgled and you may be feeling particularly vulnerable. Or, and we hope this is the case, you feel it would be commonsense to improve your home security with a visible and audible deterrent to prevent you becoming an easy target.

If you are in the first category and are unfortunate enough to have been a victim of a burglary it may be that your insurance company has insisted you have an alarm system professionally installed.

Where to go

There are many alarm installation companies to choose from, and the most successful way of choosing an installer is by recommendation from a satisfied customer. However, it's possible that your insurance company will insist on a company that is regulated by NACOSS, the National Approval Council for Security Systems. NACOSS recognised firms have to install to British Standard 4737 (for wired systems) and comply with the quality assurance standard BS5750. Their systems are regularly inspected and their working procedures must be carried out to the NACOSS code of practice. There are several other associations, including the SSA (Security Services Association) and the Electrical Contractors Association (ECA) which has a security division, the ECA Security Group, with some 50 members who are vetted for suitability and work specifically in the security field, and if you check with your insurers you may well find a company belonging to one of these will be perfectly acceptable.

In addition, if the installation or system proves unsatisfactory, you have an official organization to approach who will take up your complaint and investigate the situation.

You should obtain at least three quotes from reputable installers, and remember that the cheapest may not necessarily be the best value.

What to expect

The system offered to you should include a control panel, possibly a remote keypad, detectors (which may include passive infra-red units,

Linking up to a central monitoring station manned 24 hours a day gives you greater security and peace of mind.

magnetic contacts, vibration sensors, ultrasonic sensors or glass-break detectors), a sounder and bell box with a strobe light attached and personal attack button. You may also be offered the facility to be linked to a central monitoring station, for an annual payment, and a maintenance agreement with the installing company (the latter a requirement of BS4737).

'...Make sure there are no hidden costs...'

The alternative to a wired system is a wire-free radio operated alarm which incorporates all the elements of a wired system but uses a specially allocated frequency (173.255Mhz) to operate. The system should conform to BS6799, the Code of Practice for Wire-Free Systems. These can be professionally installed or you can buy kits (Response, Moss Security, FM Electronics, Smiths Industries and Yale are some names to look for).

Find out whether you are leasing or buying the system outright, whether a maintenance agreement is included in the price and that a 12 month guarantee is offered on parts and labour.

Make sure there are no hidden costs, such as call-out charges or a monitoring service you didn't know about, and find out exactly who is doing the work – whether the company sub-contracts and whether staff are vetted.

Many alarm systems now provide a main control panel and keypads which can be placed in any room from which you can operate the system.

Understand the system

Most important, make sure you understand exactly how the system works once it is installed. The installer should talk you through all the elements of the system and its operation and make sure you can operate it correctly before he leaves.

He should also leave you a card or a manual describing the user facilities and the action you need to take. If you or a member of your family are in any doubt whatsoever make him show you again or explain it more clearly. A very large proportion of false alarms occur simply because the owner doesn't know how the alarm system works.

Make sure you know how the alarm is operated before the installer leaves.

Doing it yourself

If you do not have to worry about insurance company demands (in many cases, and depending on the risk, good locks and membership of a Neighbourhood Watch scheme are enough to satisfy them) and you simply want the peace of mind an efficient alarm system can bring, you may consider installing an alarm yourself.

There are two ways of approaching this, buy a kit or choose the components yourself, as we have done (see Chapter 15). If you buy an alarm in a box from a security centre or one of the major DIY superstores it should comply with BS6707. Do make sure it contains sufficient cable, detectors which will suit your home and protect areas in the right way, and that overall the quality of the components is good. Make sure also that there is a 'Help hotline' in case you get into difficulties. Read the instructions very carefully, particularly those relating to wiring, and check that all the components said to be included are there before you begin.

Another way of choosing an alarm system is to visit your local security centre and ask whether they are prepared to make up an alarm kit for you. This way you are much more likely to arrive at the right solution, get the right advice and be sure of quality goods. Not all security centres offer this service but you may be lucky enough to find one that will either issue you with a set of instructions for fitting or be prepared to answer any queries over the telephone. The system we have chosen to fit was completed in this way.

> ## '... check all components are there before you begin...'

Unfortunately, neither the police nor an alarm monitoring station will accept emergency calls directly from a DIY alarm system although you will need to notify the police the system has been installed and give them the names and addresses of two keyholders. However, some systems have the facility to accommodate an automatic dialling device which will, if the alarm is triggered, repeatedly telephone a series of numbers you have chosen until it receives a reply and is able to send a recorded alarm message. Well worth considering if you have elderly or disabled relatives living in the house.

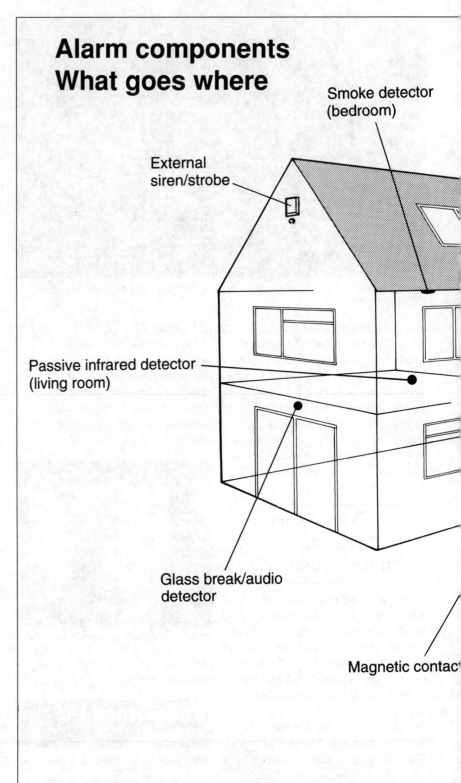

Alarm components What goes where

Smoke detector (bedroom)

External siren/strobe

Passive infrared detector (living room)

Glass break/audio detector

Magnetic contac[t]

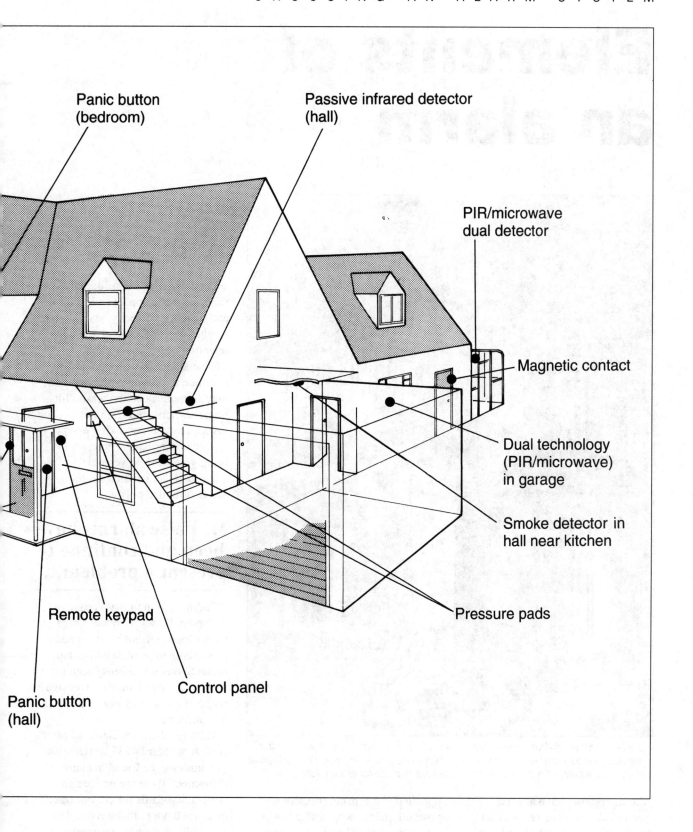

Panic button
(bedroom)

Passive infrared detector
(hall)

PIR/microwave
dual detector

Magnetic contact

Dual technology
(PIR/microwave)
in garage

Smoke detector in
hall near kitchen

Pressure pads

Remote keypad

Control panel

Panic button
(hall)

CHAPTER 11

Elements of an alarm

A bell box warns of an alarm system inside. It should be fixed as high as possible on the front of the house, and somewhere where it is easily visible to the casual passer-by. Fit an additional dummy box if locating it at the front of the house is not practical for cabling reasons.

Alarm systems have altered a good deal in recent years in an effort to help us install and use them more efficiently.

Where a single zone, keyswitch-operated alarm panel (usually an unsightly metal box) with a few magnetic contacts and a pressure mat was once a typical residential kit, today's alarm system is far more sophisticated, has considerably more aesthetic appeal and, if used and installed correctly, should give trouble-free and false alarm-free operation.

False alarms have been and continue to present a problem and may sometimes be the reason for home-owners preferring not to install a system, or taking one out if it proves unreliable. It can also bring you some unwelcome attention from irritated neighbours and disgruntled police.

> ## '…False alarms have been and continue to present a problem…'

Finding a system that is easy to understand, uses tried and tested technology and can be expanded at a later date to provide additional protection is the ultimate aim, but when presented with the extensive range of equipment available it can be confusing.

Although there are elements of British Standard 4737 which relate to features to be found in alarm equipment, there are no specific British Standards for control panels or alarm devices themselves. This may well change in due course as European Standards are being prepared and, for the first time, individual components will be required to meet levels of both performance and construction.

What exists presently are standards for testing introduced by the Loss Prevention Council for an increasing number of products, and this applies in particular to detectors (and a growing number of other security devices). However, these are likely to differ from the European Standards, so to be quite honest the scene is changing rather too rapidly for any one standard to be treated as the ultimate criterion.

Control panels

It is very important that we understand how an alarm system is operated if false alarms are to be avoided. Manufacturers have been making user instructions easier to follow to reduce this risk, and many panels now incorporate a Liquid Crystal Display (LCD) giving plain English step-by-step instructions to guide users through arming, resetting and disarming procedures.

Precautions to prevent tampering are also built in. The control panel

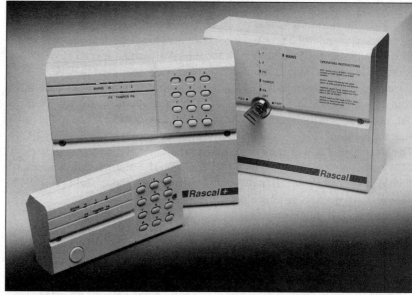

Alarm panel operating options. Choose from a keyswitch, digital code and/or remote keypad.

should incorporate an anti-tamper device to deter an intruder from trying to prise the lid or attack it in any way, and each zone, the wiring and detectors will also be protected from attack, triggering the alarm if there is any interference with the system.

The control panel will also feature a device to set the alarm and turn it off. This may be a keyswitch

(operated by key only) or a digital keypad where you will need to use a code (usually four digits) to carry out any procedure.

Most panels allow you to divide your home into zones and set all or part of the system. It will also enable you to set the entry/exit time delay, that is the amount of time you have to enter and turn off the alarm or set the alarm and close the door behind you. This will vary but can be as little as two seconds to over a minute. Make sure it is set to give you enough time to enter or exit the front door (or your final exit) and disarm/arm the system. The delay will be signalled by a sounder and can instill panic if you have forgotten the code or can't find the key to turn the panel off before the alarm proper sounds!

> ### '...most panels allow you to divide your home into three zones...'

The panel will also contain an alarm sounder of its own and should have a stand-by rechargeable

Everyday operation of an alarm system can be carried out from a neat keypad like this one. An LCD panel gives the user instructions and prompts in simple language.

12v battery which will take over powering the alarm, for at least eight hours, in case of a power cut. (If a primary battery is used as a stand-by it must be able to run the system for four hours if it is to comply with BS4737). If this runs out, however, it will trigger an alarm condition.

The alarm panel will operate using a 240v mains power supply – you should never see a professionally-installed wired alarm panel with a plug attached, it should always be wired in. In addition, alarm panel cabling and existing mains wiring should never be run in the same trunking.

'...have the control panel hidden away...'

The trend today is to have the control panel hidden away, perhaps in a cupboard where it is out of sight and not immediately accessible to an intruder. The system will have one or more remote keypads which can be used for all the day-to-day programming positioned at prominent places around the house. Usually not much larger than a lightswitch, they result in a more attractive and discreet system and a far less daunting piece of equipment to operate.

Detectors

The most popular type of detector to protect complete areas – rooms and hallways – is a passive infra-red device (known as a PIR) explained in greater detail in Chapter 12. Also essential to the system are magnetic contacts (small, flush or surface-mounted devices which protect doors and windows) and one or more personal attack buttons which activate the alarm in an emergency even when it is switched off. P.A.

buttons usually have a red circular or rectangular push button which triggers the alarm and can only be turned off with a special key.

Other devices used may be ultrasonic or, rarely used alone in domestic situations, microwave. Some detectors now combine two of these technologies, typically PIR plus microwave, in an effort to reduce false alarms, and these are proving very successful in difficult environments.

A very important addition to an alarm system is a smoke alarm. There are smoke detectors which can be wired into an alarm system (the latest Building Regulations specify smoke alarms as a standard requirement in new and newly converted homes) or you can buy a battery-operated smoke alarm, easily fitted (see Chapter 20).

Monitoring

Most modern panels are able to provide a means of monitoring the alarm. A special device called a digital communicator is installed in the control panel and is able to send a digitally encoded signal, via a normal telephone line to the central monitoring station. For an alarm to be acted upon and a message to be passed to the appropriate emergency

This particular panel from Menvier Security has a large number of options including engineer remote reset, digital communicator connection and keyswitch or keypad operation.

services (police, fire or medical) the receiving equipment must receive and acknowledge the correct sequence of signals.

Bells and sounders

The bell box can be of polycarbonate or, for high security applications, produced in aluminium and treated steel and powder coated. (BS4737 requires the housing to be of 1.2mm mild steel, 1mm stainless steel, 3mm polycarbonate or equivalent.) Bell boxes should be fixed as high as possible on the house front and may now include a strobe light which will continue to flash after the bell has stopped ringing after the statutory 20 minute maximum period. (See below.) The alarm should also trigger if the bell box is tampered with, and this is brought about by the fitting of a self-actuating bell module (SAB) which, if the mains cable is disconnected or cut, will bring in its stand-by battery to sound the alarm. Bell boxes are also increasingly being fitted with a separate timed cut out (from two to 18 minutes approximately) so that if the SAB took over operation of the sounder, it would not continue to ring, unless automatically reset by the system, for longer than 20 minutes at a time.

'...local authorities have the power to fine owners...'

There is a good reason for this. If an alarm is considered to be constituting a statutory offence under The Environmental Protection Act 1990 (Section 80) local authorities have the power to fine the owners of the alarm up to £5,000. The Noise and Nuisance Bill of 1993 increases these powers to enable officers to enter premises under certain conditions.

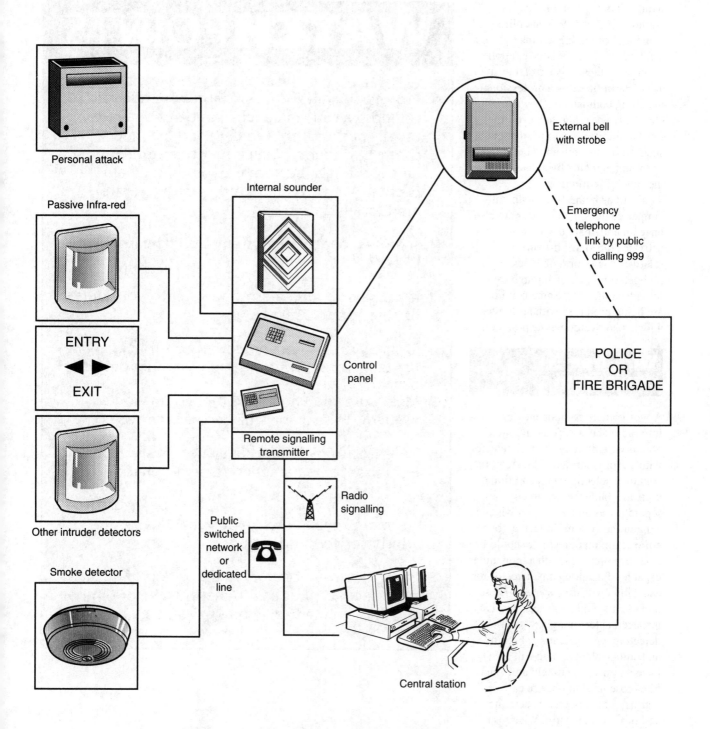

Personal attack

Passive Infra-red

ENTRY
◄ ►
EXIT

Other intruder detectors

Smoke detector

Internal sounder

Control panel

Remote signalling transmitter

Radio signalling

Public switched network or dedicated line

Central station

External bell with strobe

Emergency telephone link by public dialling 999

POLICE OR FIRE BRIGADE

A TYPICAL PROFESSIONALLY INSTALLED ALARM SYSTEM

In addition, the London Local Authorities Act 1991 can oblige owners of offending alarms to fit cut off devices. This, of course, applies as much to those systems DIY fitted as an alarm fitted by a professional installing company, so beware. Generally speaking, however, the local authorities try to resolve any such problems amicably, but it has been implemented by at least one at the time of writing.

As well as being fitted with anti-tamper devices, bell boxes may also have an anti-foam device which activates the alarm if foam, a relatively new form of attack, is pumped into the box through the louvres at the side. Some bell boxes are being produced without louvres which also overcome the problem.

Wire-free equipment

A word on the components for wire-free radio alarms. You can now obtain virtually any form of detector with a radio alarm, and kits tend to contain a selection with additional units available for you to buy separately as and when you wish to expand the system. In fact, a good radio alarm manufacturer should be able to supply you with a transmitter capable of adapting any detector for use with a wire-free system. These include magnetic contacts, passive infra-red detectors, glass-break detectors, personal attack buttons and smoke alarms. You will also have a remote hand-held unit (just like those used to operate car alarms) which is used to activate and turn off the alarm. What you won't need is much in the way of cable and cable clips!

WATCHPOINTS

1 A professionally installed alarm system should comprise a control panel, a range of detectors, usually passive infra-red (PIR) and magnetic contacts, a sounder/bell box with a strobe and a personal attack button or two. It should also be possible for it to communicate with a central monitoring station.

2 A professional alarm system should be installed to BS4737.

3 If your alarm false-alarms persistently you could be fined up to £5,000.

4 Ensure your system's detectors, control panel and the bell box are fitted with anti-tamper devices.

5 Make sure you know how the system works properly. False alarms may occur otherwise.

6 Wire-free (radio) alarms may not satisfy your insurance company's requirements. Check first.

7 You can now choose to operate your system from a remote keypad or a keyswitch. Choose whichever you find easier.

8 In no circumstances should the wiring of an alarm system, which uses a 240v mains power supply, be run in the same trunking as existing mains wiring.

CHAPTER 12

Means of detection

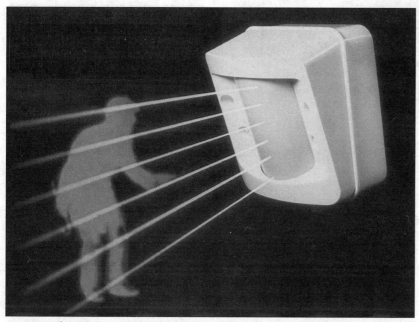

A passive infra-red detector is triggered by a person moving across a fan-shaped pattern of zones.

There are numerous detection devices available, and choosing the right one to protect a particular area isn't always easy. There is a whole range of circumstances to take into account – the size of the room, what's in it, even how it is constructed as well as what's outside or even across the road.

You may need one or more types of detectors in any one area – for example, there are bound to be doors and windows to protect as well as the room itself. There may also be very large areas of glass, such as a patio door, draughts or heating which may make it difficult to site certain types of detectors and you may have pets in the house which will mean careful positioning and directing of the detection pattern.

Magnetic contacts

The most basic detection device is a magnetic contact (or reed switch). The reed switch, fitted to the fixed section of the opening (door or window), is held in the closed position by a magnet which is fitted to the moving part. When the magnetic force is removed by the protected door or window being pushed ajar, the switch opens, cutting off the current if the alarm is set, and triggering the alarm. Contacts should be positioned carefully. They should trigger the alarm when the door or window is opened at a point within four inches. They are best positioned at the top of the door, with the contact flush mounted in the architrave a few inches in from the catch side of the door. Surface mounted contacts, easier to fit, are often provided with DIY kits. One is sufficient for each opening but it is important they are installed on well fitted and sound frames or you may end up with false alarms.

Detecting shock

Shock sensors are available in a wide variety of forms – inertia, piezo electric and vibration. These are designed specifically to detect force and sounds like splintering wood in the area that is being protected. Once again, it is very important to position these correctly.

Pinpoint the most obvious point of attack, where the intruder may gain access with the least noise; on a window this is likely to be close to the handle where the intruder may try to lever the window open. The sensor should be mounted on the window frame and set at a sensitivity level where it will not trigger the alarm other than when a real attack is detected. You should also check that other sources of vibration like a subway close by or railway lines will not affect the device.

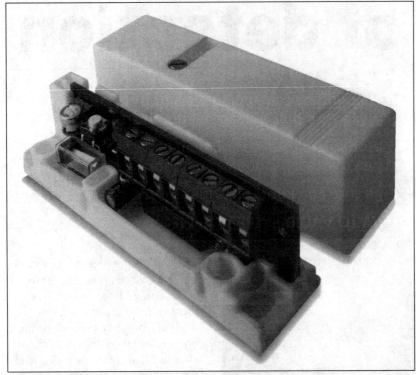

A vibration detector. This is the well-known Viper.

Independent tests on a Viper vibration sensor fitted correctly, for example, showed that it didn't react when the window was tapped on, a door knocked on or a tennis ball thrown against an adjacent partition. Even a masonry drill used on an external wall about a metre away did not activate the alarm.

Glass break

The problem with glass break detectors is that not all types will work effectively on double-glazing. There are basically two methods. Self adhesive foil strips, or tape carrying a current, can be applied to the glass. Breaking the tape triggers the alarm (although even a hairline crack can produce this and cause false alarms).

A single strip should be applied no nearer to the edge of the glass than 12 inches (300mm); the glass is held firmly and any nearer may not shear the foil. If a rectangular pattern, rather than a single strip, is used, then it must be applied no less than 50mm and no more than 100mm in from the edge. It also has to be varnished to insulate it from moisture.

'...Laminated glass may reduce effectiveness...'

The other method is based on audio (ultrasonic) technology and enables the detector to recognize the particular frequency of breaking glass. Here it is important not to position a detector close to air vents or doors where the noise of glass breaking outside may be picked up, or placed near a telephone. Laminated glass may also reduce the effectiveness of the device. However, C & K's FlexGuard system is able to measure the flexing effect of a blow on glass as well as the frequency it generates, so glass breaking outside should not create an alarm. Their units, unlike others on the market, can also be used to protect several windows at a time, rather than having to fit a device to each window separately.

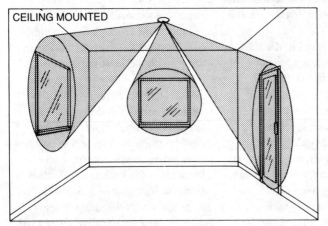
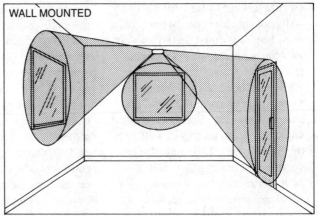

Glass break detector based on audio technology.

Panic buttons

A personal or panic attack button has to be deliberately activated manually by the person in the house. Usually it's by pressing a hand button, although it is possible to obtain adapted units which can be activated with a knee or foot (often used by retailers, banks and similar premises or by the disabled). The unit activates the alarm via a special 24 hour circuit even when the alarm has not been set and can only be turned off and reset with a special key. P.A. buttons should be sited as discreetly as possible, and are often positioned just inside the front door and by the bed.

Pressure mats

These aren't widely used today but are often included in DIY kits. Available in various sizes they are suitable for protecting staircases, (one may be positioned at the top or bottom of the stairs), immediately inside patio doors or other possible points of forced entry. Pressure mats incorporate an 'open' circuit which is completed when the intruder steps on the mat. It is necessary to have the underlay of the carpet cut away to avoid the mat showing – an expensive measure if you have to employ a carpet fitter to do it for you.

'...Pressure mats are often included in DIY kits...'

You should be careful not to place furniture on them by mistake, or to install them on uneven floors or on top of carpet tacks or other sharp objects which could pierce the plastic covered mat. They are prone to wear, which could result in a false alarm, and if placed under a thin carpet may eventually show.

Passive infra-reds

Various movement detectors have been developed, the most popular of which is the PIR (passive infra-red detector). PIRs look for a change in energy, in this case the infra-red produced by humans, and will trigger an alarm if the source of the energy (body heat) moves across a fan-shaped series of zones. In older PIRs strong sunlight could trigger the detector but most now incorporate a dual sensor system which has zones on two levels and if the source of heat is static it should be ignored. Only if the heat source moves across the PIR's range should an alarm be triggered.

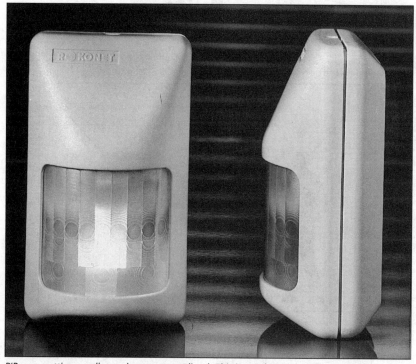

PIRs are getting smaller and more streamlined. This is a Rokonet detector.

PIRs are supplied in a choice of ranges – long, wide, corridor and curtain – and can cover as little as three metres up to as much as 40 metres. The long and corridor lenses have fewer zones across a narrow width, but can detect as far as 30 or 40 metres away. The curtain type is suitable for protecting doors or windows and particularly large areas of glass. The pattern is a vertical one running parallel with the area to be protected and creates a solid protected zone. These are also useful if the house is open plan with a mezzanine floor for the bedrooms. The pattern would be able to detect anyone jumping off the mezzanine or a break-in through the ceiling from a loft.

Pet alley patterns allow an area at ground level for pets to walk around safely without triggering the alarm. However, this means that an intruder crawling by would not be detected and it also doesn't prevent pets jumping on to furniture and setting off the alarm. The only way really to avoid this risk is to keep dogs and cats, and any other warm-blooded animals likely to roam, confined to one room where a movement detector is not in use. A room protected by contacts or shock detectors would also be pet false alarm free.

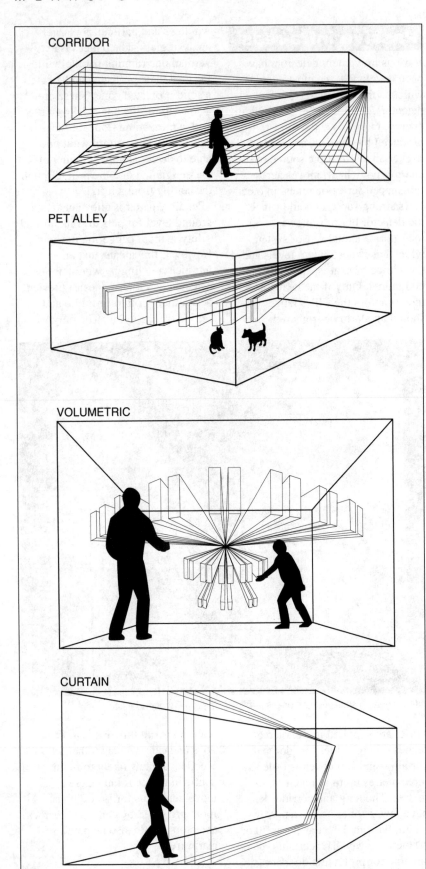

CORRIDOR

PET ALLEY

VOLUMETRIC

CURTAIN

A passive infra-red detector suitable for domestic situations, the Apollo from Guardall.

Some passive infra-red detector manufacturers now supply masks with a standard unit which enables the person installing to modify the coverage pattern, preventing the PIR from seeing 'hot spots'. This means they can be adapted to different circumstances rather than having to buy a completely different unit.

PIR's are susceptible to moisture – ensure that any used to control exterior lighting, for example, are IP rated – a grading system which shows the level of resistance to dirt and moisture; they should be at least IP44 to IP55. Insects can cause havoc if they make their way into the casing or even walk across the sensor if the optics used aren't sealed. PIRs should also be resistant to RFI (radio frequency interference).

Ultrasonic and microwave

An ultrasonic is an active, rather than a passive detector. This type of detector is particularly useful in a glass conservatory or perhaps to

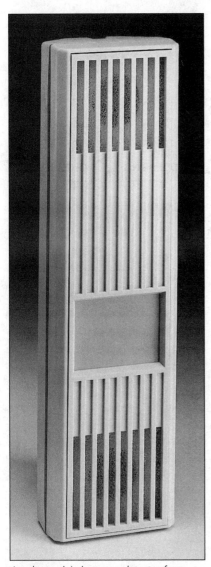

An ultrasonic/microwave detector from Aritech.

(known as the Doppler effect) and an alarm signalled. Once prone to false alarms, a new method of signal processing incorporated in ultrasonics has reduced the problem and they can be effective if used correctly. However, draughts or the effects of air conditioning equipment can affect ultrasonics.

Similarly, microwave alone has limited domestic uses, particularly in homes where its capacity to cover large areas is not widely used, and the disadvantage of using radio waves which can penetrate glass and brick and even water running down a plastic drain pipe could activate the alarm. They can be particularly tricky to site, and should really only be installed by an expert.

protect an indoor swimming pool, as the energy it transmits is easily contained within a small area; a PIR is susceptible to sun and headlights penetrating the glass and may cause false alarms in these circumstances. The device generates a low frequency of about 20KHz and incorporates a receiver and transmitter allowing it to compare the received energy with the original transmitted frequency. Stationary objects, such as furniture, will return the same frequency but if an intruder is moving within the area a changed frequency will be returned

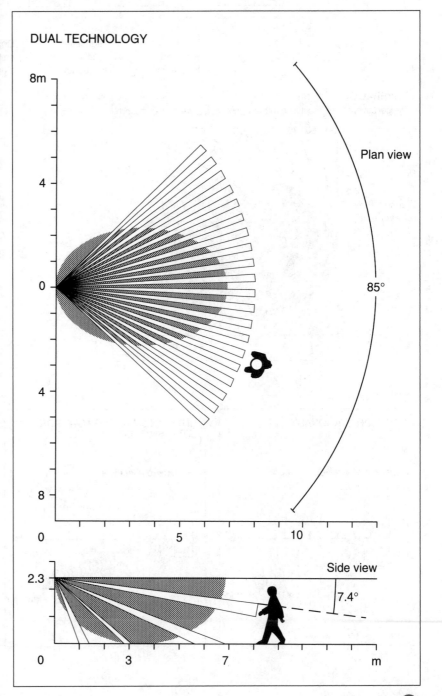

12
M E A N S O F D E T E C T I O N

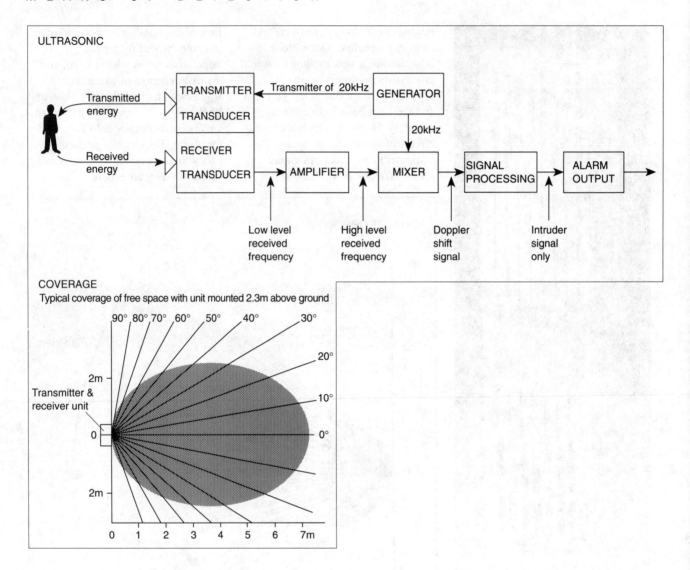

ULTRASONIC

TRANSMITTER TRANSDUCER

Transmitted energy

Received energy

RECEIVER TRANSDUCER

Transmitter of 20kHz

GENERATOR

20kHz

AMPLIFIER

MIXER

SIGNAL PROCESSING

ALARM OUTPUT

Low level received frequency

High level received frequency

Doppler shift signal

Intruder signal only

COVERAGE

Typical coverage of free space with unit mounted 2.3m above ground

Transmitter & receiver unit

MICROWAVE

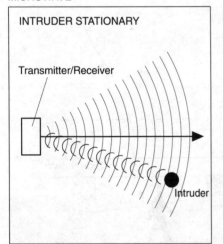

INTRUDER STATIONARY

Transmitter/Receiver

Intruder

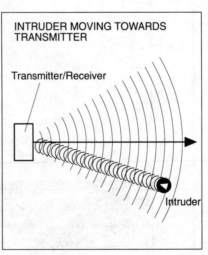

INTRUDER MOVING TOWARDS TRANSMITTER

Transmitter/Receiver

Intruder

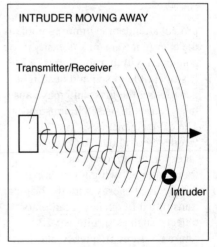

INTRUDER MOVING AWAY

Transmitter/Receiver

Intruder

FALSE ALARM HAZARDS

Source	PIR	Ultrasonic	Microwave
Change in temperature	Can be a problem	Minor problem	Usually OK
Curtains and other absorbent material	OK except if swaying	Problem	OK except if swaying
Pets	Can be a problem	Problem	Problem
Running water in plastic drainpipes	OK	OK	Problem
Thin walls/glass penetration	OK	OK	Problem
Draughts/air movement	Usually OK	Problem	OK
Sunlight	Can be a problem	OK	OK
Phone ringing, planes, and similar noise	OK	Problem	OK (if old style bell phone)

Dual detectors

A fairly recent advance is the combination of microwave (or ultrasonic) and PIR technology in one detector. If, for example, you have a detector (perhaps a PIR) which is persistently false alarming because of the surroundings, a dual detector may well solve it. A number of manufacturers are now producing these, and although more costly than a single technology unit they have been very effective in reducing false alarms as each technology is able to 'talk' to the other, checking that both sensors have detected an alarm condition before actually triggering the alarm.

A range of dual technology detectors from C+K.

WATCHPOINTS

HOW TO AVOID FALSE ALARMS:

1 Be sure you know how the alarm is operated.

2 Make sure all windows and doors are secured properly before leaving home.

3 Make sure that sensors are not obstructed with anything placed immediately in front of them.

4 Do not bring in new sources of heat, movement or sound without checking with the alarm installer first.

5 Always use the same point of entry. Switching off the alarm is the first thing to do.

6 Always go back to the alarm installer who fitted the system if you want alterations made.

7 Be careful not to damage or move wiring or detectors, particularly when decorating.

8 If you have a false alarm, let the alarm company know straight away.

9 Take up the offer of regular maintenance checks carried out by the installer. A small charge is better than a false alarm, and the police may refuse to come out if too many false alarms are reported.

CHAPTER 13

Calling for help

In an emergency it is reassuring to know that your alarm will bring help.

There are several ways to alert others to an emergency, whether it's a burglary, someone in trouble, a medical crisis or even a fire.

The obvious way is to have an alarm sounder outside the house, and a flashing light to indicate there has been an alarm situation. In such a 'bells-only' system, giving the alarm locally, the light will continue to alert passers-by after the statutory 20 minutes during which the siren is allowed to sound.

However, it may be that you are a long way from neighbours and there are very few passers-by, in which case a lot of noise may not bring the right response fast enough. Or perhaps, you may feel people are so used to hearing alarms going off they tend to ignore them. As an

alternative, or perhaps in addition to, a bells-only system, it is possible for you to 'sound the alarm' silently. This also has the advantage of keeping the burglar in the dark as he will be unaware that he has triggered the alarm.

Monitoring stations

If you have a modern alarm system, the control panel can easily be linked to a central monitoring station. This usually involves a special device fitted in the control panel called a digital communicator, which in turn can automatically 'pick up' your BT telephone line and send a digitally coded message indicating the emergency (intruder,

medical or fire) to the receiver at the monitoring station. This enables staff who are present at the station 24 hours a day to call the appropriate emergency service and get them to you as fast as possible.

'...it is possible to sound the alarm silently...'

The alarm is triggered in exactly the same way as an audible system – by detectors, panic buttons or smoke alarms. One thing to remember about digital communicators is that they 'dial' the telephone number of the monitoring station to get through. Inevitably problems may arise when telephone numbers change, or when BT decides to change the national dialling codes by adding a digit or two, something which is due to take place in April 1995. This means that, if you have a digital communicator fitted, it will be necessary for your alarm installer to reprogram it. If done in good time this should not entail a special (costly) visit, but could be done at the six-monthly maintenance check (necessary for any system with remote monitoring facilities). Don't be misled by stations who claim that using 0891 or similar 'chat-line' type numbers will avoid this

A central station offers 24 hour monitoring for your alarm system. It can receive alarm calls via a digital communicator installed in your alarm panel, Telecom Red CARE or Paknet signalling systems.

problem – they could cost you more. However, Linkline 0345 or 0800 numbers do not incur extra cost and will not be changed.

To fit a digital communicator the equipment and initial connection will cost £100 to £125, and you will need two maintenance visits from the alarm company (around £60) and there will be an annual monitoring fee of around £65 to £75.

If you decide to go for Red CARE (see below), the initial equipment and installation charge will be nearer £250, with the maintenance visits and monitoring fee as above, plus monitoring by the BT network of £109 a year which you will be billed for by BT.

In both cases, don't forget you will also need BT to fit a block terminal. This involves an engineer call-out and will total around £63 plus VAT.

High risk services

While the digital communicator is the most popular way to connect homes to a monitoring station, they may be vulnerable in higher risk areas. If the telephone line is cut or tampered with the alarm signal will not be able to get through. To overcome this problem there is an alternative system offered by BT called Telecom Red CARE. This service continuously monitors the existing telephone line, and if the line is put out of action there is an alternative secure route for the signal to follow, a parallel network which duplicates the signalling. There is no need to have a second telephone line – all the user is aware of is a small box (known as STU, Subscriber Terminal Unit) linked to the alarm panel.

'...ensure your system is installed to BS4737...'

One further advance is the use of radio to signal alarm conditions to monitoring stations. Paknet is a system based around the x-25 radio network. A radio pad fitted with an anti-tamper switch and a concealed aerial is fitted in your home, and the system automatically tunes into the best of 14 frequencies to send the signal. The great advantage of Paknet is that there are no telephone lines involved. The whole system can be set up very quickly and an alarm is received within seconds. If your premises are high risk, this alternative or BT's Red CARE system may be suggested.

'...If you have persistent false alarms police response can be withdrawn...'

If you do decide to have your alarm monitored by a central station, ensure that your system is installed to BS4737, that the station being used complies with and operates under BS5979 and that you have two keyholders with telephones available who can respond to an alarm if you are not there within 20 minutes. Although personal attack alarms are immediately passed by the central station to the police, other types of alarm have to be verified by the station by a telephone call to the user before they are passed to the police (which would be in the case of some indication of duress, no reply or some other cause for suspicion). The alarm then has to be reset by an engineer, although an increasing number of control panels enable the system to be reset from the central station if, for example, it was a false alarm and the system does not have a fault and require an engineer to put it right.

If you have persistent false alarms (over six in any 12 months) police response can be withdrawn, except for personal attacks. Response is usually restored after three months if no further false alarms occur.

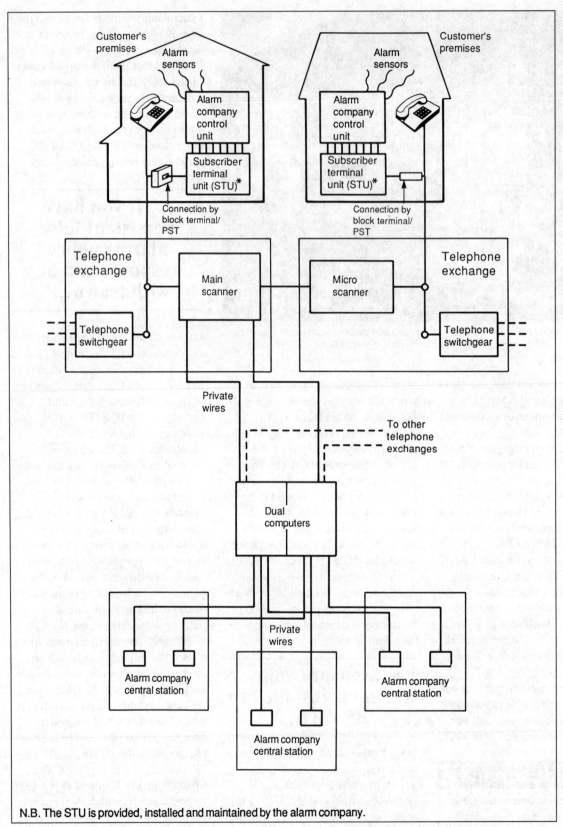

N.B. The STU is provided, installed and maintained by the alarm company.

How Telecom Red CARE works. It uses a signalling system which is duplicated to ensure the alarm gets through to the central monitoring station.

Looking after the elderly

It may not be necessary to go to these lengths to send your alarm signal to someone who can respond quickly. For those who are concerned about elderly relatives living on their own, for example, there are a number of devices which can be linked to the telephone and will automatically dial several numbers until they receive a reply and can send a pre-recorded message.

A1's Communicator, for example, is a unit designed to link up with a BT line and can be connected to any control panel. Resembling an alarm panel, it will signal intruder, fire or personal attack and communicate with up to four pre-programmed telephone numbers of your choice – perhaps a car phone or an office. The numbers can be changed whenever necessary and you can record and change your own message.

> ### '...A number of devices can be linked to the telephone...'

Smiths Industries also produce an emergency telephone dialler which plugs straight into a BT-approved wall socket and can sit neatly under the telephone. Mains operated, but with battery back-up in case of a power failure, it will dial up to six telephone numbers if triggered by a hand-held radio transmitter. The recipient has to make a return call to the phone number given by the message to ensure further dialling stops, a feature which overcomes the problem of emergency calls getting through to an answering machine.

Warden-controlled systems

If you have relatives living in sheltered homes or similar cared for accommodation, you will probably have come across warden-controlled alarm systems where a special panic button or radio-operated pendant can raise the alarm by communicating directly with a central emergency control room in the building or monitoring station. These systems are often provided by the local authority, but if the person's home does not come under their control it is still possible to have a similar system installed, even without a normal intruder alarm at the premises.

Tunstall Lifeline and Scantronic's Homelink involve the use of a special telephone which acts as a normal phone and incorporates a microphone for two-way hands-free speech. They can automatically dial pre-programmed phone numbers of relatives and friends and allow the user to answer the phone without having to get up.

Both systems can be expanded with various detectors (smoke, passive infra-red) which are wire-free, communicating with the main console by radio.

Systems that use an automatic dialling system triggered by a panic button or pendant to alert a central monitoring station or warden control centre are ideal for the elderly or infirm.

CHAPTER 14

Why wire-free?

Often professionally installed and complying with Class III of BS6799, Scantronic's 4600 system has a main control panel, and a choice of passive infra-red detectors, magnetic contacts, vibration sensors, panic buttons, remote set/unset unit and smoke detectors.

Traditional alarm systems are normally hard-wired, that is communication between the main panel, detectors and alarm bell box is via special security cabling and powered by the mains electrical supply. Radio, however, means you can install an alarm faster and more easily and you can take it with you if you move.

In the mid-1980s the Department of Trade and Industry issued a special radio frequency on which alarm systems could operate, 173.225MHz. The majority of radio alarms now use this frequency, although there are some exceptions. The legal frequencies include spot frequency 458.825 and bandwidth 417.9-418MHz, but beware of anything else – products which haven't been approved for operation in these frequencies are illegal. Approved equipment will carry a label with an identifying number.

The British Standard Code of practice for Wire-free intruder alarm systems (BS6799: 1986) grades complete systems in line with the degree of monitoring they achieve. Class 1 requires detectors/devices to transmit an alarm signal, and for low battery warning to be given. Class II should, in addition to these requirements, be able to indicate at the control panel which of the detectors/devices have been triggered. Class III is for more sophisticated systems which are able to monitor the transmission channels and detect any interference which could jam the signal for over 30 seconds providing a fault indication at the controller.

Class IV and V, as well as fulfilling the requirements of all the other grades, are for higher risk alarm installations and are known as 'supervised' inasmuch as the signals are periodically checked by the system.

Other British Standards you may see referred to include the Electrical Safety Standard BS3535 and the BS for intruder alarm systems for consumer installation (that is, DIY), BS6707. Anything else is probably not very relevant and mentioned merely to impress.

'...Radio means you can install an alarm faster and more easily...'

You should also check with your insurance company before installing a wire-free system in preference to a wired system. They may insist on a wired system if the risk is high or they have specifically asked you to install an alarm. (A sixth class has recently been approved by the Association of Chief Police Officers (ACPO) which, in meeting their requirements, will be responded to by police if an alarm is triggered.)

Advantages

The big advantage of wire-free systems is that they are simple and quick to install. There is no need to disrupt your decor, channel out plastered walls or chisel woodwork. If you move, you can take a wire-free system with you, or if you extend the house or move things around it is a simple task to alter the position of detectors and other devices. Setting up the more sophisticated systems (such as those from Scantronic, FM Electronics and Electronics Line) may require professional installer help, but if the level of risk isn't too high and the likelihood of interference or tampering with the system relatively low there is no reason why you should not install a wire-free radio operated system yourself.

Ready-to-go kits, such as those from Response, Smiths Industries or

Another kit from Moss Security is widely available and reasonably priced.

Moss Security, all operate on 173.225MHz and use much the same setting-up procedures. They are becoming more sophisticated and can now include a wide choice in detectors (including smoke, passive infra-red, magnetic contacts, glass-break and panic alarm) as well as a wired bell box and even an automatic emergency dialler. All the detectors will be fitted with a battery and a transmitter. This sometimes makes them a little larger

than the traditional detectors, and early systems had the aerial outside which made them look rather bulky. However, most today integrate the aerial in the casing, which also prevents them being tampered with or moved by mistake.

'...certain things may reduce the range...'

The range of a radio alarm should easily cover a typical house – about 300 feet in 'free air space' is often quoted. However, you must be aware that certain things may reduce the range of the signal – low-power, walls and steel-girders, for example, may prevent a signal getting through. Other things to watch for are metal water pipes and mains cables, and you should avoid mounting the control unit close to computers or fax machines. It is a good idea to do a 'walk-test' before finally positioning the sensors, and most systems will allow you to do this to check that the system works effectively before finalizing it. Look out for 'dead' spots. These can be overcome by moving the transmitting unit a few inches. FM Security and Scantronic, whose

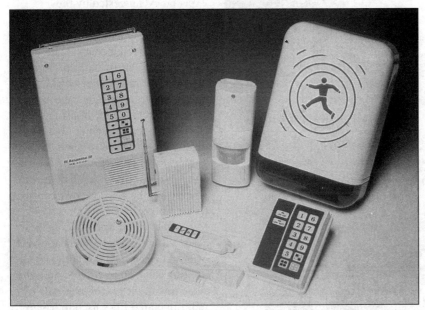

The Response RE3000, designed for DIY installation, can be expanded from this basic kit to cover more than one zone.

systems are to the higher Grade III, produce a portable test receiver for this task.

The control panel will have to be plugged in (kits usually provide a transformer for this purpose) or wired into the mains, with a stand-by 12v battery which will maintain the system if there is a power cut. (Systems complying with BS6799 must not use a plug and socket for connection to the mains.)

Setting the house code

The usual practice is for a house code to be set which will be repeated throughout the system where a transmitter is incorporated with a detector. This is usually achieved quite simply with a series of small switches in each unit; some systems will also allow you to set a zone code so each detector or group of detectors can be allocated to a different zone enabling you to quickly identify which has alarmed.

The system may have several zones allowing you to part-alarm the house, and it should have a variable

Smiths Wireless control unit can be table top or wall mounted.

entry/exit setting to give you enough time to enter and exit before the alarm is triggered. Detectors should also trigger a low-battery warning light at the control panel, and it is important that you regularly change the batteries according to the life-expectancy suggested by the manufacturers. When you are setting the code in the detectors, make sure that the control panel is switched off, as the detector will have an anti-tamper device fitted and will therefore trigger the alarm when you remove the housing!

Wire-free alarms can easily be extended. A workshop, shed or garage could be brought into the system by simply fitting a detector and setting the same house code (preferably a magnetic contact rather than a PIR as these can be susceptible to changes in heat levels or bright lights). And security lighting can also be brought into the system with the use of external radio-operated PIRs used to trigger existing lamps.

Wire-free alarm systems are particularly easy to install.

CHAPTER 15

DIY alarms

(A1 Security do several comprehensive kits) available from DIY multiples or security specialists, or you can visit the latter for advice and purchase individual components to make up an alarm system that will exactly meet your specific requirements.

'...By buying components individually you can achieve a more sophisticated system...'

Depending on how much you pay, a standard DIY kit may include only the absolute basics for perimeter protection, such as a simple control panel, bell box, magnetic contacts for doors and windows, and possibly a panic button. It may not offer devices to detect movement inside the home. By buying components individually you can achieve a much more sophisticated DIY system which, for example, incorporates a superior control panel offering a number of zones, passive infra-red detectors to sense movement, and vibration detectors. Obviously price will determine the final system – but the result should

Professional alarm installations offer a number of benefits. The installation should be neat and tidy, with wires tucked away out of sight. The work involved should cause little inconvenience and upheaval and, provided the installer shows you how to operate the alarm correctly, you should not have problems with false alarms. But professional installations can be expensive and, if cost is prohibitive, a competent DIY enthusiast with knowledge of wiring and electrical work, should be able to install a fairly comprehensive do-it-yourself intruder alarm in a weekend.

With DIY alarms you have two options. You can either buy a kit

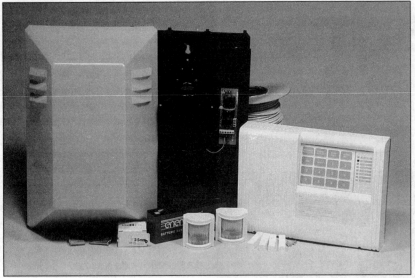

With DIY alarms you can either buy a kit like the expandable AJ600 from A1 Security, or you can purchase individual components to make up a system.

be a professional alarm system without the installation costs.

So, where do you start? First you will need to draw a floor plan showing both upstairs and downstairs, and all windows and doors. Think about your particular requirements. If you live in a flat or bungalow, you may only require what is known as a single zone system, with windows and doors protected, and a panic button by the bed. If the property has an upstairs you will probably require at least two zones which can be controlled independently. This would enable you to secure the downstairs only, when the family is asleep at night, or would allow you to alarm all the external doors and windows, whilst disarming interior protection devices when you are at home during the day.

'...First, draw a floor plan...'

Think also about other family members; if there are children in the house you may want a control panel that is particularly easy to operate. Or if there are pets you will not want a PIR guarding areas where they have free access when the alarm is set.

The number of zones which your control panel offers will, to a large extent, govern the level of protection which your system provides. If, for example, you want to install several passive infra-red detectors to protect a number of rooms, each will require a separate zone. The installation sequence at the end of this chapter uses a six-zone panel for greater flexibility and ease of installation.

Once you have some idea of your particular requirements, take your floor plan along to a specialist security centre where experienced staff will be able to discuss your requirements in detail and also point out vulnerable areas that you may not have considered. It may be worth phoning and arranging an appointment first to make sure an experienced installer has time to talk you through your options. He will be able to show you where best to site the detectors, bearing in mind the concealment of cables and ease of fixing the detectors. He will also point out potential sources of false alarms.

A security centre may be prepared to offer advice, based on your floor plan, and show you a range of alarm components from different manufacturers. If you choose to install a DIY kit it should conform to BS6707, the British Standard for Intruder Alarm Systems for Consumer Installation. A BS6707 approved alarm should have an audible alarm which will cut out after 20 minutes; failure to limit the amount of noise emitted by an alarm system can lead to prosecution for noise nuisance. If your alarm is made up of individual components it will not conform to BS6707, as this is only for complete systems. Components, however, should conform to BS4737; in which case you should not come across problems with component compatibility when installing your system. You should not attempt to start installing a system until you have ascertained the components you require, and the siting of each.

There are a number of points to bear in mind when considering

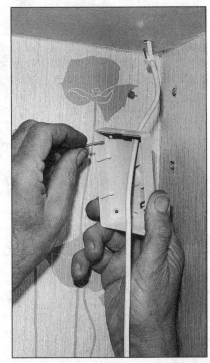

Site components carefully.

siting to reduce the risk of false alarms. Make sure that the distance between the control unit and your exit door can be easily covered in the time delay between setting the alarm and the system becoming operational. Keep the control panel accessible, but out of reach of young children. Make sure doors and windows fit securely and do not rattle or vibrate in response to high winds or heavy traffic. If there is a 'nightset' zone (i.e., leaving the upper floor unarmed for night-time convenience), make sure the family know where they can and cannot go, and banish pets from armed areas. The ideal mains supply for an intruder alarm system is direct from the consumer unit, on its own fused spur. This can be prepared before beginning the installation but must not be connected until installation is complete. The control should not be wired into a lighting circuit, or a ring main into which appliances with electric motors are plugged. Motors generate mains surges which can cause the microprocessor to momentarily malfunction. If in any doubt about the installation, contact a competent electrician.

Locate the control panel as close to the mains supply as possible.

Installation

Once you have decided on the position of each detection device, you then need to plan the route of the cables from those devices and the external sounder to the control panel. DIY kits are often supplied with cable, mounting screws, wall plugs and cable clips, but by buying extra cable you can achieve a more professional installation, running concealed cables the long way round rather than having short, visible cables which will make your alarm installation look amateur. Easily concealed under carpets, cables should be run alongside gripper rods to protect them from being crushed. Alternatively there

may be a gap under the skirting board, wide enough to accept the cable. They can also be run under floorboards or buried in the wall, but test the circuit before covering the cables.

For ground floor movement sensors, cable can be dropped down from the first floor. Visible cable should be concealed with plastic trunking, or secured with clips at frequent intervals (every 150mm).

The control panel should be firmly fixed to the wall with the mains supply taken, if possible, directly from the consumer fuse box and via a 2 amp fused spur. Door contacts can be fitted anywhere along the opening edge of the door or on the top of the door within 150mm of the opening edge. Always use a surface mounted contact on the final exit door. Passive infra-red detectors should be fitted to a flat surface in the top corner of a room, in a position where they will deter intruders and protect a likely point of entry. They must not be sited over a heat source, nor looking directly at a window, and the alarm cable must not be run near mains cables. Do not use PIRs where large

air movements are likely, such as a garage, or where warm air heating is in use. Each PIR must be connected to its own zone, with no other devices on that zone. Personal attack buttons should be sited near the front door, and/or in a bedroom, and out of the reach of small children. If there is more than one personal attack button on the circuit, they should be wired in series.

'...Each PIR must be connected to its own zone...'

The sounder enclosure, or bell box, should be fitted in a prominent position where it cannot easily be tampered with. Its visibility can be extremely effective in deterring intruders. The bell box should contain a self-actuating bell which will power the sounder in the event of its disconnection from the control panel. The connecting cable from the sounder should be taken through the wall directly behind the enclosure and run to the control panel.

Instructions for your DIY system, or control panel, should take you through testing of the complete system during and after installation. This will ensure that components are installed and operating correctly, and will minimize the risk of false alarms. Once the installation is operational, make sure each member of the family knows how to use it. Appoint two keyholders who will be able to see to your system should an alarm condition occur while you are out. They must know how to operate and silence the alarm. Notify the local police station that you've installed an alarm and give them the names and addresses of the keyholders so they can be contacted in an emergency.

'...Notify the local police station...'

For greater security, you may be able to link your alarm to a communicator like the Communicator 3000 from A1 Security. This provides low cost 24 hour monitoring of your alarm system by, in the event of an alarm situation, sending programmed alert messages to up to four contact telephone numbers selected and programmed by the user. Smiths Industries Environmental Controls offers the Security Autodialler. A complete system, it works on a normal British Telecom line in conjunction with magnetic alarm contacts secured to doors and windows. In the event of an intrusion it will automatically dial up to six pre-programmed telephone numbers to alert neighbours, family, friends or colleagues. It continues to dial these numbers until one is answered and will then relay a spoken emergency message. Battery back-up ensures continued operation in the event of mains failure.

Stand-alone systems

The term DIY alarms can also encompass simple battery-operated or plug-in devices which require little in the way of installation skills.

Battery or mains-operated stand-alone devices can be used to protect one room, or can be sited to detect intrusion through a door or window, or positioned in a hall to protect several rooms. These devices normally incorporate a passive infra-red detector to sense movement, and in response, trigger a loud in-built sounder which can operate as a deterrent. These alarms are no substitute for a comprehensive, built-in system but do offer benefits in the fact that they may be moved around from room to room. They are ideal for protecting garages, greenhouses, sheds, workshops, caravans or boats and provide relatively low cost protection, with

prices ranging from £20 up to about £100. A new low-cost model from Superswitch is so small and lightweight that it can be carried around to provide protection for personal belongings in hotel rooms.

Other simple DIY systems are designed to operate via the ring main; components are simply plugged into 13 amp sockets around the home via adaptors. The single-unit SAS02 from Smiths Industries and the Spacewatch Alarm from A1 Security operate on this principle, detecting break-ins by sensing changes in air pressure caused when doors or windows are opened or broken. The devices can also be linked to an external sounder for greater protection and the Spacewatch can be expanded to protect outbuildings via the addition of magnetic contacts, patio door contacts or passive infra-red detectors.

More comprehensive is the S.O.S. System from A1 Security. The basic

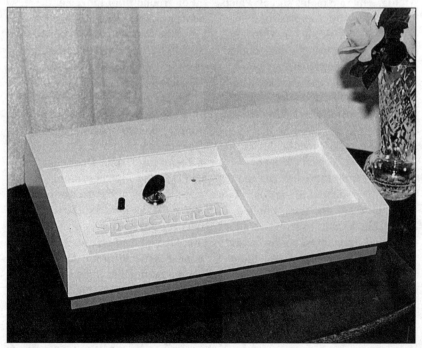
The Spacewatch alarm from A1 Security.

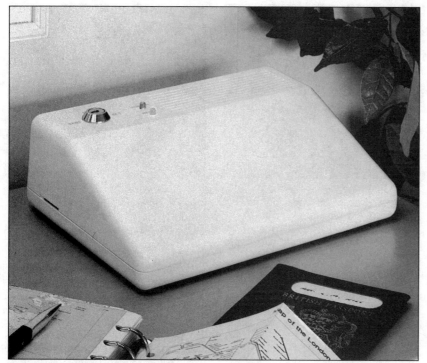

The single unit SAS02 from Smiths Industries is an installation-free, air-activated alarm system which detects break-ins by sensing changes in air pressure caused when doors or windows are opened or broken.

Electronics both offer systems which, it is claimed, are easy to install. Wire-free systems will probably work out slightly more expensive than a wired DIY installation.

Whilst a DIY installation will undoubtedly save you money it will be a false economy if the installation is faulty and continually causes false alarms. Not only will it upset your neighbours but, at the end of the day, you will probably stop using it altogether, leaving your home vulnerable. Make sure that if you attempt an installation you have the knowledge to carry it out effectively. Bear in mind also that a DIY installation is very unlikely to qualify you for a discount on your house contents insurance. This is normally restricted to installations carried out by an installer recommended by your insurer, or one who is NACOSS or police-approved.

kit comprises a master alarm unit, slave unit and two infra-red movement sensors to provide coverage for at least two points of entry in the home. Each unit plugs into a 13 amp socket and they 'communicate' via the regular mains wiring. The system is easily expanded with a range of additional detectors and an external siren and strobe. Dependent of electrical conditions, security can be shared with a neighbour via this system. By installing a slave unit and alarm enhancer in the neighbour's home they will be alerted should someone break into your home, and vice versa.

The final option for a comprehensive DIY system is the wire-free alarm which uses radio transmission between detectors and the control unit. Although many of these are designed for professional installation there are kits available specifically for the DIY market – Smiths Industries and Response

WATCHPOINTS

1 Set aside a weekend to carry out the installation.

2 Use individual components for a more comprehensive system tailored to suit your requirements.

3 Plan your system and consider your requirements carefully before buying.

4 Make sure your chosen control panel offers an adequate number of zones.

5 Kits should conform to BS6707; components to BS4737.

6 Make sure that each member of the household knows how to operate the system.

7 Stand-alone alarms can be used for additional security in garages, sheds, greenhouses and caravans.

8 Remember that a DIY installation is unlikely to qualify you for a discount under your house contents insurance policy.

15
DIY ALARMS

▼ Fitting a DIY alarm

1 We fitted an ADE Optima XM six-zone panel (rear), an ADE Sonade external siren/strobe (rear left), an Intellisense Omni 5030 passive infra-red/glass break detector from C & K Systems and their 4040T passive infra-red (which has two optional lenses to alter the detection pattern if necessary). Also pictured, in the foreground are C & K's dual technology microwave/passive infra-red detector which is suitable for a conservatory or other difficult environment, and the FlexGuard glass break detector (front, right). You could also fit magnetic contacts to doors and windows where required, but this particular system had good perimeter protection with the use of glass-break detectors.

First plan your installation, pinpointing the most vulnerable points. For example, you may need detectors upstairs if you have a flat roof outside a bedroom window. The next job, and this can be a lengthy one, is planning and running the cabling. Ideal places are lofts, runs through airing cupboards, bedroom cupboards, under floor boards etc. You will need to connect the mains supply to the control panel using a fused (not a switched) spur. If in any doubt about this at all use the services of a qualified electrical engineer.

2 Our wiring took us into the loft, a bedroom cupboard and under the floorboards. It is important to isolate the alarm cabling from the house mains wiring. The special alarm cable is metal screened to protect it from the magnetic field generated by currents flowing through mains wiring which, if too close to the alarm cable, would generate a voltage which could give a false alarm. The mains cabling is on the left, the new alarm cable on the right.

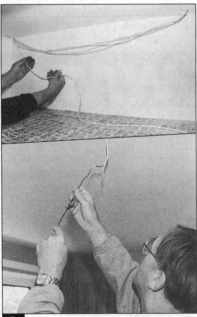

3 Routing the ceiling detector cabling (one for each device) through a bedroom cupboard. You will need two people for this job. The lower cable is being fed through a hole in the base of the cupboard to below the floor boards and through the ceiling of the room below. Take care when you are handling alarm cable, especially when pulling it through pre-drilled holes – it can be easily damaged. The other detector cables will be routed around the house from the detector units to the control panel downstairs.

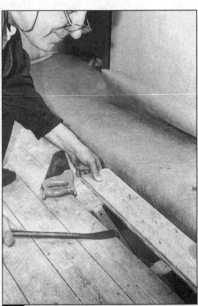

4 Saw across the end of the floor board (and down each side if tongued and grooved), lever up the floorboard carefully and lift the sawn off section away. Here we were unlucky and exposed bracing struts which get in the way. If you are lucky, the joists will run parallel to the direction you want your wire to go, but in this case they didn't! Consequently it was necessary to drill a hole in each joist to feed the cable through. Laying the cable along the top of the joists is not advised as it would be in danger of being crushed.

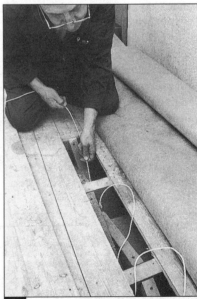

5 Gently pull the cable through for the ceiling detector. A 'mouse' made from an unravelled coat hanger can be attached to the cable to make it easier to pull through.

6 The housing removed from the siren/strobe (bell box) unit, showing the circuitry, the cable entry holes and fixing bolt holes. It is possible to remove the circuit board (just disconnect the sounder and the battery first) for safety.

8 Drill the holes for the fixing, and drill the wall for the cable entry hole (from either side) at an angle of 30°. This prevents water entering the hole and pouring into the house when it rains! It may be easier to use a straight hollow metal tube, if available, (or even a straightened coat hanger) attached to the cable from the other side to feed the cable through, particularly if you are drilling through a cavity wall where it will be prone to drop down.

10 Bolt the sounder and strobe housing securely to the wall.

7 Mark the position of the fixing bolt holes and the cable entry hole for the siren/strobe unit. It is best to centre the hole for the cable over mortar as it will be easier to get the cable through.

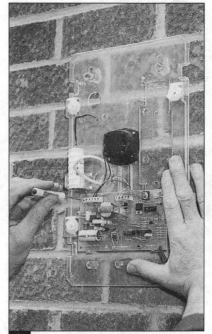

9 The cable from the siren/strobe will be connected to specially allocated terminals in the control panel. The manufacturer of both the siren/strobe and panel has ensured these are co-ordinated but this may not always be the case.

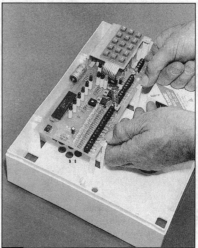

11 To fix the panel to the wall first remove the cover and unscrew the low voltage wires from the AC terminals, and the speaker wires from terminals 13 and 14. Lift out the circuit board (PCB) by pushing down on the holding clips and lifting the board clear.

15
D I Y   A L A R M S

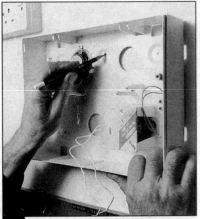

12 Mark the fixing holes for the panel. The main cable will come in from the spur and the alarm cables from each detector. There are knock-out holes in the panel housing which should be cut out with a junior hacksaw to allow entry.

14 Use a separate connector block, available from most good electrical shops, to connect the tamper leads from each device.

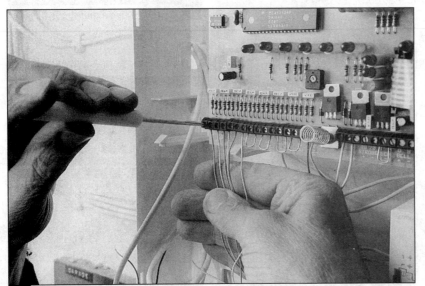

13 There are seven pre-fitted links which are inserted in the zone inputs, PA and tamper positions. It is possible to test the panel before wiring it up by connecting the 12v battery wires to the terminal. However, the detectors must be fully installed and wired correctly to achieve this. You will need to enter the factory code given in the instructions to allow you to override the 'tamper' alarm condition which is given when you open the housing. Leave a little slack cable in case you have to remake the connections. Wrap them in a cable form, and leave them tidy.

15 Wiring up the ceiling mounted glass-break/passive infra-red detector (the C & K Intellisense Omni 5030). Remove the cover with a small flathead screwdriver and separate the two parts. Remove the circuit board from the unit and press out the knock-outs for fixing the unit.

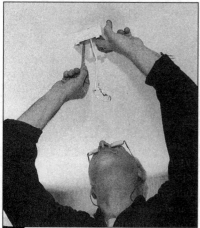

16 Use the rear housing as a template for marking the holes for the mounting screws and wiring.

19 The unit has been surface mounted, but it is also possible to flush mount it with the special recess bucket and retainer ring packed with the device.

21 This PIR has jumper positions to allow you to set the detection sensitivity.

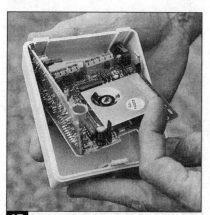

17 The PIR sensitivity can also be adjusted, for high, medium and low. An LED can be set to operate or not, as preferred, to show that the PIR has alarmed. Two to four normal steps across the PIR pattern should light the red LED to indicate an alarm.

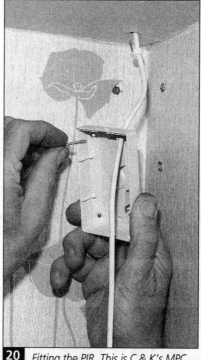

20 Fitting the PIR. This is C & K's MPC 4040T which gives a 12m x12m coverage. It can be mounted in the corner, as we have done, or be fitted on the wall at a height of between four and ten feet. Here we have removed the front cover and the circuit board to feed the cable, which has come from our run above, through the entry knock-outs. Mark the fixing screw holes, centre punch them to ensure accuracy and drill carefully having checked there are no cables or pipes behind the drilling area. You will need four screws to fix it firmly.

22 It also has various notches for positioning the circuit board, which enables you to adjust the range.

18 The glass break detector sensitivity can be adjusted.

23 Set the PIR to the correct range and sensitivity required, clip the circuit board back into position and wire the terminals according to the manufacturers' instructions.

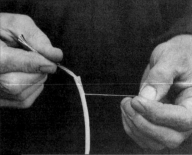

27 *Most alarm cable employs a neat method of paring the cable back to reveal the wires – a piece of string is incorporated to split the insulation to the required level, helping to protect the cable from the heavy handed!*

26 *Use the housing of the panic button to position the unit. This particular model features a dual button, a safety feature which ensures the alarm will only be activated if both are pressed together.*

24 *The PIR neatly in position with the front cover in place. There is also a choice of lenses, one to exclude small pets, and a barrier lens for narrow areas (such as hallways)*

28 *Test the panel fully once you have all the detectors installed and operating correctly.*

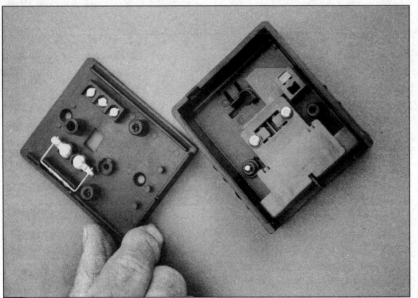

25 *The panic button is wired in the same way as any other device and incorporates a simple relay. It is connected to the PA terminal at the control panel.*

CHAPTER 16

Make your mark

Police always check recovered property for visible identifying marks. An ultra-violet lamp is used to detect invisible marking.

Security marking your valuables offers two major benefits. Marked property is more difficult to dispose of and, therefore, can deter the would-be thief from stealing your possessions. It also ensures that, should the worst happen, your lost or stolen possessions stand a better chance of being returned to you if they are recovered by the police. As such, property marking is a very worthwhile and inexpensive security measure, and one in which the whole family can become involved.

Up and down the country police are inundated with recovered stolen goods which cannot be returned to their rightful owners simply because there is no means of identifying them. Police always check recovered property for visible identifying marks, and with an ultra-violet lamp for invisible marking. If an identifying code is found, the police can easily decipher it and return the property to the rightful owner.

'...Police always check recovered property...'

Somehow this identifying mark has to be unique to you to ensure that it enables you to be traced easily by the police. The recommended method of security marking property, therefore, is to use your postcode – which narrows your location down to a specific geographic location – followed by the number, or first two letters of your house name. For instance, if you lived at 7 New Road, Anytown AN14 3BR, the mark you code your property with would be AN14 3BR 7. If you lived at 'Beechwood', New

Road, Anytown AN14 3BR, your code would be AN14 3BR BE.

If you are not sure of your postcode, your local Post Office will be able to tell you; or check in your local Thomson Directory.

Should you move house, of course, your property will then show an incorrect postcode. Rather than trying to remove the old code, simply put an 'X' by the side of it and then mark your possessions with the new postcode. This allows the police to trace the history of ownership if necessary.

'...There are companies who offer computerized marking services...'

Of course if you rent a home, or move home frequently, using your postcode may not be an appropriate security marking method. In such cases there are companies who offer computerized marking services by subscription. Each subscriber is normally allocated a personal code number which is stored on a computer with the subscriber's name and address and other necessary details for police reference. The company supplies marking stencils and materials to enable you to mark your property. Should your property be recovered, police will note your code number and check it via the computer. Computer marking companies are best sourced via your local police station to find a reputable firm.

Marking methods

There are various methods of marking property. You will probably need to adopt several in order to mark a variety of surfaces. Nowadays, many police stations have comprehensive property

Local police often organize cycle coding and property marking events when you can take items along for marking.

Die-stamping is best used for large metal objects, including bicycles, lawnmowers and tools.

marking kits which you can borrow, or a Neighbourhood Watch scheme or Residents' Association may like to get together and buy a kit to be shared by members. Both the BodyGuard Security and Markitwise International offer a comprehensive range of security marking products. Police also frequently organize bicycle coding days when you can have your bicycle die-stamped. Property marking pens should also be readily available at a relatively low cost from security centres, DIY superstores, department stores and newsagents.

On most surfaces the best form of marking to use is visible marking. There are various methods including etching, die-stamping, branding, identification paint and indelible ink.

Die-stamping is best used for large metal objects, such as bicycles, lawnmowers and tools. Even if a thief files down the mark, it can usually still be detected by forensic tests. Similarly, identification paint can be used on bulky objects where appearance doesn't matter.

Sandblasting is carried out professionally to apply the registration number to car windows and headlamps.

Etching leaves a permanent mark on hard surfaces. Use a stencil to achieve a neat finish.

Etching is ideal for hard surfaces, such as televisions, video recorders, cameras or hi-fi equipment. There are two methods. The first requires the use of a hard-tipped engraving pen, usually supplied with a stencil to help you obtain a neat, legible mark. The second method is acid-etching, or sandblasting which is carried out professionally to apply vehicle registration numbers to car windows. Retainacar, for instance, will mark vehicles with a Security Protection Number which links them to a National Security Register (see also Chapter 22).

Ceramic markers may also be used to mark hard surfaces such as glass, porcelain or china. However, unlike engraving pens, ceramic markers do not scratch into the surface but deposit a permanent metal compound. Again these are easy to use, and usually supplied with a stencil. To apply a mark keep the area moist. If the tip of the marker

begins to blunt it can be sharpened with a carborundum stone available from hardware stores.

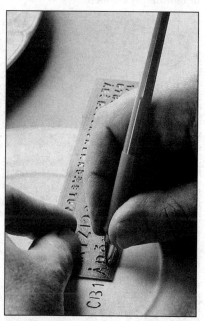

Ceramic markers deposit a permanent metal compound – ideal for marking glass, porcelain or china.

Invisible ink

When the concept of security marking was first introduced, the most popular method was 'invisible' marking, which utilizes ultra-violet fluid, normally contained in a pen for ease of use. This can only be detected under ultra-violet light. Whilst still a good marking method for specific surfaces, uv marking does have disadvantages. It's important to remember that a uv mark is not permanent. Exposed to natural or artificial light the mark will fade over a period of time. It is important, therefore, that the mark is checked every six months and reapplied as necessary.

Having said that, however, it is a useful means of marking valuable articles of clothing, leather goods and other objects which you do not wish to deface, although it is always a good idea to test the pen on a hidden area first as the ink may lightly etch some surfaces, or be visible in direct sunlight on non-porous surfaces. Also, remember to reapply the mark each time an item of clothing is cleaned.

WATCH POINTS

1 Security marking helps to ensure that lost or stolen property may be safely returned.

2 Use your postcode and house number, or first two letters of its name, to provide a unique code.

3 To invalidate a code, put an 'X' by it and write the new code.

4 Look out for security marking days organized by the police.

5 Don't forget tools in the garage and/or shed.

6 Remember to check and reapply ultra-violet marks where necessary.

7 Never mark antiques without expert advice.

8 Display 'Marked Property' stickers in your windows.

9 Keep a visual record of small items, with identifying marks.

10 Keep written records, with serial numbers and receipts.

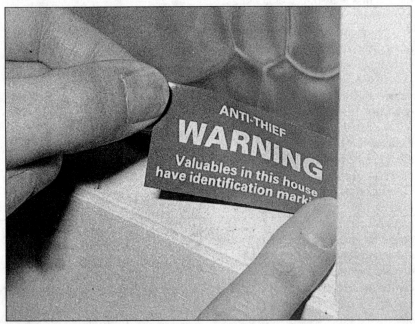

Remember to display 'Marked Property' stickers in your windows to deter would-be thieves.

Antiques or other items of considerable value should not be marked without obtaining expert advice first in case it reduces the value.

'...advertising the fact deters would-be thieves!...'

Once you have marked your possessions it's worth advertising the fact in order to deter would-be thieves! Most property marking pens are supplied with 'Warning – Marked Property' stickers to put in your window, alternatively they may be available from the Crime Prevention Officer at your local police station.

Small items

Of course, some articles are too small to write your postcode on, but items of jewellery are a popular haul – and often difficult to describe when they go missing.

The best way to improve their chances of a safe return is to keep a visual record of each item. You can either take photographs or use a video camera to record items on tape. Each one should be logged in colour against a plain background, and next to a ruler to give an idea of scale. Keep a written record of any distinguishing marks or features such as hallmarks, crests, initials, and even cracks, chips or dents.

Written records

Keep a written record of all your property, along with serial numbers and, for insurance purposes, values (it's always a good idea to keep receipts for this purpose). Make a copy of the list and leave this and your photo negatives or duplicate video tape with a relative, neighbour, or solicitor just in case you lose the originals.

Time consuming it may be, but if you're ever faced with a room full of recovered, stolen property and you're trying to identify your own possessions, you'll be pleased that you took the trouble to make your mark.

CHECK LIST

Use this form as a guide to make a checklist of security marked property, and keep it in a safe place. List jewellery separately, with hallmarks, distinguishing marks or features and a photographic record.

ITEM	MAKE	MODEL	SERIAL NO	VALUE	WHERE MARKED	PHOTOGRAPHIC RECORD y/n?
Television						
Video						
Hi-fi						
Home Computer						
Printer						
Typewriter						
Camera equipment						
Camcorder						
Clocks						
Antiques						
Other valuables						
Fridge						
Freezer						
Microwave						
Washing machine						
Dishwasher						
Food processor						
Bicycle						
Tools						
Lawn mower						

CHAPTER 17

Making a safe choice

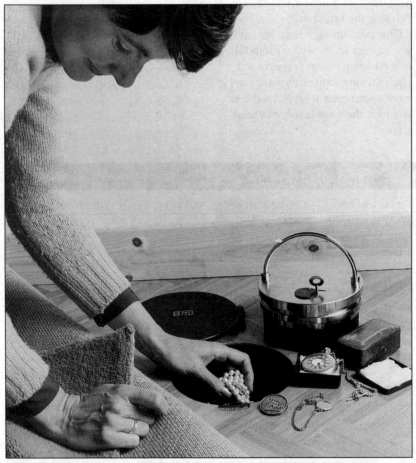

An underfloor safe, conveniently concealed, is ideal for securing family heirlooms and jewellery.

We may laugh at the idea of granny hiding her money under the mattress yet most of us do very little better.

We all have valuables we would hate to lose. While they may be of purely sentimental value, any amount of insurance could not compensate for the loss of handed down jewellery or medals, ornaments, collections of stamps or coins. Valuable documents, such as passports and deeds, computer disks or cash which needs to be kept safely, should never be left lying around where the opportunist could find them, in an unlocked drawer or tucked behind the clock on the mantelpiece.

Valuable jewellery placed in insecure, if decorative, boxes which a child could open, and cash left in pockets of clothing or tucked under a saucer in the kitchen to pay the milkman are all quickly located and easily snatched by the opportunist. A safe will ensure these items aren't left lying around to tempt the potential burglar.

'...A safe should be hidden, but avoid the obvious...'

When deciding where to put your safe it is important to bear a number of points in mind. Ideally it should be hidden, but avoid the obvious, such as fitting a wall safe behind a picture. It can be hidden behind window curtains, for example, but must not be closer than 225mm to the edge of the opening in the wall where the window fits (that is, the reveal). It should also be positioned where limited space would make it difficult to attack – with the swing of a sledge hammer, for example. Depending on the type of safe you choose, you could fit one in a cellar or the attic, both places a thief may not care to venture in case he is trapped. Freestanding safes can sometimes be fitted in a wardrobe or cupboard or under the stairs – you could even disguise one as a window seat or a television stand! – and underfloor safes should, ideally,

A range of wall safes from Churchill. It's surprising how much they will hold, but check cash ratings carefully.

resist oxyacetylene torches. The locks are designed to be more difficult to pick and are usually reinforced with steel plates.

That doesn't mean it's not possible to buy a good quality second-hand safe, but make sure it isn't pre-1945 which would be virtually useless. Some locksmiths who specialize in safes re-condition them, and if you buy from a reputable company, such as a member of the Master Locksmiths Association you can be sure that the safe itself and the lock that's fitted will be up to standard.

Safes can be free-standing and bolted to the floor, underfloor and sunk in concrete, flush fitted in brick walls, concealed under floorboards and fitted between joists, or simply be steel containers which are disguised to resemble have furniture placed over them.

There are a number of popular misconceptions about safes. For example, an old safe, however hefty it looks, is often far from effective, constructed in materials easily overcome or penetrated with today's tools, and fitted with low security, unprotected locks. Today's safes are built with specially developed barrier materials, layer upon layer, with the highest grades able to

A free-standing safe can be bolted to the floor of a wardrobe. This is a Chubb Heritage.

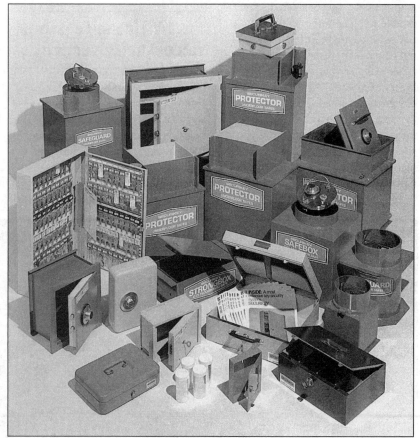

This popular range covers virtually every round and square lid underfloor safe. Securikey also produce free-standing and wall safes, cash boxes and key cabinets.

Two types of novelty hide-away safes, the Vent-Safe and Strongpoint, from Ashley Security Products.

other items – an electric socket or even a can of hair spray!

There are also fire safes and cabinets which, although fine for protecting valuable documents from damage in a fire, should not automatically be considered secure or able to resist forceful attacks. Likewise a safe built for security is not necessarily resistant to fire.

Fire safes are built of several layers of material which are designed to spread and disseminate the heat. Their resistance is usually measured in hours, something you should look for if you wish to store material such as computer disks or tapes. They come in various forms from a simple document safe resembling a cash box, a hanging file unit or free-standing unit which can be bolted to the floor. Other units are designed to accommodate computer disks and are often referred to as media safes.

'...A fire safe is not necessarily secure...'

There are basically two types of safe. Those providing a high level of security and resistance to determined attacks and those which rely on disguise and are intended to conceal items of lower value – which, if discovered, would probably offer little resistance. Most domestic safes, except the low security hide-away types, have the capability to resist cutting, drilling or grinding tools – sledge hammers, chisels, drills or angle grinders, for example.

First decide precisely what you want the safe for. If you are fitting a safe because your insurance company says so, then you should establish what level of insurance rating is necessary – two figures will be given, the cash rating and jewellery rating and you will find most safe manufacturers are able to quote these in relation to particular models. A cash rating of £3,000, for example, will provide a jewellery rating of £30,000. Make sure before buying

If you want to avoid this happening to important documents, use a proper fire-resistant cash box like this one from Sentry who offer a wide range of fire safes and files, some of which are also suitable for computer software.

the safe that your insurance company will be happy with your choice.

An underfloor safe is considered the most secure and there is a wide range of sizes available. Smaller units can be used for cash, passports, credit cards, jewellery and other items, while the larger models are capable of holding boxes of jewellery, cameras, ornaments, stamp collections and hand guns. (We cover gun cabinets and the requirements for guns later on.)

Features to look out for, apart from the insurance rating and level of security or fire protection claimed for the materials used in the safe construction, are the number of bolts, that the interior is lined with felt or velvet to protect jewellery or ornaments from damage and to prevent condensation (not just to look pretty!), that the safe has at least a seven-lever lock and preferably one that retains the key if it isn't actually locked so that you cannot walk away with the key if you forget to lock it.

If you are in the habit of mislaying keys, a combination lock may be the answer, or even an electronic digital lock, although this will inevitably add something to the cost of the safe.

Also look out for safes that have a re-locking mechanism which jams the bolts in the locked position if the safe is attacked.

Underfloor safes

You can choose a square door safe or a round door (some round door safes have a deposit tube which is suitable for inserting cash without having to lift the entire door, and are often used by retailers who prefer not to hand the safe keys to their staff). One thing to watch is that the people using the safe are strong enough to lift the heavy door to open it. A gas-pump (also referred to as a strut) assisted door makes it much easier to lift out, and there are

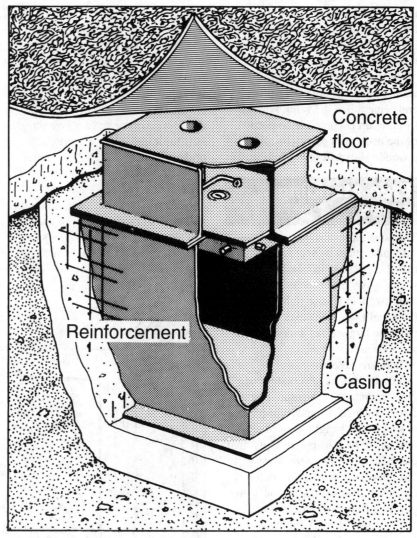

Underfloor safe

many models, often with interchangeable doors with different types of lock, number of bolts etc., and a choice in body sizes so you can choose one that gives the appropriate features. Other models offer a hinged door, but this may limit access.

Fitting an underfloor safe involves burying it in concrete, reinforced with steel mesh or metal reinforcement rods and, depending on what type of floor you have, this can be a messy business.

If you have a concrete floor already you will need to drill a hole, using a 'demolition' hammer such as a Kango or Makita, at least six

inches larger and three inches deeper than the safe. Layers of concrete are then built up around the safe, compacting each layer (each about three inches deep) with a one-inch square steel rod. The concrete mixture must be allowed to cure for seven days in a damp atmosphere and, to prevent rapid drying, it should be covered with polythene sheeting, sealed around the edges. Once dry it is advisable to paint the surface with a liquid lino paint to stabilize it and reduce the risk of dirt and grit entering the safe mechanism.

While the safe is being installed, the safe door should be placed well away from the site to avoid any form of contamination. Fill the safe itself up to the neck with crumpled newspaper to protect the interior.

The final screed of half-an-inch should be a mixture of sharp sand and cement in a 4:1 ratio. When the installation is complete no portion of the neck or deposit tube should protrude above floor level.

Free-standing safes

The advantage of a free-standing safe, other than its accessibility, is that it is possible to take it with you if you move. They come in sizes from two feet square right up to bank vault size. However, don't presume larger sizes are necessarily more secure.

There are several ways of installing free-standing safes but most important is to ensure that the floor on which it stands will be able to support its weight. Don't forget it also has to be transported to its final place, so make sure your floor will also take the weight of the delivery men (say 20 stone per person!). A concrete floor will probably be fine but you may need to reinforce a suspended timber floor.

Anchoring is usually through the base of the safe, and the most popular method of fixing the safe to a concrete floor is with an expanding steel sleeve which is inserted into a drilled hole in the concrete, fixed with a steel bolt, which is then passed through the base of the safe and screwed into the expanding sleeve. There may be one or two of these fixing points.

If the floor is wooden, a special fixing anchor with a rubber expansion sleeve moulded over a threaded insert is placed in the hole. The safe is positioned on top and then the base fix bolt is inserted through the safe into the sleeve and tightened, expanding the sleeve to

form a strong anchor. Alternatively a base fix plate may be used in conjunction with countersunk screws which has a threaded boss which will align with the safe base fix hole.

Wall-safes are designed in brick sizes – two, three or four (we show how to fit one in our picture sequence at the end of this chapter) and will hold a surprising amount of small items, such as jewellery, documents and cash. They, too, may have an insurance rating, so check this with your supplier. Names to look for include Chubb, Securikey and Churchill. Expect to pay from

£85 to £130 depending on the size of safe, and more for one with a combination lock and a shelf.

Alternatively you could fit a 'floorboard' safe such as Securikey's Strongbox or Churchill's Treasure Chest, especially designed for DIY and fitted between the joists of any suspended floor. These are relatively easy to fit and make a good, fairly secure hiding place. You will need to remove sections of the floorboard to expose the joists (look for the rows of nails on the floorboards to locate the joists). There should be a distance of 16

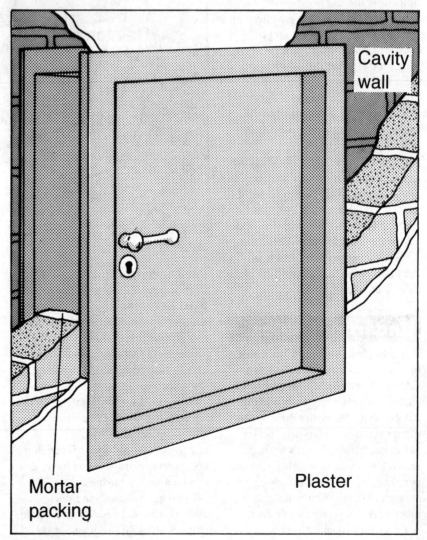

Cavity wall

Mortar packing

Plaster

Wall safe.

Always keep weapons and ammunition in a safe place. Gun cabinets should comply with the Firearms (Amendment) Act 1988.

inches between the centre points of the joists – if not, you will need to nail or screw a piece of timber to them to make the gap measure 14 inches. Then, having marked the area, use a wood chisel to chisel out ⅛ inch of the timber from the top of the joists for the flanges of the safe – some models don't require this and are built to match the standard floorboard thickness. This allows the box to drop flush so that the top of the safe is level with the top of the joists, and it also allows the floorboards to fit flush with the surrounding floor. Then mark the positions of the four coach screws through the holes provided in the safe walls. Remove the box and drill the four starter holes – no less than ¼ inch diameter and no more than one inch deep. Replace the box and

secure it in position with the coach screws provided. Various sizes are available and the smallest will cost from around £70 or £80.

Securikey and Churchill both produce 'above floor' safes. The Securikey Safebox is suitable for DIY installation, and prices start from around £189 for the 10 inch high by 10 inch wide model. It is fitted with a seven-lever lock, or a combination lock, along with construction which should satisfy most insurance companies (depending on the risk), and Securikey supply a certificate of installation which must be signed and forwarded to the insurance company.

Churchill's Housemartin has a round door and a cash rating of £3,000 if fixed suitably – a wooden

fixing kit is available as an extra. Measuring 12 inches wide by 9 inches deep the safe retails at around £258.

Gun cabinets

The Firearms (Amendment) Act 1988, means that shotgun certificate holders must keep their guns securely in a locked gun cabinet or similar secure container. Prior to the Act over 700 shotguns were reported stolen annually and could easily have fallen into the wrong hands.

Gun safes come in various sizes and can accommodate several guns; larger units containing a lockable compartment for ammunition. Usually of 2 to 3mm continuously welded steel, they should also have two high security locks (at least seven levers) reinforced with steel plates, be resistant to jemmy attacks and other forceful measures, and have protected hinges, preferably concealed. They will need to be anchored to the wall and should be pre-drilled to enable easy fitting. If coach bolts are difficult to fit – they would show on the other side of the wall – use screw bolts (10 x 80mm or ⅜ inch x 3¼ inch) and self-tap their thread into soft brick or blockwork, once an 8mm pilot hole has been made.

Some manufacturers produce disguised gun cabinets which can be built into furniture or are ready made to look like a tallboy or chest of drawers.

Simple DIY

Often the simple ideas are the most effective and, depending on the level of security you require, there are some neat, cost-effective ideas which effectively conceal cash and jewellery, particularly if you are travelling. For example, SAS produce a range of look-alike cans of household products. The top or bottom of the cans twist off to reveal a storage area, but look and weigh just like a full can of, say, household cleaner or polish.

Another company producing look-alike safes is Ashley Security Products. One looks like an air vent (Vent-Safe) and the other (the Strongpoint) an electrical socket (see pictures). Both have a six lever lock and conceal a steel box which makes up a drawer section. They are designed to be fitted between courses of brickwork or in standard cavity walls and can easily be DIY installed.

Look-alike cans offer a convenient hiding place

WATCHPOINTS

1 Keep irreplaceable family valuables in a safe.

2 Ensure the cash/jewellery rating is adequate. Check with your insurers.

3 Make sure the safe you are using is not too old, is strong enough to resist today's break-in tools and has adequate security locks.

4 Fire resistant safes and cabinets may not be resistant to forceful attacks.

5 Keep computer disks and other media in a specially designed safe with resistance to fire as well as security.

6 Choose a safe that is easy for you to use. No use having one you don't use.

7 Make sure you can lift the door of an underfloor safe. Or choose one with a gas-strut assisted door.

8 If you are prone to mislay keys, choose a model with a combination lock.

9 Keep guns in a special cabinet complying with the Firearms (Amendment) Act.

10 When installing a safe, choose a place in limited space where it would be hard to attack.

11 Do not take a risk and use 'hide-away' safes for permanent storage. They are great for holidays, in caravans or chalets, for example, but fit a real one for greater security.

▼ How to fit a wall safe

Wall safes, available in brick sizes, are not difficult to fit, but there are points to consider. The size of the safe you can install is restricted by the thickness of the walls. A solid wall must be at least 9 inches thick, or it may be fitted in an 11 inch cavity wall. It is quite likely that the only walls of sufficient thickness will be outside walls. Remember also that building blocks do not provide a secure fixing, and that safes should be installed away from 'weak spots' such as the edge of a wall.

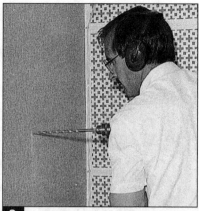

2 *Next step is to drill a small hole through the wall. This will indicate whether or not the wall is of sufficient thickness for the installation of the safe.*

5 *Use a drill to weaken the bricks so they can be removed more easily. An alternative method is to drill rows of holes all the way round so the block falls out more or less in one piece.*

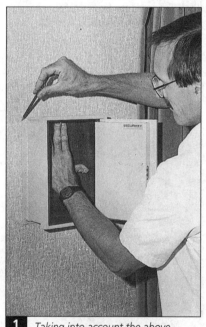

1 *Taking into account the above advice, select a suitable site for your wall safe. Ideally it should be hidden, but also positioned where limited space would make it difficult to attack. Make sure there are no wires running where the safe is to be installed. Mark the required position of the safe with a pen or pencil.*

3 *The hole in the wall must be an inch bigger on all sides than the actual safe. Drill a hole in each corner and use a hammer and chisel to remove the plaster.*

4 *A tip from the experts at Locksecure Services – spraying the opening with plenty of water keeps dust down to a minimum.*

6 *Take care to ensure that rubble does not fall down the cavity as this can lead to problems with damp. Line the cavity with newspaper to prevent this.*

7   *Remove as much dust as possible, and wet the wall thoroughly to ensure that the mortar will stick.*

8   *Check the fit of the safe and then mix up some sharp sand, cement and grano (one part cement to three parts sand and grano) to secure it. Grano is available from builders' merchants and will make the mortar much harder.*

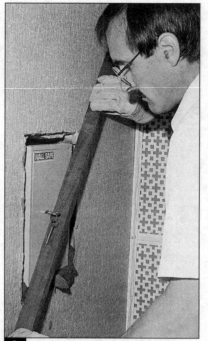

9   *Lay a neat pile of mortar at the bottom of the hole and place the safe on top with a wedge positioned underneath. Use a piece of wood or a spirit level to make sure it is straight.*

10   *Tape up the side of the safe to protect the hinges, and cement it in place, pushing the mortar well back.*

11   *For a smooth finish cut back the mortar and cover it with a layer of plaster or smooth cement.*

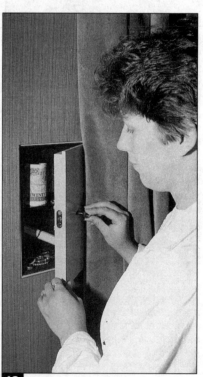

12   *With installation complete, our Securikey wall safe in four-brick size provides ample room for the safekeeping of passports, legal documents and items of jewellery.*

▼ Underfloor safes

1 Fitting an underfloor safe involves burying it in concrete. If you have a concrete floor you will need to drill a hole (using a 'demolition' hammer) at least six inches larger and three inches deeper than the safe.

2 The reinforcement grid supplied by Hamber Safes is ideal for a home handyman's installation.

3 After the safe and grid have been lowered on to the level concrete base of the hole, further layers of concrete, well mixed with polystyrene fibres, are stamped down into position. When the installation is complete no portion of the neck or deposit tube should protrude above floor level.

CHAPTER 18

The light approach

if you switch it on every night. So don't just put in any old bulb, think about using the longer life lamps which will cost you less in the long run and you won't have to change them so often.

'...Longer life lamps will cost you less...'

Good street lighting has been shown to effectively reduce fear of crime on large residential estates, and generally makes people feel safer and less worried about coming home to an empty house at night. If you are unhappy about the lighting in your street, or perhaps a particular area close by, such as an underpass or an alleyway, bring the matter up with your local Neighbourhood Watch scheme or the local authority. They may well be able to improve the situation, particularly if it is encouraging vandals, car thieves, burglary or similar criminal or unsocial activities.

You can do a great deal to improve your own lighting indoors and out, and it is important to identify where it can be most effective. While it is a good idea to have a light in the porch, it is equally important to illuminate dark corners at the side and back of the house. Be careful when you position the lights, it is

A home that looks occupied, with lights on, immediately feels more secure and far safer than a house in darkness. Well positioned and cleverly operated lighting is not only welcoming for you but will encourage the passing opportunist burglar to move on to a home where he can work in the shadows.

The simplest way to make the house look occupied is to leave a light on with the curtains drawn when you go out. And it really doesn't cost that much to keep a 60 watt bulb burning for a few hours. Even better, a modern compact fluorescent lamp bought for around £5 will cost about £4 per year to run

Good street lighting can make a neighbourhood feel more secure and safer to live in

easy to create more shadows. At the front door the light should be mounted on the wall so that the caller is well lit. If it is mounted too high, not only will you find it awkward to change the lamp but also it may create a shadow. Ideally, the householder, when he or she comes to the door, should be in shadow, while the caller is bathed in light. If you have a door viewer fitted it is pointless if you cannot see the caller well enough through it at night.

If you have an existing outdoor light with mains wiring in place, then the job of fitting another light is very simple. If not, and you are starting from scratch, you may prefer to use a qualified electrician to do the initial work of providing a power supply. If you feel confident to tackle it yourself (but remember electricity is dangerous and can cause serious injury or death) then it is certainly possible to do all the work. Normally you can take power from the downstairs lighting circuit or, depending on where you want the light to be fixed, from the upstairs lighting circuit from the junction box or last loop-in ceiling rose. Before you start, ensure that you have turned off the electricity and isolated the circuit by removing the fuse from the consumer unit.

Using existing lights

If you have an existing light that you particularly like, you can transform it into an automatic security light, switching on when someone approaches. This will involve fitting an internal controller which will allow you to set how long the light remains on for (a few moments or all the time) and to adjust light sensitivity. This operates with a passive infra-red sensor fitted outside to detect movement, and both are wired to the existing light unit.

A PIR can control existing lighting.

Smiths SL032 Night Protector, a halogen floodlight operated using a passive infra-red detector.

A photocell-operated bulkhead light fitting from Superswitch.

A number of sensors, which can be sited at various points outside, can be linked to one control unit, and these may also have the ability to switch on a number of lights. Do check the switching capacity, however, they vary from as low as 60W to 100W (for one light only) to 2,000W. Sometimes manufacturers are a little optimistic in their recommendations, so stay well within them. The sensors should

also be fitted with a device called a photocell to prevent the light switching on in daylight. This device also offers an alternative to passive infra-red automatic lighting, and when incorporated in self-contained light units (ranging from lanterns to bulkhead lamps) allows them to come on automatically as light falls and switch off at dawn. This means they are on all night rather than triggered when someone approaches.

Built-in sensors

As well as adding sensors to control existing lighting you may prefer to fit a light which has a sensor built in. These range from floodlights (usually with 500W halogen lamps) ideal for lighting up the garden or a drive, to decorative coach lamps in different finishes – most popular are brass, white and black models.

If you feel that you need something with a bit more resistance to attack, particularly for a vulnerable side of the house where, perhaps, late night revellers may pass, choose a bulkhead light with

vandal resistant housing of polycarbonate, and with concealed screws. Some floodlights can be supplied with protective grilles.

The passive infra-red units can usually be adjusted to alter the coverage provided. This is carried out by tilting the sensor head itself or by stick-on tapes provided by the manufacturer which enable you to mask the detection beam. For example, you may not wish people walking up the pathway next to your drive to switch on your light, so you can adapt the angle to allow for this.

> ### '...PIR units can be adjusted to alter the coverage provided...'

To check that the light is operating correctly most units will enable you to carry out a walk test before the unit is finally programmed. This will allow you to adjust in daylight the sensitivity angle and length of time on. Sensors vary in their pattern of detection – most will have a range of at least 10 to 12 metres (30 to 36 feet) and pick up movement across an angle of up to 180°, others may have a narrower angle and a shorter range. The manufacturers should make this information available on the packaging or literature.

As well as features which resist attack you should look for an IP rating which indicates the level to which the unit when fitted outside will resist the effects of moisture and dirt. The rates vary from IP33 at the lowest end to IP55 for the better models.

We show you how to replace an existing lantern with an automatic passive infra-red operated model and a floodlight with a separate sensor in the picture sequence at the end of this chapter.

The Guardall Excalibur control unit for converting existing lights into automatic operation. A passive infra-red fitted outside triggers the system.

Controlling indoor lamps

There is a wide range of devices which can control internal lighting. Plug-in timers allow you to control an electrical appliance (lamp or radio, for example) to make the house look and sound occupied. They are plugged into the normal

Turn indoor lights into security lights by simply replacing the light switch:
(Top) *The Audioswitch detects the sound of someone entering the room and switches the lights on.*
(Centre) *A miniature passive infra-red detects movement to trigger the light.*
(Below) *This unit simply repeats the light switching pattern of the previous 24 hours.*

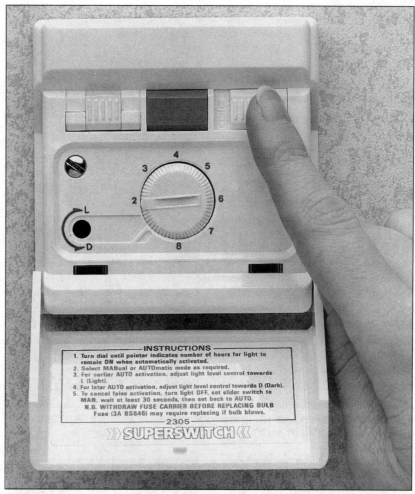

This lightswitch incorporates a photocell which turns the light on for up to eight hours after dusk.

socket and the appliance then plugs into the timer. Some repeat the same switching patterns over 24 hours, or can vary it from day to day on a seven-day cycle. Or there are timers designed to switch appliances on and off at pre-set times. Other units will switch on and off at random intervals.

Then there are replacement light switches. These replace the existing light switch and allow the lights to be activated by a variety of methods. For example, some can be programmed, just as the plug-in timers, while others remember when you switched on and off the day before and repeat the pattern, or they will switch the light on if a sound is heard or the device, using a passive infra-red detector, detects

movement. They should include a photo-cell to ensure they don't come on during the day, and should allow you to switch back to manual control if necessary.

'...units will switch on and off at random...'

These switches have until recently been limited to working with normal bulbs, but a recent innovation is a fluorescent light adaptor from Smiths Industries for use with strip lighting (such as that often used in kitchens) and their range of automatic light switches.

There are also units – reacting to

A plug-in timer shows the times you have programmed in for the lighting (or other appliance) to be switched on and off.

Another way of controlling a lamp. These units plug into the lamp between the bulb and the socket.

sound, or with an in-built program – which plug into the bayonet of the lamp itself. The bulb then plugs into the device and is controlled by it.

Sunshine, size and simple installation!

Developments are reducing the size of sensors and making the units increasingly energy efficient. If you prefer to save your electricity, how about a light unit which uses the sun to power a rechargeable battery and is fitted with a long life (five years, it is claimed) fluorescent bulb. It's a passive infra-red operated unit from Siemens and is able to provide up to 14 days power with no sun. Many other lights can now use energy-saving bulbs, so it's worth shopping around. For possibly the smallest unit on the market, look at the passive infra-red operated Trimalert from Homeguard UK. It's about the size of a compact camera, so can be fitted neatly beneath guttering. Wiring, too, is becoming less complex with two-wire systems and low-voltage options making the handyperson's job much easier.

Small enough to fit under a gutter, this is the Trimalert, a 150W floodlight linked to a passive infra-red detector, from Homeguard UK.

▼ Fitting an automatic lantern

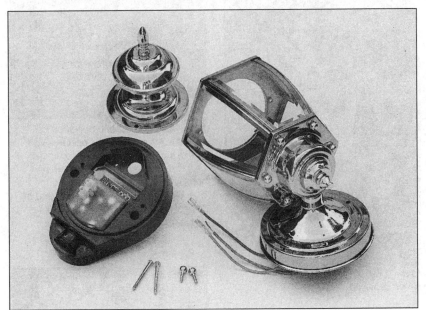

1 We fitted Smiths Industries SLO43 Brass Sensor Lantern, an automatic security/courtesy light which incorporates a miniature passive infra-red detector. It has an 8 metre detection range with a 180° coverage pattern and will switch the lantern on for 2½ minutes. You can override this so that it is on permanently.

2 Unscrew the existing lantern and plinth, leaving the mains cable in position. It is wise to check the position of the new lamp – allow for its height if you have any overhanging porches or gutters. In this case we had to drop the cable down to the brickwork below the wooden fascia to accommodate the new lantern.

3 Using the lantern's plinth itself or the template provided in the kit, mark the new position and the screw fixing holes. Drill the holes using a suitable drill bit depending on what you are drilling into.

4 Having drilled the holes, if working with brick, knock plugs in with a hammer.

5 Press the rubber sealing grommet into the cable entry hole on the plinth base; a small screw driver (or use your fingers) should squidge it into position!

6 Having cut the mains cable to length, leaving enough to make the connections, run it into the plinth through the grommet. Screw the plinth into position with two No. 8 1½ inch (40mm) brass screws. Tack the cable with cable clips neatly into position.

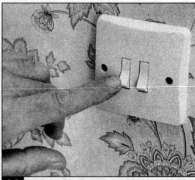

11 *The walk test and operation is controlled from the mains operated light switch indoors. After an initial walk test period the lantern should set itself in automatic operation mode. To change the operation mode a sequence of on and off switching can be carried out to walk test or give manual override.*

7 *Connect Live, Neutral and Earth from mains supply to lantern terminals (see manufacturer's diagram). (The mains cable should be double insulated 3 core PVC sheathed cable 0.75 – 1.0mm².)*

9 *Swing the lamp upright and secure to the plinth with the two brass No. 8 screws provided.*

8 *Then connect the lantern itself by pushing the Live and Neutral leads on to the spade connections on the plinth base and secure the Earth lead to the Earth terminal. The lamp will be hanging upside down at this stage!*

10 *Fit a bulb up to 100W and remove the two brass cover screws from the top of the lantern base. Place the top cap in position and re-secure using the brass screws.*

12 *The kit includes masking strips so you can adjust the detection range and angle. However, it has its limitations, so do a careful walk test, particularly if you have a 'front' door at the side of the house! It responds better to people walking directly towards the sensor and also should be mounted at a height of no more than 1.6 to 2 metres.*

▼ Fitting an automatic halogen floodlight

We fitted Smiths Night Protector (SL22), a fully automatic quartz halogen security floodlight which has a passive infra-red attached. It has an adjustable detection range of up to 15 metres with a coverage area of 180°. It can also switch up to 2,000W of additional lighting, so you could add more floodlights or lamps to the same system.

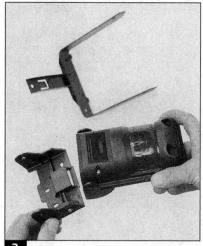

3 *The passive infra-red unit slots into the brackets provided and sits below the floodlight.*

5 *Having clicked the brackets for the sensor unit and lamp together, and ensuring the lamp fixing holes are at the top of the bracket, mark the wall for drilling the fixing holes. Make sure it is square or it could look a real eyesore!*

1 *This was the old lamp at the rear of the house. Its only good point was that the mains wiring was already available!*

4 *The brackets for the passive infra red and floodlight also slot together.*

6 *Drill the holes using a suitable drill, and plug if into mortar.*

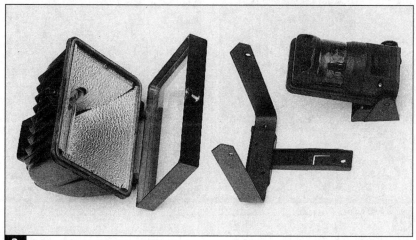

2 *The components of the Night Protector.*

7 *Remove the top cover on the halogen lamp. The cable which links the sensor to the halogen lamp is supplied. Strip the wires first.*

8 Connect the Neutral, Live and Earth from the sensor unit to the lamp unit by feeding them through the grommet in the lamp unit and connect earth link to tab screw by squeezing with pliers. Remove the terminal block for easier installation. Then connect the Live and Neutral wires.

9 Screw terminal block back into position and replace cover.

10 Connect the cable from the lamp to the appropriate terminals as marked in the sensor housing.

11 Screw the lamp and sensor bracket into position on the wall.

12 Using the hexagon nuts provided, secure the lamp to the bracket; the sensor will be hanging below it.

13 Clip the sensor into its bracket below the lamp.

14 Bring the mains cable to the sensor unit, and wire as indicated (the two earth wires will be in the same terminal).

15 *Screw the cable clamps into position to hold the wiring in place. The grommets provide protection against weather and a seal prevents dirt getting in.*

17 *You can adjust light level sensitivity and the length of time the lamp stays on by turning the controls with a screw driver.*

16 *Fix the sensor housing with the two screws provided.*

18 *The installed floodlight is adequate to illuminate a small garden, and additional lights can be run from the same system.*

CHAPTER 19

Outside security

The importance of external security is often overlooked. It's all too easy to concentrate your attentions on fitting locks to windows and doors and to forget external considerations altogether.

First, you need to consider the landscaping of your property to prevent intruders from having places to hide, and security lighting to eliminate any 'black spots' (see Chapter 18) for the same reasons,

and you need to consider the security of outbuildings.

Take a typical shed or garage. These probably contain all the tools a burglar would need to break into your home – no matter how well-secured it might be. Neglecting the security of such outbuildings will undo all the hard work you have put into securing your home.

Not only that, but signs around your property that you are security-conscious will go a long way to

deterring a thief from attempting a break-in in the first place. If external security is up to scratch, chances are the protection for the home itself will also be to a high standard. Even stickers in your windows showing that you belong to a Neighbourhood Watch scheme, or that you have security-marked your property may make an intruder think twice. 'Beware of the Dog' signs and dummy bell boxes also have a role to play.

Design to fight crime

Landscape design is a very important security consideration and one which, until recently, was seriously overlooked. With the introduction of the 'Secured by Design' concept for new housing projects more thought was put into estate design, and many of these ideas can be adopted by the individual home owner.

Perimeter protection

The type of property you live in will determine the level of perimeter protection required. A detached house for instance, usually offers access to the rear of the property on both sides and at the back, requiring

Keep fences low if your property can clearly be seen by neighbours or passers-by. (Fence by Jacksons Fine Fencing)

barrier and, at the same time do not inhibit surveillance. Do make sure, however, that the bars are sufficiently close together – after all, it could be a ten-year-old child attempting access. Railings or a rose trellis can also be used to increase the height of a brick or stone wall. Wooden or wire fences provide little protection. They can easily be cut or kicked down.

'...Shrubs with thorns or spikes provide protection...'

Plants and shrubs can also be used to deter intruders. Roses or thorny shrubs can be planted in front of vulnerable windows, and shrubs with thorns or spikes can provide excellent perimeter protection. Remember to keep them low to the ground, to provide clear views from neighbouring houses and pathways. Paths to and from the house can also be used to improve security. A gravel drive or pathway makes a silent approach to your home impossible, increasing the burglar's risk of being spotted.

Side and rear access gates should always be firmly secured. However,

a higher level of perimeter protection. A terraced house, on the other hand, is more likely to provide limited access and a greater risk of being observed. If you live in a residential area or along a busy road where your home can be clearly seen by neighbours or passers-by, it's important to keep hedges or fences low so that any suspicious activity is likely to be observed. Landscape design can also be used to protect more remote properties by restricting access, although obviously the home is more vulnerable if a burglar is not likely to be spotted attempting a break-in.

Homes which back on to open land, car parks, schools, or where there is easy access to the rear of the property, are particularly vulnerable. In such instances perimeter protection may be provided by dense shrubbery, hedges, walls or fences. A solid brick or stone wall built to the maximum height permitted by the Local Authority will provide a good level of protection, provided it does

not feature decorative effects such as alcoves or projecting bricks which a burglar could use to scale the wall. Tempting as it may be, avoid topping the wall with broken glass or spikes. If there were an injury you may be liable.

Alternatively you could install iron railings. These provide a reasonable

For security and convenience this gate has been fitted with an Autogate from Jacksons Fine Fencing, allowing automatic operation from the comfort of your car.

traditional garden gates offer little in the way of security, with fixings and bolts that are normally weak and easily overcome. Gates should be at least the same height as the surrounding wall or fence, and should provide minimum clearance at the bottom to prevent someone crawling under. Ideally, the gate should be made of strong wood or metal, capable of standing up to a brute force attack, with no bars or rungs which a burglar could climb. Wrought iron gates often provide a ready-made climbing frame! Wooden gates should be secured with a five-lever mortice lock or a rim deadlock. Alternatively you could use a close shackle padlock in conjunction with a hasp and staple (also known as a padbar).

'...Wrought iron gates can provide a climbing frame...'

For large remote properties, security and convenience can be combined if you can afford the luxury of gates that open automatically. When these are linked to a closed circuit television camera and/or audio visual entry panel, they enable you to view the caller and grant or refuse entry from the comfort of your own home. They also prevent a burglar from gaining vehicular access to your grounds, loading up and driving away. Ideally, any CCTV system should be linked to a video recorder so that, if a break-in is attempted, the intruder will be captured on film. Cameras can also be strategically placed and linked together to provide surveillance for vulnerable areas around the home. Dummy CCTV cameras are also available to make a thief think that a system has been installed, or to make an existing system look more comprehensive than it really is.

Drainpipes

Drainpipes can provide a means of access to upstairs windows. Old metal drainpipes may be strong enough to climb and, provided the house is not listed, should be replaced with plastic versions. An alternative is to coat the drainpipe with anti-climb paint which should be applied from about six feet upwards. This nasty, sticky substance will not dry and not only makes the pipe impossible to climb, but will also leave the intruder covered conspicuously in paint that is very difficult to remove.

Garages

As we remarked earlier, the garage or shed probably contains all the tools a burglar would need to break into your home; not to mention items of value such as expensive garden equipment, sports equipment or DIY tools.

On all types of garages you will need to ensure that both the vehicle and personal access doors are secure.

If you have an integral garage it should be secured as part of the home. The door leading from the garage to the house should be treated as a final exit door and should ideally be secured as a back door with a five-lever mortice lock and possibly hinge bolts and mortice bolts.

Detached garages should be secured with a five-lever mortice lock or deadlock on the personal access door. Vehicular access metal 'up-and-over' doors are often supplied with inferior locking devices which are easily overcome. These can be supplemented with a multi-purpose door bolt for metal or wooden doors which incorporates a steel locking bar designed to engage in a fixed frame, and is secured by a key mechanism. Some up-and-over doors are now supplied with multi-point locking systems. Alternatively fix a padbolt to each side of the metal door (use rivets to prevent tampering), with the bolt shooting into the surrounding framework. The bolts can then be secured in place with a close shackle padlock.

Garage doors can also be secured

If you have an integral garage it should be secured as part of the home, with a 5-lever mortice lock and, ideally, mortice bolts and hinge bolts.

Garage doors can be opened and closed from the inside of your car with an automatic door opener.

with a remote-controlled automatic opener if your budget will stretch to it. Double leaf doors may be secured with a cylinder rim lock, but make sure that the door is in good condition – not weak or rotten. The second leaf should be fitted with bolts top and bottom, and hinge bolts should also be fitted to each side.

Garages and workshops may be alarmed to provide greater protection. If they are part of the house they may be linked in to the home alarm system, or can be incorporated easily into a wire-free system. Alternatively, a battery-operated stand alone intruder alarm may be used. Selmar has recently introduced one which offers additional protection by incorporating contact switches to protect doors and windows; and an additional siren which can be fitted to the exterior of the garage, or wired up inside the home to alert occupants to an intrusion.

For sheds and garages the Beta-Thief alarm incorporates two sirens – one to be used inside the protected property and the other fitted externally to be heard from nearby houses.

Sheds

By their very construction, sheds are not designed for security. If a burglar wants to break in he will. The opportunist can often be deterred, however, by a stout close-shackle padlock and padbar fitted to the door. Suitable window locks should be fitted to shed and garage windows – again make sure that the frames are in reasonable condition.

Tools should be locked away in the shed or garage at all times – even if you are only popping out for a few minutes – so that they cannot be used for a break-in or vandalism. Items should also be security marked. Ladders in particular should be kept safely out of reach. If they cannot be locked in a garage, secure them to an outside wall with a padlock and chain.

Don't leave ladders propped against a wall. Make sure they are properly secured.

resistance against attempts to cut or saw through the shackle. A shackle which is easily accessible (i.e., an open shackle padlock) and which isn't manufactured from hardened steel provides an inferior level of protection as it is easily tampered with. To prevent tampering, the padlock and padbar should not have any exposed screws or bolt-heads (unless they are clutch head or security screws).

Sheds and greenhouses can be protected with a portable alarm like the model 6000 from Superswitch.

'...For maximum security choose a padlock with a concealed or close shackle...'

To ensure that the padlock is adequate for your requirements, look for the British Standard 'kite mark' which guarantees that it has been manufactured to meet the requirements of the British Standards Institute, or one which is 'insurance-approved'. Beware of very cheap padlocks as they may offer little in the way of security. Expect to pay around £20.00 upwards.

Greenhouses

Even the garden greenhouse is not immune to the thief. Expensive plants can always be sold on – with no questions asked. Again a padlock on the door will help, but if your plants are really valuable to you, you could use a portable battery-operated alarm to provide interior protection. This will sense an intrusion and sound a loud built-in alarm to alert the householder or neighbours.

Padlocks

Padlocks vary tremendously in quality and, at the end of the day, you get what you pay for. You will need not only a padlock, but also a padbar which comprises a lock staple fitted to the door frame, and a hinged hasp which is fitted to the

door. For maximum security choose a padlock with a concealed shackle or, next best, a close shackle and high shoulders. A concealed or close shackle provides much greater

Fit good quality hasps and padlocks, ideally with a concealed or close shackle like the Diskus from CK Abus.

WATCHPOINTS

1 Make sure your house can be clearly seen by neighbours and passers-by.

2 Houses which back on to open land should be secured with high walls or dense shrubbery.

3 Use prickly shrubs outside windows to deter intruders.

4 Make sure gates are the same height as the surrounding wall and provide minimum clearance at the bottom.

5 Secure garage doors, gates, sheds and greenhouses with adequate locking devices.

6 Ideally, use higher security close shackle padlocks.

7 Replace metal drainpipes with plastic ones if they provide easy access to upstairs windows.

8 On an integral garage treat the personal access door as a final exit door and secure with a five-lever mortice lock.

▼ Fitting a garage door lock

One of the most successful ways of securing an up-and-over garage door is with a padbar and stout padlock fitted to each side of the door. For greater convenience, ask a locksmith for two padlocks that are keyed alike, i.e., can be operated with the same key.

1 *Mark and drill holes on the garage door for the padbar.*

2 *Secure bar in position with bolts that cannot be undone from the outside.*

3 *With the bolts holding the padbar firmly in position, a the rivet gun to shoot rivets through remaining screw holes.*

4 *Using a pencil or sharp instrument, mark the position of the bolt hole on the garage wall and drill.*

▼ Lock up your ladder

If ladders cannot be safely locked away, they should be firmly secured to a wall. This method, involving a roll bolt, length of chain and padlock, provides a very strong fixing.

1 *Select a suitable site for the roll bolt, indoors or out, and drill hole.*

3 *Once the fit is correct, insert the roll bolt and secure in place by tightening the nut.*

5 *Shoot bolt into the wall and secure in place with a stout padlock. Repeat for other side of the door.*

2 *Insert the bolt to check fit – the drill hole must be just the right size to accept the bolt.*

4 *Loop chain through the ring on the bolt, around the ladder several times and secure in place with the padlock.*

CHAPTER 20

Fire fighters

Cooking appliances are the most frequent cause of accidental fires in the home.

Every home contains many potential fire hazards. Some – such as cooking with hot oil, smoking in bed and carelessly guarded open fires – are quite obvious; others are less so. But, no matter what the source, a fire in the home is devastating, not to mention potentially lethal.

Each year in the UK there are over 50,000 accidental fires in the home, and many people are injured. An early warning and a contingency plan for what to do in the event of fire are important considerations which could go a long way to minimizing damage and, more important still, preventing injury or death.

Kitchen hazards

Cooking appliances are the most frequent cause of accidental fires in the home. Care should be taken with saucepans on the cooker, particularly if there are young children at home, and handles should be positioned so that they don't overhang a hot ring or burner, or the edge of the stove. Never lean over the hob when it is switched on, and make sure that tea towels do not overhang the cooker.

Chip pan fires are a particular hazard. Once switched on, chip pans should never be left unattended. Never fill a pan more than one-third full with fat or oil, and do not insert wet chips. When you have finished cooking, turn off the heat and remove the pan from the heat source. If a fire does start, do not attempt to move the pan. Turn off the heat, if it is safe to do so, cover the pan with a lid or damp cloth and leave to cool for at least half an hour. If you cannot control the fire, shut the door and call the fire brigade immediately. Safer than a chip pan is a thermostatically controlled fryer which can be purchased from most electrical stores.

Smoking

Many deaths and injuries result from carelessly discarded cigarettes and matches. Lighted cigarettes or pipes should never be left lying around; they could easily fall on to upholstery and start a fire. Always make sure you have plenty of deep ash trays around, and check

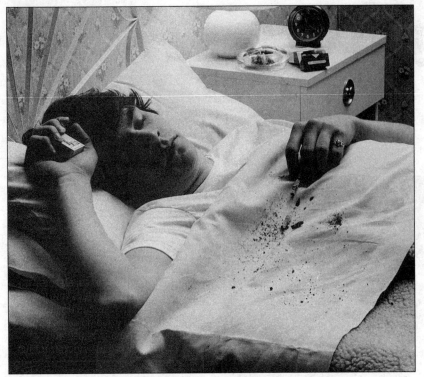

Never smoke in bed – dozing off while smoking a cigarette or pipe could cost you your life.

Electric blankets can be very dangerous when misused. They should be kept dry and flat and should be serviced every two or three years (you can ask the shop you bought it from to arrange this for you). Buy a blanket which conforms to British Standard BS3456, and preferably one that has over-heat protection. An electric underblanket should always be switched off before getting into bed. Some overblankets are designed to be left on, but check the manufacturer's instructions.

Heaters

With a return to more traditional decor, open fires are again seeing a return in popularity. Chimneys should be swept at least twice a year if you burn ordinary coal, once a year if you use smokeless fuel. If

upholstery for cigarette ends before going out or to bed. Empty ashtrays last thing at night – preferably into metal bins with lids – and make sure they are properly extinguished. Never smoke in bed – dozing off while smoking a cigarette or pipe could cost you your life. Finally, make sure matches and lighters are kept out of the reach of children.

Electric appliances

Fires caused by electrical faults, accidents or misuse of electrical equipment are very common. Maintenance of house wiring and appliances is vital for safety. Wiring should be checked regularly. If your home still uses round pin plugs, or if the wiring is over 25 years old, it probably requires replacing. Indications that wiring is dangerous include plugs and sockets that are hot to the touch, and fuses which blow for no apparent reason. Wiring should be checked by your local

electricity company, or by an electrician on the roll of the National Inspection Council for Electrical Installation Contracting (NICEIC). Appliances should also be checked regularly, and frayed flexes replaced. Flexes should never run near hot surfaces, or under carpets where they could be damaged without being noticed. Always use the correct fuse for equipment. Make sure that your home has enough electrical sockets to avoid having to use multi-way adaptors and wires trailing across the floor. When joining flex, use purpose-made connectors – never twist the wires together. Never cover light bulbs with fabric or paper, and remember always to switch off electrical appliances when not in use, and remove plugs from sockets. If you suspect that an appliance is faulty, do not use it until it has been properly checked. Never attempt any electrical jobs unless you know exactly what you are doing.

A portable heater should be kept well away from inflammable materials and areas where it could be knocked over, or where something is likely to fall on it.

you think the chimney is on fire, call the fire brigade immediately and remove any materials that could catch fire. Always put a fire guard in front of the fireplace, using a British Standard approved all-enclosed guard, particularly if there are children or elderly people at home. Remember to damp down the fire before going out, or off to bed.

Portable heaters should be kept well away from flammable materials and areas where they could be knocked over, or where something is likely to fall on them. Do not use portable heaters to dry clothes.

Gas appliances

When lighting a gas cooker or heater you should always be ready to light the burner before you turn on the gas. If you have an appliance with a pilot light it should light immediately. If it doesn't, turn off the gas and check that the pilot is alight.

If you smell gas, extinguish cigarettes and never use matches or a naked flame. Do not operate electrical switches. Open doors and windows and then check to see whether a tap has been left on, or a pilot light has gone out. If you suspect a gas leak, turn off the main gas tap (usually located next to the gas meter) and call the gas company immediately.

Gas appliances should be serviced regularly and should be installed by British Gas or by a member of CORGI.

Bottled gas should always be stored in an outbuilding, never in the home, and must be protected from heat and frost. Cylinders should be changed outdoors or in a well-ventilated room. If you suspect a leak, test by brushing soapy water over the joints and connections. If bubbles appear the cylinder is leaking and should be capped and placed outdoors until it can be checked by an engineer.

Safe at night

Many serious fires are those which start at night, taking hold before they can be discovered. It is crucial therefore to have a bedtime routine.

Before retiring to bed, switch off all electrical appliances (except those designed to be left on) and remove plugs from sockets. Empty ash trays, making sure that their contents are extinguished and discarded safely, and check furniture for cigarettes and matches. Damp open fires down. Finally close all doors, so that if a fire does break out it is less likely to spread quickly to other parts of the house.

Smoke detectors

Should a fire break out, your chances of survival will be much greater if a smoke alarm is installed. By providing the earliest possible warning, this gives you a vital extra few minutes to escape.

The fact that more and more people have fitted smoke alarms in homes has not only reduced the number of deaths in fires, but also increased the number of fires

detected early on, before they take hold. The number who died in fires in the home has now fallen to the lowest figure since 1971, and domestic fires where smoke detectors have given early warning have risen by 164 per cent since 1988.

Nevertheless, 75 per cent of deaths in fires are in the home and most of these are fires caused by the misuse of cooking appliances. Half are started in the kitchen, and a third of all deaths are caused by smoking and smokers' materials.

Choosing a smoke detector

So, if you don't have a smoke detector, now is the time to fit one. There are several types on the market, ranging in price from under £10 to over £20. Models use either ionization or photoelectric detection, and can be mains or battery-powered. Make sure they conform to BS5446 Part 1 1990 and display a British Standard kitemark, as this shows they have been adequately tested.

Ionization units contain a tiny amount of harmless radioactive

Smoke detectors are saving lives every day by detecting fires at an early stage.

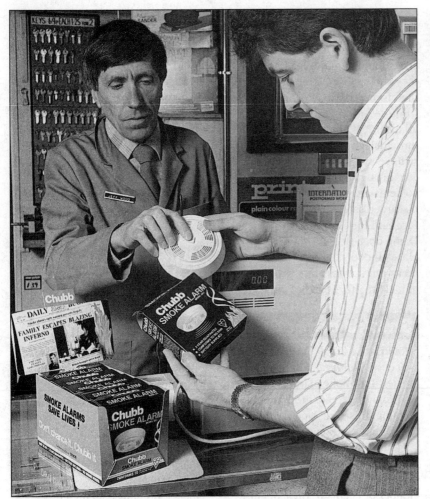

Choose a smoke detector with a BS kitemark.

Ideally, fit one alarm on each floor of your home, and if you are only fitting one make sure it is between the sleeping and living rooms – the lounge or kitchen.

A smoke alarm should be fitted on the ceiling in the centre of a room or a hallway. If you have to fit the alarm on a wall, it should be around six inches from the ceiling so it can detect smoke as it rises. If the room has a gable, the alarm should be fitted about three feet from the highest point. If you can, also fit a detector at the top of the stairs and in or outside each bedroom.

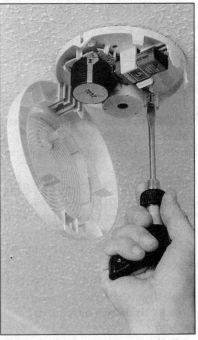

Fitting a smoke detector is very simple. Fit the battery, and screw the unit to the ceiling. A ratchet screwdriver can be handy here.

material (said to be less radioactive than a house brick) and can detect tiny changes in an electric current flowing in the chamber caused by smoke particles in the air. They are able to respond quickly to flaming fires.

Photoelectric alarms use pulsating light beams which 'see' smoke and are claimed to respond more quickly to smouldering fires.

Mains-powered alarms

Recent legislation means that new and newly-converted homes must be fitted with mains-powered smoke detectors and, while these have been regular stock for professional alarm

installers and electricians, they are now being made more widely available. These must be interconnected and can be powered by either mains electricity, mains electricity with battery back-up or low voltage via a mains transformer.

Battery-operated models, using a 9v battery, are perfectly acceptable for existing homes, however, and these are available from most DIY and hardware stores and security specialists. They are very simple to fit with just a battery to insert and two screws to secure the unit to the ceiling. Be careful where you fit the device, however, as ionization units are sensitive and may trigger if you burn the toast or are grilling lamb chops, for example.

Don't fit a smoke detector in the garage where exhaust fumes could set off the alarm or where insects could get into the unit, or in bathrooms and kitchens where condensation or cooking fumes could affect it. Battery-operated detectors don't usually work in

A smoke detector should have a test button. Sometimes these can be operated using a torch so you don't have to climb on a chair or steps.

extreme temperatures – below 40° F (4°C), or above 100°F (38°C) – so don't fit them in a conservatory, boiler room or cold store room.

If fitting a detector at the top of the stairs means testing the unit or changing the battery could be difficult or dangerous, find another suitable spot, or choose a unit which can be tested with a torch (First Alert produce a unit that can be tested by shining a torch beam across the test button so you don't have to stand on a chair or stepladder, and Dicon's Micro 300 has an extra large button which can be pressed using a broom handle or walking stick). You'd still have to reach it to change the battery, of course, something you should do at least once a year, although the unit will give a low battery warning. Make sure you always have a spare battery – fire chiefs have pointed out that while many people have fitted smoke detectors, quite a large percentage aren't in operation because they haven't bothered to change the battery. A long-life alkaline battery can last up to three years.

Special features

Some detectors are fitted with a light which comes on automatically when the alarm is triggered. This is designed to help you make your escape in smoky conditions, and if there is a power failure. Others are fitted with a 'pause' button which allows you to silence the alarm and reduce its sensitivity for around eight minutes – so you can finish burning the toast! These are suitable for caravans or similar confined areas. The alarm should automatically reset after the stated time. Some smoke alarms can be interlinked so that if one alarms others elsewhere in the house are triggered at the same time.

Recent developments include a portable detector (not intended to replace permanent devices) and, bearing in mind the need for mains-operated alarms, intruder alarm manufacturer Scantronic has come up with a smoke alarm which is designed to fit in place of a ceiling rose. It can be fitted directly into the existing house lighting circuit without the need for additional wiring and without interfering with the normal light switch operation. The switch can, however, be used to test the alarm and provide a 'pause' facility. Rechargeable, stand-by lithium batteries provide at least a ten year life.

You can now buy smoke detectors which can be interconnected so that if one is triggered the others elsewhere will alert people in other parts of the house.

Extinguishing the flames

A fire extinguisher can be worth having around, but do make sure you choose the right type and you know how to use it properly. The old halon filled canisters are no longer being produced because of their ozone depleting affects (the manufacture of halon gas has been banned since early 1994) and other alternatives are being developed. However, powder, foam, water and CO_2 gas cover most eventualities, with powder the most suitable for the home.

A fire blanket is very useful in the kitchen, particularly for smothering chip pan fires, still one of the largest causes of fires. They can also be wrapped around a person to smother the flames. Usually wall-mounted, made of woven glass fibre and with quick release tabs, they should conform to BS6575: 1985.

Which Extinguisher to Use

Class of fire	Water	Spray foam	CO_2 Gas	Powder
Type A Paper, Wood, Textile & Fabric	●	●		●
Type B Inflammable liquids		●	●	●
Type C Inflammable gases			●	●
Electrical hazards			●	●
Vehicle protection		●		●

Chubb do special dual packs of a fire blanket and fire extinguisher for use in the home.

A fire blanket is ideal for smothering chip pan fires in the kitchen.

Making an escape

If a fire does take hold you will need to get yourself and your family out of the house as quickly as possible. It can take less than 60 seconds for a small fire to fill your home with highly poisonous smoke and fumes.

It's a good idea, therefore, to plan an escape route in advance. Try to plan two escape routes from each room, and make sure that all windows and doors can be opened easily. Keep a torch handy to use during your escape, and keep keys to hand to allow a prompt exit.

If a fire does break out, close the door of the affected room to delay the spread of fire and smoke. If closed doors feel warm do not open them, as you will release the fire. Get everyone out of the house and do not go back in to save possessions. Phone the fire brigade from a neighbour's home or from a phone box. Warn neighbours if your home adjoins others. If you are cut off by the fire, try to get everyone into a room at the front of the house; close the door and use bedding or other materials to seal any gaps. Go to the window and try to attract attention. If the room begins to fill with smoke, stay as close to the ground as you can.

> ### '...less than 60 seconds for a fire to fill your home with poisonous smoke...'

If the fire is so severe that you must escape before the fire brigade arrives, climb out through the window, breaking the glass if it is jammed. Remove jagged glass and cover the lower sill with a blanket. Drop bedding or cushions on to the ground to break your fall and climb out, feet first, lowering yourself to the full length of your arms before dropping. This should only be attempted from first floor windows.

If you live in a flat, never use the lifts in the event of fire – always use the main or escape staircases.

If clothing catches fire, lie down immediately and roll across the floor. If someone else's clothing is alight, force them to the floor and wrap a blanket, rug or carpet round them. Call medical help as soon as possible.

It can take less than 60 seconds for a small fire to fill your home with highly poisonous smoke and fumes.

One other fire safety device you may like to consider is an escape ladder. Several manufacturers have introduced these, including the Eliza Tinsley Res-Q Ladder, the Firefly from Red House Marketing and Phoenix Safety Ladders. Make sure the ladder has stable brackets which fit inside the window, a spacer which keeps you away from the building as you climb down, and has strong enough rungs (of steel which should be resistant to heat and non-corrosive). Some units can be stored in a cabinet in a room where exit is most likely, or be folded away beneath the window. Typically the Eliza Tinsley ladders range in price from £45 to £70.

An emergency escape ladder like this one from Eliza Tinsley could help you make a safe exit.

WATCHPOINTS

1 Keep portable heaters away from anything combustible, such as furniture or curtains.

2 Do not place a clothes horse near a fire or the cooker.

3 Always stub out cigarettes in a deep ashtray.

4 Never smoke in bed.

5 Surround heaters and fires with a large guard.

6 Do not stand portable heaters where they could be knocked over.

7 Do not use a candle or naked flame for lighting.

8 Store inflammable liquids in a cool, safe place (out of sunlight), in clearly labelled containers.

9 Make sure loft insulation is non-combustible.

10 Buy flame retardant nightwear and bedding.

11 Make sure upholstered furniture conforms to safety standards.

12 Buy a fire blanket and a suitable fire extinguisher.

13 Fit a smoke detector which has a BSI kitemark and conforms to BS5446 Part 1 1990.

14 A smoke alarm should not be fitted in the kitchen, bathroom, garage or in areas likely to experience extreme heat or cold.

15 Interconnectable smoke alarms can be used to ensure everyone in the house will hear the alarm.

16 A newly built house or a newly converted home must be fitted with mains-powered smoke alarms.

17 Change the battery in your smoke alarm regularly.

18 Test smoke alarms every month.

19 Once a year, remove the cover and dust or vacuum the inside of the smoke alarm to ensure insects are not trapped.

20 If fitted on a wall, a smoke alarm should be no less than six inches from the ceiling.

21 Do not fit a smoke alarm in the peak of a gabled room.

CHAPTER 21

People in glass houses

- Easily accessible ground floor rear windows and doors which are out of sight of neighbours or passers by.
- Replacing louvre windows.
- Glass panels in the front door, or to the side of the door which allow a burglar to break the glass, put his hand through and release the catch.
- Leaded lights – burglars can gain access by leaning on these to stretch the lead, then lift out the small panes, undo the catch and climb in. Double glazed units with a leaded light effect cannot be attacked like this.

Types of glass

Annealed glass
In homes, most windows are fitted with ordinary annealed glass (unless they have been fitted with toughened or laminated glass for safety purposes). Annealed glass, which is also known as float or plate, breaks very easily, producing long, sharp-edged splinters which can cause horrific injuries. It is very vulnerable to the thief who may break a small area of glass near a lock or handle to gain access. He is less likely to smash a large glazed area as the resulting noise could attract attention.

Home security is most often viewed in terms of fitting better locks and bolts. But one of the weakest areas of any building is often overlooked – its glazing.

Glass is very vulnerable. The wrong sort of glass fitted in the wrong place increases the number of weak points in a building. In 21 per cent of all domestic burglaries, the intruder breaks glass to gain entry. Secure locks and bolts will act as a deterrent – especially against the opportunist. But, if you are considering replacing windows or glazing for reasons such as safety or energy efficiency, it may be worth fitting glass which offers greater security in several particularly vulnerable areas:

Annealed glass breaks very easily, producing long, sharp-edged splinters which can cause horrific injuries.

Wired glass

The appearance of wired glass can be misleading, with the wire mesh making it look stronger than it really is. In most cases it is simply annealed glass with a thin steel mesh embedded. The glass is easily fractured but the mesh is designed to hold the glass in place, acting as a barrier until the mesh is sheared. Once this occurs the glass will just fall away leaving jagged fragments and the additional risk of injury from protruding wires. With sustained pressure the glazed area can be removed from the surrounding beading. Wired glass is mainly used as a fire retarding material, providing resistance for up to one hour, or more in some special cases.

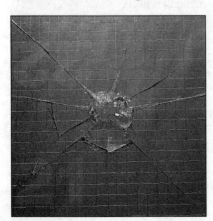

Once wired glass breaks, severe injuries can be caused by sharp splinters and protruding wires.

However, Pilkington Glass has introduced a safety wired glass which combines fire resistance with impact resistance. This is provided by a specially developed electrically treated steel wire mesh. It is classified as a Class C safety glazing material in accordance with BS6206 and satisfies the fire requirements of Part B of the Building Regulations.

Toughened glass

Toughened, or tempered glass is annealed glass which has been subjected to a heating and fast cooling process to give much greater strength. Greater impact is necessary to break it, but when it does break, the glass will shatter into tiny pieces. These particles are not sharp like annealed glass so injuries are much less severe, but, once broken, it does provide the burglar with a safe entry and exit.

When broken, toughened glass will shatter into tiny fragments, ensuring that injuries are much less severe.

Because of the manufacturing process, toughened glass cannot be cut to size on site and must be ordered to size from a glass merchant. Any measurements, therefore, must be accurate.

Laminated glass

Laminated glass is an excellent safety glass and, unlike other types of glass, can, depending on the thickness used, provide a very high level of security. It is made by bonding together two or more panes of ordinary float glass alternated with a plastic interlayer called polyvinyl butyral (PVB). The outer layer of glass will break almost as easily as ordinary glass, but the pieces remain bonded to the interlayer so there are no dangerous splinters or glass fragments. By using sheer brute force an intruder may eventually break through the interlayer, depending on the thickness of the glass, but the amount of noise and length of time required should be a sufficient deterrent.

With laminated glass any shattered fragments adhere to the plastic interlayer, avoiding injury and prohibiting entry.

The number of glass and pvb layers is varied according to the application. In the home, laminated glass with a thickness of 6.4mm or 6.8mm is most commonly used. This is known as a safety glass which also incorporates an element of security. Glass with a thickness of 7.5mm or more is known as security/anti-bandit glass and is used in retail and commercial applications. Anti-bandit glass has thicker interlayers than safety laminated glass, and special glazing techniques are usually employed.

Laminated glass fitted to easily accessible ground floor windows and doors will deter intruders.

Installation

Annealed glass used around the home is normally 4mm thick, so when installing laminated glass the extra thickness must be taken into consideration, particularly when framing; it may be a problem with existing fixtures. Laminated glass for use in interior windows and doors can be installed using putty, although laminated glass in exterior installations should be fitted using a silicone-based sealant to prevent moisture penetrating between the glass and frame as, on rare occasions, the moisture can cause delamination. Because of its construction, the glass must be cut from both sides. It is as easy to fit as ordinary glass, bearing in mind the thickness and cutting requirements, but you would be well advised to contact a glazier for advice and have the glass cut to size.

In addition to security and safety, laminated glass offers further benefits, cutting out damaging ultra-violet rays to protect furnishings from fading, and providing insulation against noise. It can be used successfully in double glazing, and if only one of the two panes of glass is laminated, this should be installed on the inside of the unit to maximize safety benefits. The cost of laminated glass differs from glazier to glazier so it's a good idea to obtain several quotes. Generally, laminated glass costs approximately half as much again as ordinary glass, but when it is installed or replaced complete with new frame and glass, the additional cost of laminated glass will only be 20-30 per cent at most.

Plastic films

An alternative to reglazing is the application of an adhesive plastic film on to an existing pane of glass. These films are designed to cut down the amount of sunlight getting into a room, to reduce heat loss and to make vulnerable areas of glass safer and more secure. Some films offer a one-way mirrored effect to increase privacy, allowing the occupants to see out, but preventing anyone outside looking in.

Films are available in a variety of thicknesses to protect against accidental impact through to vandalism and even terrorist bomb attacks. Buy a good quality film which is scratch resistant and UV stabilized. It should be tested to BS6206. Thinner films for use around the home, and where the area to be covered is not too large, are suitable for DIY installation. Bonwyke, for instance, offers a DIY film in two feet widths which, they claim, is probably the largest width that should be applied without specialist training.

'...Buy a good quality film...'

The installation process is quite simple but it can be difficult to apply the film smoothly. Fitting requires spraying the surface of a previously cleaned pane of glass with water, removing the protective liner and sliding the film on to the wet surface. With the Bonwyke film the adhesive does not adhere immediately so the film can be positioned accurately. A squeegee is then used to iron out air bubbles and excess water. Edges may be trimmed using a straight edge trimming guide and a Stanley knife. Films take about four weeks to dry properly, after which time it should be virtually undetectable.

When buying glass it is advisable to approach a glazier who is a member of the Glass and Glazing Federation, in which case the GGF logo will be displayed on the premises. A good glazier will ask you where the glass is to be sited and, if the application is potentially dangerous, should insist that you fit safety glass.

Safety

According to latest figures released by RoSPA (The Royal Society for the Prevention of Accidents), every year 40,000 people have to be treated in hospital after accidents in the home involving glass.

With the revised Building Regulations of June 1992, it is now a legal requirement to install safety glazing in certain critical locations. Glazing with which people are likely to come into contact while passing through a building should, if broken on impact, break in a way which is unlikely to cause injury, resist impact without breaking, or be shielded or protected from impact. In the home this would include areas such as fully glazed doors, door side panels, shower screens and glazing in wet areas, low level glazing, glass in furniture, conservatories and patio doors.

'...assess the safety of glazing...'

Remember that these regulations apply to glass which is installed in new buildings, including extensions and conservatories, or in areas where glazing did not exist previously. In homes built before this date it's important to assess the safety of glazing, particularly if there are young children at home. Check any areas of glass which could be potentially dangerous. This includes internal doors, full length windows, patio doors, porches, conservatories, front and back doors, glass doors at the bottom of stairs, glass-topped tables, full length mirrors and glass roofs and skylights.

If you move to a new home it's worth asking whether safety glass has been installed. Each pane of safety glass should be marked in one of the corners, but sometimes the marks can be concealed in the framing. The mark should incorporate the words BS6206 which shows the glass conforms to the relevant British Standard for safety in buildings. It will also feature the letter 'T' for toughened or 'L' for laminated glass, as well as the registration number of the company which supplied the glass. If in doubt, call in a glazier for advice.

If non-safety glass is fitted in potentially dangerous areas, either remove it and replace it with safety glass, or place wooden battens across to prevent anyone falling against it. Safety films can also be used but, on the advice of the Glass and Glazing Federation, the installation should be carried out professionally. If the film is applied correctly the combination of glass and film can reach BS6206, but check with the supplier that this is the case.

In all cases remember that some glass or plastic glazing materials can present a serious obstacle to emergency escape. Every room must have a window which can be opened and is large enough to climb through. Keys for security locks must be kept readily to hand.

British Standards

BS6262 – Glazing for Buildings
BS6262 identifies areas in the home where safety glazing should be installed to reduce the risk of injuries resulting from broken glass.

BS6206 – Impact performance for flat safety glass.
BS6206 was introduced to define a safety glass. Using an impact performance test devised by the British Standards Institution, a glass is defined as Class A, B or C relating to the level of protection it gives. A, the highest grade, is strong enough to resist the impact of a 14-year-old boy running at the speed of a four-minute mile.

WATCHPOINTS

1 Security glass will give greater protection on vulnerable windows and doors.

2 When buying glass, go to a member of the Glass and Glazing Federation (GGF).

3 It is now a legal requirement to install safety glazing in certain critical locations in new buildings, or areas where glazing did not exist previously.

4 Check glass in your home for marks which illustrate whether it is safety glass.

5 Replace any areas of glass which could be potentially dangerous, especially if there are young children at home.

6 Make sure that fitted safety films reach BS6206.

7 Ensure that each room provides an emergency escape.

CHAPTER 22

Careless means carless!

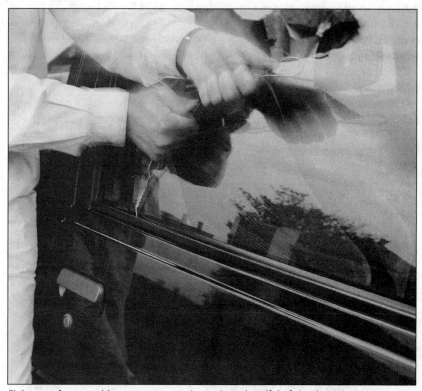

Eight out of ten car thieves are opportunists, using a handful of simple tools.

Although the increase in vehicle crime had reduced in 1992 there were still 1.5 million reported thefts. This means more than a third of all reported offences are vehicle related, cars either being stolen or being broken into for items left inside.

The 1992 British Crime Survey, which includes unreported crimes as well as those recorded, puts the figure much higher at 2.5 million thefts from vehicles and over 500,000 thefts of vehicles.

In 1992 the Home Office launched a new media campaign to fight car crime. The image and sounds of a hyena were used to represent the scavenging car thief, who would laugh in an eerie, evil fashion at yet another motorist who had left his car unlocked with valuables on display, even leaving the ignition key in the lock.

The apathy of the motorist was very evident and well documented; this remarkably careless attitude would often result in his becoming carless!

A NOP poll revealed that 30 per cent of motorists didn't do more to protect their cars because of the expense, and 18 per cent put it down to apathy. In addition, 75 per cent of motorists said that they might well leave their car unlocked in a petrol station while they were paying for petrol, with a further 24 per cent admitting to the possibility of leaving it unlocked if they 'popped into a shop'.

Over 8 per cent said they had left their car unlocked in a public car park in the last month; they probably didn't realize that 20 per cent of all car crime (and up to 40 per cent in some areas) takes place in car parks. Nevertheless, 63 per cent said that security was 'very important' when choosing a car.

'...The apathy of the motorist is very evident...'

Car manufacturers have certainly been improving the security of cars, if only after nagging by government and, more particularly, because of the influence of insurance companies. With the revision in Group insurance ratings (there are now 20 compared to nine previously) and the publication of the Thatcham Report which specifies the levels of security a manufacturer must achieve before a car is allocated a particular rating, there is considerable pressure on manufacturers to ensure that premiums are kept down by meeting the criteria. Naturally, if a premium is too high for the type of car and its intended market, it is likely that the manufacturer will sell considerably less of that model.

It would seem, at last, that there is now less emphasis on the speed with which the car will go from 0 to 60 and more on how long it is likely to stay in your possession. Standard equipment being fitted by manufacturers now includes high security door locks, alarms and immobilizer systems, glass etching, coded audio equipment, locks for alloy wheels and visible VIN numbers.

Keeping valuables

Car radio manufacturers have had to fight to keep ahead of the ICE (in-car entertainment) thief. As a result, security coded radios, removable radios and removable radio fascias have been introduced. There are also lockable protective steel housings which can be fitted over the radio itself to conceal it and give it protection. Removing it completely is, of course, the most effective method.

While car radios were once the top target, mobile telephones are now just as vulnerable. Just as the car radio manufacturers have had to invent new ways of protecting and keeping their product in the rightful owner's possession, so the cellphone makers are also having to look at ways of making their phones less attractive to steal. Mobile phone thefts were running at around 10,000 a month in 1993 and the Metropolitan Police indicated that over 40 per cent of car break-ins within Greater London are related to such thefts. The thieves use the stolen phone for 'cloning' (rechipping so that an unsuspecting customer receives a bill for air-time he or she did not use) or for resale where they are rechipped in order to reconnect them to a network.

Measures being considered and introduced include invisibly marking the phone, and a registration system.

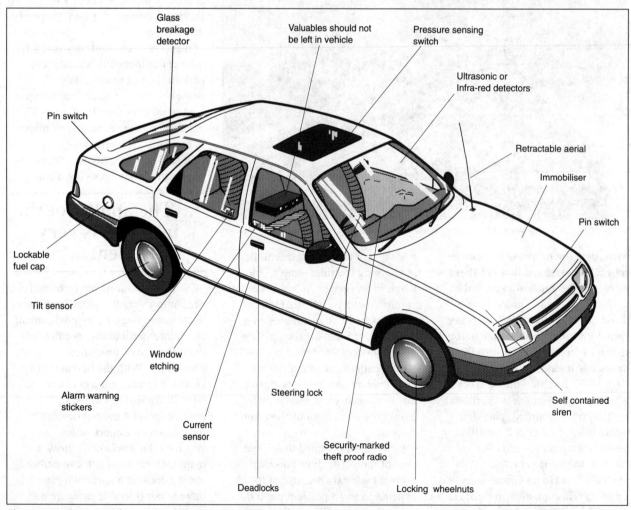

There are many means of improving car security. This vehicle has been fitted with a wide range of physical and electronic options.

Choose wisely

If you are buying a product to fit to your car, how do you know how effective it is? A new organization, Sold Secure PACT, an initiative by Northumbria police, is now spreading nationwide via police forces and comprises a network of installers and retailers who are able to sell and fit tried and tested products which can then be used to help police trace any stolen vehicle fitted with a recognized product.

A technical committee assesses the product – an alarm or lock, for example – and will only recognize products that are able to withstand a criminal attack for five minutes, a time scale arrived at from police working knowledge of how long a thief is prepared to work on stealing a vehicle. The issue of a certificate for each product fitted in accordance with specifications allows the police to set up a database for tracing if ever necessary.

'...Fit tried and tested products...'

You should also be aware that there is a British Standard for vehicle alarms. BS6803 Part 2 is a code of practice for systems installed after vehicle marketing, and this covers components and installation of an alarm. If you have an alarm installed, make sure the fitter complies with this standard.

AU209 is a standard covering other aspects of vehicle security, including locking systems, security etching, marking of car hi-fi equipment, and it may well include the use of laminated glass in cars. A section on immobilizers is also in preparation.

There are many initiatives up and down the country fighting car crime. Elsewhere we have mentioned another growing scheme, Vehicle

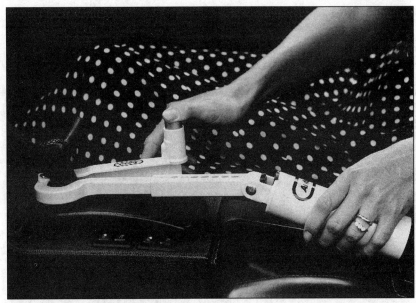

Use a visible deterrent like this device from Autolok which secures the handbrake and gear lever.

Watch, which allows the police to identify cars on the road at unusual times. Do check to see if your police force operates a scheme like this. Look, too, for car parks that have a Secured Car Parks gold or silver award. These will have built-in security, such as closed circuit television, regular patrols and good lighting.

If the latest 1992 figures are anything to go by, perhaps the small reduction in the increase in car crime is slightly encouraging. However, it is only by thinking twice before we leave our vehicles, and what's on the back seat, that we can ensure we don't become one of those statistics.

Beat the car thief

Eight out of ten car thieves are opportunists, using a handful of simple tools and very little in the way of skill. In many cases, all it takes is the opening of an unlocked door, or a hand reaching in through an open window. The statistics for car crime are staggering, yet few drivers take even simple steps to protect their vehicles.

By increasing the time it takes to break into your vehicle, simple security devices can go a long way towards safeguarding your car and its contents. But it's important also not to make your car an attractive target in the first place. Take desirable items with you or, at the very least, lock them away out of sight in the boot. If you own an estate car, make or buy a load cover for the luggage compartment. Never leave vehicle documents, or cash and credit cards, in your car.

Even if you are only leaving your car for a matter of seconds, it pays to take precautions. Keep your car locked at all times – even when you are just at the petrol station. Always take the keys with you, and close the windows. Remember, it only takes a few seconds for an opportunist to reach in and make off with your camera or wallet. Make sure, also, that the steering wheel lock is engaged, otherwise the lock could be smashed by a thief forcing the steering wheel. On older cars you can also immobilize the vehicle very easily by removing the rotor arm. Modern cars often have a screw-retained cap or no distributor

The Gearlock from Euro Mul-T-Lock is bolted to the vehicle floor and incorporates a high security padlock secured around the gear lever.

at all. Some cars do not even have HT leads.

With growing public awareness of the importance of vehicle security, manufacturers are increasingly building security measures into new cars; research shows 75 per cent of car buyers are prepared to pay for built-in anti-theft features. But it is not just new cars which are targets for the thief. Older cars may not have security measures built in, and rely on the owner fitting secondary security – something which many seem loath to spend money on. In many instances it is these cars which are most at risk. At the end of the day any car without some sort of security measure is a target. It may be taken by joyriders or broken into for a radio, or desirable items left on show. With new MoT regulations, there is even a growing market for stolen windscreens.

Additional security can be as cheap, or as expensive, as you want it to be, but you get what you pay for. There is a wide range of physical security devices on the market which require little in the way of installation skills, and offer

good visible deterrent value. Included amongst the visible deterrents are hook locks linked between the steering wheel and the brake pedal, the steering bar that locks on to the steering wheel to prevent it being turned, locks which fit over the handbrake lever to prevent it being released, and the locking bar that immobilizes the

gearstick and handbrake. All these devices may be carried in the car, and easily locked into place when you leave the vehicle. Another device which operates on a similar principle, but requires professional installation, is the Gearlock from Euro Mul-T-Lock. Bolted to the vehicle floor, this incorporates a high security padlock, operated by a registered key, which is secured around the gear lever in neutral position, to prevent the car being driven away.

Other physical security devices protect individual items fitted to the car. For example, petrol locking caps to keep the joyrider within catching distance, locking wheel nuts to protect expensive alloy wheels, wheel clamps, and lockable covers which fit over the stereo system. Most car audio manufacturers are also taking steps to improve security, with stereos which will only operate when a unique code, known only to the driver, is keyed in if the power is disconnected, and radios which can be removed easily and carried with you. If you must leave valuables in the car, there are vehicle safes you

Lockable covers are available which protect the car radio. This one is from Arjan.

Locking wheel nuts are widely available from motor accessory stores.

can purchase which are bolted to the vehicle floor. Automobile Inparts for example, offers the 'Vault X' safe, available in two sizes to protect pull-out stereos, car phones and other valuables.

Lock logic

Locks fitted to older cars are particularly vulnerable and easily overcome, even by less experienced car thieves. Additional deadlocks, or a central locking system, can be fitted to overcome weak locking devices. Simba offers additional mortice security deadlocks and, for DIY enthusiasts, Safeways Security Products offer additional or replacement locks which, they claim, can be installed by a competent handyperson in an afternoon. Those who would prefer a professional installation should contact a local garage or auto-security specialist for advice.

To discourage the professional thief, have all windows etched with the vehicle registration number – etching pens and stencils are available for you to do this yourself, but for a more professional finish, contact a company like Autoglass who use a sandblasting technique, or ask your local police if they are

planning to organize a property marking day when vehicle windows and contents can be marked. Alternatively windows and headlamps can be marked using the Retainacar system, with a unique Security Protection Number (SPN). This is then kept on a confidential database called the National Vehicle Security Register (NVSR) which enables a prospective purchaser, or the police, to check ownership and/or mileage within minutes. Remember to security mark your car internally, as well as the contents (see Chapter 16).

Vehicle Watch

Vehicle Watch is a relatively new scheme set up by police forces, in an increasing number of counties, in a bid to combat vehicle theft on a local level. Members of the scheme – i.e. car owners – display stickers in front and rear windscreens which indicate the times when the vehicle is likely to be on the road. For instance, cars which are not normally driven at night might display yellow stickers. By displaying these discs, the motorist invites police patrols to stop the vehicle if it is found on the road between midnight and 5 a.m., and

check that the driver is the owner of the vehicle, or someone authorized by the owner.

Immobilizers

Immobilizers are designed simply to prevent someone from stealing your vehicle. They will not sound an alarm to alert passers-by, neither will they protect the contents of your vehicle. Ideally, therefore, they should form part of, or supplement, a vehicle alarm system – most are easily linked to compatible systems. There are many available on the market ranging from basic systems to more sophisticated designs like the Foxguard Immobilizer which incorporates dummy cut-out circuits to confuse the thief, and Simba's Digital Pulse Immobilizer (DPI) which will immobilize the vehicle 30 seconds after the engine stops, even if the key is not removed from the ignition.

Vehicle alarms

Over the years, car alarms have gained a poor reputation. These days they are far more sophisticated and, properly installed, should not fall prey to false alarms. These were frequently caused by poor quality shock sensors which were designed to detect violent movement or attack, but which frequently reacted to movement caused by wind, or passing cars. With modern alarms more sophisticated movement detectors are employed which are less prone to false alarms.

Vehicle alarms vary considerably in price from £50 for a DIY system, right up to £1,000 or more for a highly sophisticated, professionally installed alarm. To ensure you are buying a reliable system, look for the British Standard for vehicle alarm systems – BS6803. Part I covers original manufacturers'

Suitable for DIY installation, the AT125 Remote Control Car Alarm from Sparkrite includes ultrasonic sensors, engine immobilization, separate siren and a windscreen receiver with armed warning light.

a Proximity Sensor which allows Cabriolets to be left with the top down. It constantly scans the space inside the passenger compartment with high frequency invisible beams, ensuring that any intrusion or body movement inside the car will activate the alarm. In addition to one or more of these sensing devices, an alarm may also incorporate a back-up battery which means that the alarm will continue to operate even if the car's own wiring is interfered with. The alarm may also be linked to the car's own headlamps or hazard warning lights to provide visual indication that the alarm has been activated.

To deter would-be thieves, opt for an alarm which incorporates a small flashing light mounted to the windscreen or dashboard to indicate that the alarm is in operation, and apply warning stickers to windows to draw attention to the alarm.

systems, and Part II, after-market installations.

The simplest type of alarm offers ignition cut-out linked to the car's horn or, preferably, a separate siren which is less vulnerable and can be hidden away. Operation may be via exterior key operation, or a 'hidden' switch inside the vehicle. Such alarms offer only minimal protection and, with car crime statistics as they are, you would be advised to install a system which offers greater protection than this.

'...a separate siren is less vulnerable...'

An alarm ought to cut out the ignition but also incorporate devices that will detect attempted entry to the vehicle. This may be done by detecting a drop in voltage or change in current, with the alarm sounding in response to operation of the car's door/boot/bonnet courtesy lights, or in response to a change in

electrical load. Make sure, however, that the alarm allows for the vehicle's electric cooling fan to cut in without activating the siren. Pressure sensing switches activate the alarm when a drop in pressure inside the vehicle is detected – when a door, window or sunroof is opened, for example. Depending on its sophistication, you may find that your alarm also offers ultrasonic detection – or with DIY kits this may be available as an optional extra. Ultrasonic modules emit sonic waves inside the car which, if disturbed by movement, will trigger the siren. Microphones are also offered with some systems, activated by the frequency of noises produced by a forced entry.

For convertibles, where ultrasonic protection with its air movement sensitivity would not be appropriate, alternative detection methods may be used. These include infra-red detectors which send out beams across the car, or microwave sensors. Clifford Electronics offers

'...Modern alarm systems are becoming increasingly sophisticated...'

Alarms can be armed in a variety of ways. The most basic requires the setting of a switch situated in the car, or less frequently in modern systems, via an exterior key switch. For the forgetful motorist there are 'passive' alarms which activate automatically a short time after the ignition has been switched off. A popular method these days incorporates a radio transmitter key fob to remotely activate the alarm. However, cunning thieves now carry scanners which can be used to capture the correct code when transmitted by the unsuspecting driver. Some cheap alarms can be 'cracked' in this way. Manufacturers are responding by incorporating anti-scan and anti-grab features into their vehicle alarms.

Modern professionally-installed alarm systems are becoming increasingly sophisticated. Options available range from a 'panic' device which, operated from a remote key fob or a switch in the car, is designed to sound the alarm in order to summon help from passers-by should you or the car be attacked, right up to 'anti hi-jack' facility. This enables the thief to drive a short distance before the engine cuts out and the alarm sounds. Security systems can also be linked in to central locking circuits and electrically-operated windows and sunroofs, locking them automatically when the alarm is armed.

Pagers

Pagers which 'tell' you when your car is being tampered with, or if the car phone is ringing, are another option, although these should be viewed as additions to alarm/immobilizer systems. Some, like LCB Radio Pagers' PG500, are supplied with a siren, while on others a siren is an optional extra. Remember, however, that pagers do have a limited range, with manufacturers claiming distances from 75 metres up to 2,000 metres.

A new system, which has been introduced from the United States, enables police to track stolen vehicles. Vehicles are fitted with a hidden electronic homing device programmed with a unique code number. If your car is stolen you simply report it to the police, with the code number. The police computer then switches on your car's tracking device which emits a radio signal inaudible to the thief, but which allows police cars equipped with a programmable tracking unit to trace your car. Systems currently available include Tracker, which is available to all motorists through the AA, and TrakBak which incorporates Securicor's proven Datatrak automatic vehicle tracking technology.

When you are choosing an alarm system, consider your options very carefully and take time to look around at what is on offer. Visit motor accessory centres if you are keen on installing your own system, but it also pays to visit an auto-electrician or specialist alarm installer to find out what is available on the market, and whether more sophisticated systems may be within your DIY capabilities. Make sure you pick a system that suits your car and yourself, and consider what you carry in the car, and even where it is parked regularly. For instance, if you have a sophisticated radio installed, you will probably want an alarm that offers internal ultra-sonic protection. If you live in a noisy area you will need an alarm with a loud siren, and which operates the hazard warning lights.

> ## '...A new system enables police to track stolen vehicles...'

Take your time before you make a choice. It may even be worth contacting a few insurance companies beforehand, as some are now teaming up with alarm manufacturers to offer substantial discounts on equipment to policyholders wishing to protect their vehicles.

Tips for two-wheelers

Theft of motorcycles has reached alarming proportions. In the UK a machine is stolen every seven minutes, frequently for spare parts or resale. Simple precautions can help – park in well-lit, busy places, never leave any valuables behind, and take your helmet with you. Cycles may be secured with a top quality chain and padlock or large 'D-ring'-type padlocks – Euro Mul-

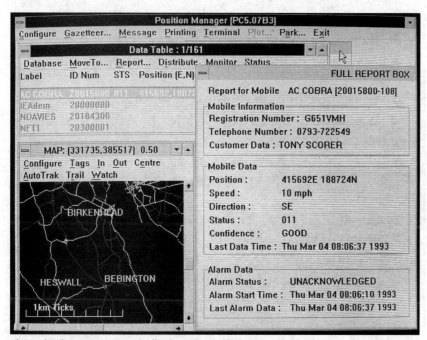

The TrakBak system automatically alerts the TrakBak control bureau (operated by National Breakdown) if a fitted out vehicle is moved without permission.

T-Lock offer high security versions. Immobilization is another precaution, either by having an electronic immobilizer fitted or a concealed cut-out switch that breaks any of the low-tension wires to the coil, or by simply removing the coil wire.

> ### '...A machine is stolen every seven minutes, frequently for spare parts or resale...'

To tackle the rise in theft, the motorcycle industry is supporting an inexpensive tagging system to help police trace stolen bikes and to deter thieves. The Datatag system, which is marketed by UK ID Systems, uses coded electronic implants which remain passive until activated by police scanners. A pack of transponders and DIY fitting instructions are available through motorcycle dealers. Tags are glued in concealed positions and injected into soft components such as seats to make them difficult to find. A thief, therefore, can never be sure whether a motorcycle has been 'tagged'. The police are supplied with scanners to locate tags and can check ownership by contacting a central database.

Alarms are also available. Solartrack plc has designed a range of remote controlled alarm systems specifically for motorcycles, scooters and mopeds. The SLA-807 remote controlled motorcycle alarm system for DIY installation incorporates a built-in alarm, adjustable shock sensor and remote panic facility. There is also a high specification system, the SLA 808, designed for professional installation.

WATCHPOINTS

1 NEVER leave keys in the ignition.

2 Always lock all doors and close the windows.

3 Never leave your vehicle documents in the car.

4 Lock all valuables out of sight, or carry them with you.

5 Try to park in well-lit, well-populated car parks. Look for a Secured Car Park logo for greater peace of mind.

6 In car parks where you pay on the way out, take tickets with you to prevent a thief driving away.

7 Always make sure the steering wheel lock is engaged when you park.

8 Fit a security device to the car stereo, or buy one you can remove and take with you.

9 Install an alarm and an immobilizer.

10 Security mark all windows and contents, such as car stereos and mobile phones.

▼ Fitting a car alarm system

Although car alarm systems are a better DIY proposition than they ever have been, it's not worth having a go yourself unless you are totally confident. Ask the shop assistant to show you the bits inside the box and the fitting instructions. It will give you an idea of the amount of work required, and the scope of the instructions.

One of the latest DIY alarms to appear is the American Code-Alarm Anes 75 'Cop in a box'. This is a good example of a sophisticated DIY alarm which has an excellent line up of features and includes a how-to-fit video tape. This makes it superbly easy to get things right.

The 75 costs no more than about £120 in the High Street stores or can be fitted for about £30 extra. Bear in mind that if you decide to fork out the extra cash, it's the installer's problem if something goes wrong. Code-Alarm do a simpler system, the Anes 50, with less features, which is priced at £90 (about £100 fitted).

Opening the box of the Anes 75 is a good lesson in what to expect for your money at this level. The alarm has several interesting features, and has plenty of options. At the basic level it provides an alarm which only needs a few simple connections and it will work very efficiently. Anyone who wishes to go further than this can connect extra wires for interior light turn-on when the alarm is disarmed. It can also be set up with or without auto-arming and voltage drop sensing, depending on whether you cut, or leave intact, small wire loops hanging out of the back of the siren.

An alarm with voltage drop sensing means that it will react to the current draw of a boot light, which means that it's not necessary for instance to run a wire to a boot pin switch (although this has the advantage on some alarms of tripping instantly). On the down side, if the battery starts to go when the car's standing around, there's a good chance of a false alarm.

Alarms can often be foiled by forcing the bonnet and snipping wires (often this is accompanied by plausible cursing and waving of arms to please passers-by!). This can be combated most effectively by a self-contained siren unit with its own battery.

Cheaper systems without batteries can be made more effective by bolting the siren securely in a position where it's hard to get at the wiring (from above and below), and taping all alarm wiring onto existing looms. Also, make sure that the battery terminals are securely tightened.

Alarms generally seem more reliable than they used to be. Any trouble you may have will be down to the quality of installation or adjustment. Two of the biggest sources of trouble experienced in this area are using a 'voltage drop' trigger system and setting too much sensitivity on an ultrasonic detector.

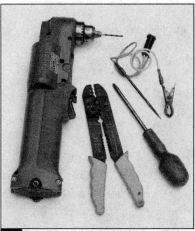

2 *Most DIY alarms only require simple tools, apart from some installations requiring a right-angle drill or adaptor for a conventional type. A simple 12V test lamp will be needed.*

1 *Code-Alarm's Anes 75 'Cop in a box'. A sophisticated DIY alarm with an excellent line up of features, including a how-to-fit video tape.*

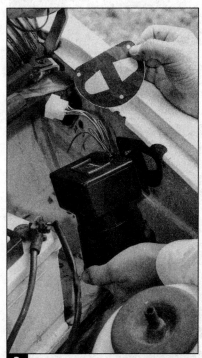

3 *The first action is to check the siting of the unit. It should be away from manifold heat, face down to prevent water collecting, and high enough to be out of reach from under the car.*

4   *A template is supplied with the Anes to simplify the drilling of the holes for the mounting plate. Always check behind the panel before drilling to avoid piercing wires or brake pipes!*

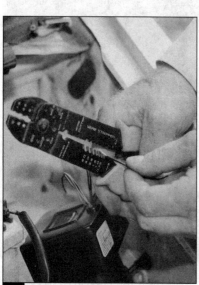

5   *Some wires can now be prepared for eyelet terminals, such as the earth wire which can be fastened under one of the bracket mounting screws. Use a star washer to maintain a good contact.*

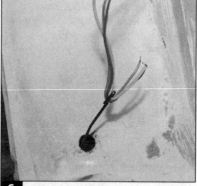

6   *A piece of stiff wire can be used as a 'mouse' to pull the wires that need to go through into the car, such as the interior light-sensing wire and the leads to the 'armed' warning light.*

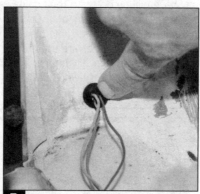

7   *The wiring can either be pulled through an existing loom grommet, or a new hole could be made (check behind!). Always use a grommet sealed with mastic to keep out water.*

8   *The wire threading operation through the bulkhead had to be completed before we could fit the siren unit to its bracket. Mounting must be solid to allow shock sensor to work properly.*

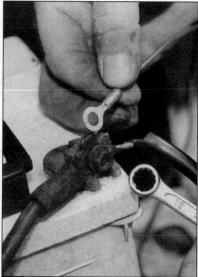

9   *Never complete the circuit with the power lead fuse fitted – this is the last item. The eye terminal can be fitted to the battery, though. Try to keep it tucked in with the other wires.*

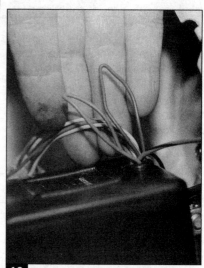

10   *The Code-Alarm has options for auto-arming and voltage drop sensing. The option loop can be cut if alarm is connected to interior light circuit to reduce chance of false alarms.*

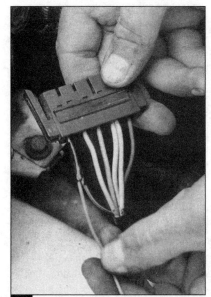

11 The parking or indicator light circuit (depending on the type of alarm) is found using a test bulb to trace the live circuit. An alarm wire is connected to flash lights on arming/disarming.

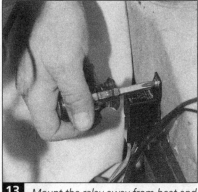

13 Mount the relay away from heat and spray. The starter trigger wire should not be confused with the heavy gauge main cable to the starter.

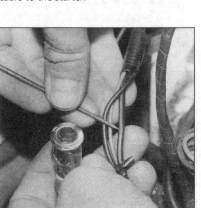

14 The starter trigger wire can be located by earthing the test lamp and probing the insulation with a sharp point. It should only light while the engine is being turned.

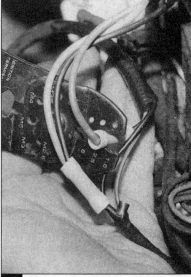

15 The starter wire can be cut and the relay leads spliced in using crimping butt connectors. A high current flows when starting, so keep the leads as short as possible for reliability.

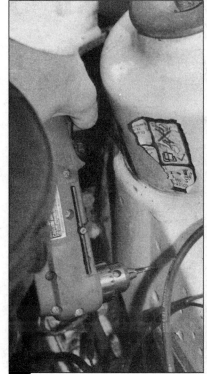

12 The Code-Alarm is supplied with a heavy duty relay to immobilize the vehicle's starter circuit. We drilled a mounting hole under the bonnet, but it can be mounted near the ignition key. Check behind panel before drilling

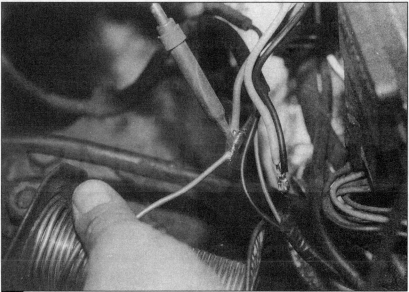

16 If you are confident with a soldering iron, soldered joints are preferable to crimping. The starter wire joint can then be wrapped in insulating tape, making it difficult to find.

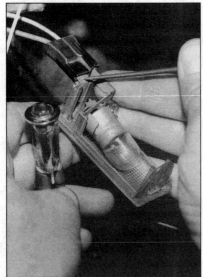

17 Inside the car, the interior light wire is usually easy to trace and can be bulb-tested to check polarity. The Code-Alarm will connect to either polarity – always check instructions here.

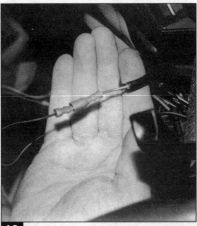

19 ... the column casing, which is a convenient spot, and earthed to a nearby switch-retaining screw. Where the casing is removable, it's a good idea to provide connector termination.

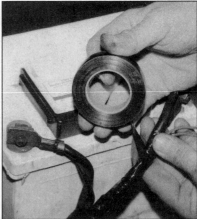

20 Once the wiring is complete and tested, it can be taped up generously, preferably with matching loom tape, to make it difficult to get to the alarm leads and fuses.

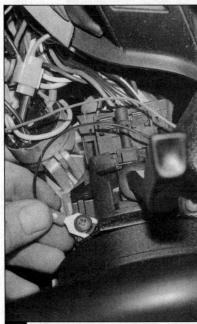

18 The arming warning light can also be wired to earth or live, depending on the type of alarm. Most warning lights are a push fit into a single hole. Ours was fitted to the top of ...

21 Part of the checking procedure will, in some cases, involve the self-programming of the remote controls. The Code-Alarm can also be remotely set up for shock sensor sensitivity.

CHAPTER 23

Lock up your leisure

The theft of bicycles, caravans, boats and their contents is big business these days. When you stop to think about it, it's hardly surprising. Leisure equipment such as this is extremely vulnerable; it's portable, valuable – boats and caravans can be worth many thousands of pounds – and, left unattended for weeks on end, it presents an easy target.

If you saw somebody on a garage drive, hitching a caravan up to a car in the early hours of the morning, you probably wouldn't think for one moment that it was being stolen. Similarly, you wouldn't think there was anything suspicious about someone at a lake or riverside, mounting a boat on to a trailer and towing it away. That illustrates how simple theft of such equipment can be without raising any suspicion. But leisure equipment *can* be protected by using commonsense and simple security devices.

General advice

The aim of the game is to send a thief away in search of an easier target. The more obstacles you put in his way, the longer it will take him to steal your boat or caravan, and consequently, the greater his chance of being observed – which, of course, is the last thing a thief wants.

All property should be security marked, ideally with your postcode and the number, or first two letters of the name, of your house. This can be etched on to equipment using an etching pen or written invisibly with an ultra-violet pen (remember that ultra-violet marks must be checked every now and again and reapplied).

> ### '...All property should be security marked...'

Maintain an up-to-date description and inventory of the contents of your boat or caravan and keep it in a safe place. To help the police you should record details such as the make, length, colour of your boat or caravan and, in the case of the former, type – such as sail, cruiser, inboard, outboard, etc. The inventory should include all valuable equipment, with details of the manufacturer, brand name, model and serial number, description, value, and the location of any security marking. It might also help to keep a photographic record.

For the protection of caravans, the National Caravan Council has

Valuable equipment can be locked away in a safe like the Vault 'X' from Automobile Inparts.

devised CRIS – Caravan Registration and Identification Scheme. Under the scheme every tourer produced from 1992 is visibly marked on the main chassis and up to ten windows, with a unique identity code called VIN (Vehicle Identification Number). The 17-character VIN gives precise information about the tourer, including the country of origin, the manufacturer, the National Caravan Council identification code and the year of manufacture.

The VIN and other details of the tourer are recorded on a 'Touring Caravan Registration Document' which is sent to the registered keeper by CRIS and must be kept in a safe place – not in the caravan. All details are then held on a central computer to enable owners of stolen or abandoned tourers to be easily traced. Details of further dealer or private sales are easily registered on the computer.

When unattended, equipment of value should be kept hidden or, better still, locked away out of sight. You may even want to consider installing a safe – the Vault 'X' from Automobile Inparts Ltd is suitable for cars, caravans, motor

homes and boats, but make sure that the floor or walls would provide a secure fixing, and try to mount the safe somewhere out of sight. In the case of boats, bear in mind that there may be likelihood of corrosion, too. Make expensive equipment more difficult to steal by bolting things in place, and burring over the threads to prevent easy removal with a spanner. If the boat or caravan is to be left unattended for long periods, make sure that,

externally, it is well secured, then strip it internally, removing anything that is portable, or valuable. Leave all the curtains, cupboards and drawers open to show a thief there is nothing worth breaking in for.

Boats

Often left unattended for long periods of time, boats are particularly vulnerable; with an estimated £60m worth of boats and marine equipment stolen in the UK each year, security measures are vital if you are to stay afloat. Smaller vessels, as well as windsurfers, surfboards and canoes can be locked away out of sight in a well-secured garage – and again should be security marked with your postcode. Larger boats, however, are often kept in their owners' gardens or driveways, where they remain for most of the year. Mounted on a trailer it is simplicity itself for a thief to hitch your boat up to his vehicle and drive away in seconds. Your main priority, therefore, must be to ensure that your trailer cannot be towed away. This is achieved very simply by

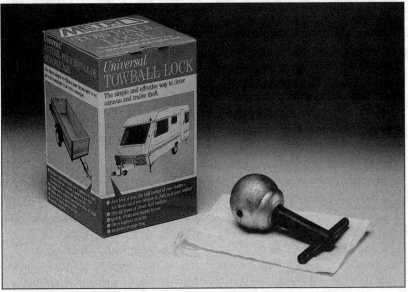

This towball lock from Metro Products locks into the ball socket of a trailer to prevent towing.

using a dummy ball which fits into the hitching socket and locks in place, or a hitch lock which slips over the hitch socket and again is locked in place. Any padlocking devices such as these must be sturdy – don't stint on quality.

Other devices which prevent towing include the wheel clamp which, though bulky, provides a strong visual and physical deterrent, and will take considerable time to remove. You could also remove a wheel – an effective, but inconvenient deterrent.

One of the most convenient ways to secure boats left in your garden or driveway, is to install an anchor post. Bolted or cemented into the ground, these can be locked in place, and can only be removed by the keyholder.

Brazen thieves are bold enough to remove small boats, boards and canoes from roof racks if the owners don't secure them properly. Use chains and padlocks to improve security; but to be really safe, avoid leaving equipment unattended.

Use waterproof padlocks for marine security, like this one from Eliza Tinsley & Co.

'...Brazen thieves are bold enough to remove small boats from roof racks...'

If possible, outboard motors should be removed from the boat and locked away safely. If the outboard is difficult to remove, the engine must be bolted firmly in place. Special locks which shroud the securing nuts are available from marine centres. Motor-powered vessels can easily be immobilized by interrupting the supply of power to the engines. This can simply be achieved by removing the distributor's coil wire, which prevents the motor from starting. Alternatively, a keyed battery switch can be installed, prohibiting anyone other than the keyholder from accessing the vessel's battery power.

Keel boats are particularly susceptible to theft as, even if the engine is immobilized, a thief could still sail away. With both dinghies and keel boats, spare sails should be stowed away safely in a locker, and foresails should be reeled in. For greater security the boom could be chained to a deck fitting to prevent the boat being sailed away. Other options include removing the tiller, or securing the steering wheel with a chain and padlock. Make sure you are adequately insured for the boat and its contents.

Standard door and window locks can be fitted to provide additional security, but an intruder alarm may provide the best protection; contact a marine or specialist boating shop for advice. Make sure that any alarm is unaffected by exterior movement – the last thing you want is an alarm that is activated by river currents or tide change. The system will probably consist of a control panel – which should be water and shock-proof – a siren and a range of sensors designed for marine use. The sensors should include surface and flush mount sensors to protect doors, windows and hatches, and others to protect the boat while it is moored, or to protect the outboard motor, and instrument sensors to protect expensive on-board marine instruments. By fitting a strobe light in addition to the siren, you can increase the likelihood of your alarm being recognized and acknowledged. Fire detection can be provided by the incorporation of smoke detectors, with gas and water detectors also a wise investment.

If your boat is moored at a marina, an intruder alarm can often be linked via radio to the marina office, or to a central station to provide 24-hour protection – and peace of mind!

A new development in marine security is the introduction of tagging systems. Tags, which incorporate a unique identification number, are placed on a vessel in two or three locations, or injected into the glass fibre hull. The vessel and registered keeper are then logged on to a central computer database which can be accessed by harbour and river police, Customs and Excise and other approved groups. These approved organizations are issued with scanners which, from certain distances, are able to read the tag and ascertain ownership. This tagging system is proving very valuable for the security of personal watercraft (jet-skis), with all new craft from 1993 onwards sold with these tagging systems already fitted.

'…DIY tagging kits are easy to install…'

Purchasers of second-hand craft, or existing owners, can buy DIY tagging kits, which are very easy to install and reasonably priced at under £60.00 – including the kit and a year's free membership to the Personal Watercraft Association (PWA). Owners of tagged craft are also entitled to reduced insurance premiums. If the craft is sold on, the new owner can obtain a re-registration form and re-register for only £5.00

To improve security at marinas and on rivers, some police forces are working with boat owners to set up Boat Watch schemes – run along similar lines to Neighbourhood Watch. Generally speaking, boat owners are encouraged to watch out for each other's vessels and report any suspicious activity to the police, to mark property and generally become more security-conscious.

Your choice of marina should be made carefully, and security should be an important consideration. Ask the marina's management what security measures they offer, and

check with fellow boat owners whether a certain marina has a good reputation for security. Ideally there should be a security guard at the premises. Also check whether public access to the boats is limited. If it is stored in a compound, make sure the area is well-protected by good fencing and is well-lit at night.

Caravans

Most touring caravans spend much of their life on the owner's front drive or in a compound. Like boat trailers, they need to be immobilized to prevent theft, and hitch locks, dummy balls, wheel clamps and anchor posts, available from caravan and motor accessory shops, will all provide good protection against unauthorized towing. The National Caravan Council recommends heavy duty 3mm thick steel wheel clamps are used, preferably hardened with a built-in high security enclosed lock. The clamp must encompass the tyre and project into the wheel well, covering at least one of the wheel nuts to prevent removal of the clamp by tyre deflation – this level of security may be a condition under

some insurance policies. When not in use, the caravan wheels may be removed and stored securely away from the caravan.

Wheels and tyres can also be protected with locking wheel nuts, and there are also devices available which prevent the caravan stays from being raised. Fitted to the two rear stays, these make towing the caravan virtually impossible. Another low-cost method of immobilizing the van is to drill a hole in the chassis, close to a wheel and thread a length of plastic-covered chain through the chassis and wheel and secure it with a padlock.

When you are out and about, the contents of touring caravans may be protected with an alarm system. Battery-operated alarms normally using passive infra-red detection can protect the interior, but these often rely on an internal siren, which may not be heard if the caravan is situated at some distance from passers-by. Some, however, can be linked to an external siren for greater protection. DIY alarms are also available from caravan centres, and normally comprise a control unit, a waterproof, tamperproof

Wheelclamps, like this one from Lionweld Kennedy, provide a strong physical and visual deterrent.

siren for external siting, magnetic contacts and vibration sensors that detect any movement inside the caravan, or of the caravan itself. Alarms may be powered using rechargeable batteries, or the car battery when touring.

One alarm for caravans from Safe & Secure Ltd is based on a small electronic safe bolted to the frame of the caravan, which communicates with various sensors via radio signals. Control of the sensors and operation of the safe is achieved through a touch-key pad fitted to the front of the safe. The system may be linked to an external siren or light to alert site security or passers-by to an intrusion. Central monitoring is also available via the site office or, if there is a telephone line available, a national security monitoring centre.

Stolen bicycles at Oxford. The police check for security marks but few can be easily identified.

'...Motor caravans can be immobilized...'

On some sites sophisticated systems are installed which use sensors to detect unwanted visitors. Other sites may employ man and dog patrols or install closed circuit television. Sites which provide mains electricity hook up points can accept caravans fitted with mains-operated intruder alarms. Caravans should be alarmed and immobilized even when left for only short periods. Time switches can be fitted to lights to give the impression that the caravan is occupied after dark.

If the caravan is not kept at home, it should be stored in a securely locked and alarmed building, or in a properly fenced, well-lit, patrolled and securely-locked storage compound – again a requirement under some insurance policies.

Static caravans are equally vulnerable, if not more so, being left unattended for long periods of time. They should be immobilized and

alarmed in much the same way, with curtains open and cupboards and drawers empty and open to deter thieves. Like Boat Watch schemes, some caravan owners have got together to form Caravan Watch on sites around the country.

Motor caravans can be immobilized by removing the engine's rotor arm, fitted to the distributor; by removing a couple of spark plug leads, or by fitting (usually under the dashboard) a simple immobilizing switch which prevents electrical current from reaching the coil or distributor. Better still, fit a vehicle alarm with additional sensors to protect the interior of the vehicle.

Fire protection

Modern caravans should be manufactured to meet stringent fire regulations. National Caravan Council member manufacturers and dealers must ensure that new and second-hand caravans are fitted with smoke alarms, manufactured to British Standard 5466. A fire extinguisher is also recommended.

Bicycles

With cycling becoming more popular, and bicycles becoming more sophisticated – and expensive – they are proving a popular target with thieves. Nearly a quarter of a million bicycles are stolen each year – and, of the small percentage that are recovered, most are auctioned because the rightful owners cannot be identified.

There are several simple measures to take to prevent your bike becoming another crime statistic. These days many bicycles are fitted with quick-release saddles and, by removing the saddle whenever you leave your bike, you can ensure that a thief would look very conspicuous should he try to ride away. Similarly most bicycles are also fitted with quick release wheels so the front wheel can be removed, or locked to the frame and back wheel when not in use.

Security devices are a must. Bicycles should be kept locked up with the best lock you can afford. Ideally it should be a 'D'-type shackle lock comprising a loop of

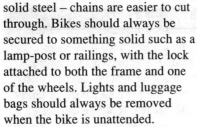

Bicycles should be kept locked up whenever they are not in use.

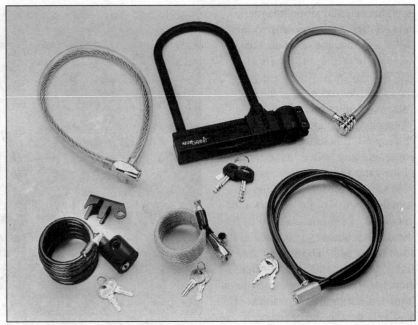

Buy the best bicycle lock you can afford. CeKa offer the Abus range.

solid steel – chains are easier to cut through. Bikes should always be secured to something solid such as a lamp-post or railings, with the lock attached to both the frame and one of the wheels. Lights and luggage bags should always be removed when the bike is unattended.

With bicycles, security marking comes into its own, providing a means of instant recognition. Your postcode and house number, or first two letters of its name should be stamped on to the frame in several places, and a Coded Cycle sticker attached to warn off potential thieves. Die stamping can be carried out through the cycle dealer, or the police, who often arrange local cycle coding sessions. Even if a thief files down the mark, or paints over it, it can still be detected by forensic tests. If you are buying a second-hand bike, try to ensure it isn't stolen. Ask for proof of purchase and the bike's handbook, and look out for frame numbers or registration marks that appear to have been tampered with. Also ask questions if it looks as though it has been resprayed. The Home Office

has produced a form, available from police crime prevention departments and bicycle shops, on which comprehensive details and a

photograph of the bicycle can be kept. If the bicycle does get stolen, the record form can be passed on to police to assist identification.

WATCHPOINTS

1 Security mark property.
2 Maintain an up-to-date description and inventory of the contents.
3 Keep valuable equipment locked away out of sight.
4 Bolt expensive, fixed items in place.
5 When unattended for long periods, secure externally and strip the boat or caravan internally.
6 Lock smaller vessels in a well-secured garage.
7 Use dummy balls, hitch locks or wheel clamps to prevent unauthorized towing.
8 Remove outboard motors if possible.
9 Bicycles should be chained to something solid, and should be security marked.
10 Make sure you are adequately insured.

CHAPTER 24

Protecting your family

Although the likelihood of becoming a victim of violent crime may be remote, the fear of it can be very real; and for some people it can even lead to them becoming prisoners in their own homes. Women and the elderly tend to feel the most vulnerable, though in reality it is more likely to be young men who are victims of violent crime. Children, too, by their very innocence and trusting natures, can be seen as easy prey.

Of course, everyone should have the right to be able to come and go as they choose – at any time of day or night. What is important, however, is to think ahead; think about what you would do in the event of an attack; be alert and go about your everyday life with confidence. Remember that violent crime is largely about power, and an attacker's need to dominate his victim. Research has actually shown that people are more likely to become a victim if they walk along looking nervous and vulnerable. Someone who appears confident and self-assured is less likely to be attacked.

Obviously it doesn't pay to take unnecessary risks, and simple forward planning and commonsense precautions can often prevent a potentially dangerous situation and make you feel safer when out and about.

Out alone

If you are going to be out late on your own, always take steps to ensure that you can get home safely. Arrange a lift home with friends, or book a taxi in advance. Try to use a firm you know well, or a licensed cab company. If you must use an unlicensed minicab, when you phone, ask for the driver's name and call sign and the type of car he will be driving. When he turns up check that he knows your name. Always sit in the back and, if you do feel uneasy, trust your instincts and ask him to drop you off at the nearest busy place.

If you are going to be out late on your own, always take steps to ensure that you can get home safely.

Never accept lifts from someone you have only just met – no matter how genuine he may seem, and never, never hitch-hike; far better to travel home with someone you know well. If your house is empty, ask your friends or the taxi driver to wait until you are safely inside. If you regularly have to work late, ask your company whether they can arrange transport for you, or arrange a lift rota with colleagues.

If you must travel home alone at night always avoid short-cuts through dimly-lit, deserted areas and alleyways. Walk in the centre of the pavement, keeping away from bushes and dark buildings, and walk facing the oncoming traffic. This makes it impossible for a kerb-crawler to follow you. If you regularly go out walking or running, it's worth varying your route and the time that you go, so that people do not get to know your routine. Choose well-lit, well-populated routes and avoid using a personal stereo; not only will it prevent you hearing someone approaching, it could also leave you vulnerable to a snatch-thief.

Handbags should be kept closed and carried close to your body, and should never be left unattended in public places. Purses should be pushed towards the bottom of the bag to guard against pickpockets and sneak thieves. Similarly, men should never carry their wallets in rear trouser pockets. Expensive-looking jewellery should be covered up until you reach your destination.

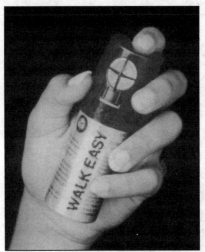

Consider carrying a personal alarm – like the 'Walk Easy'.

Many women feel safer by carrying a personal alarm. In the event of an attack the alarm can be operated easily to sound a piercing screech – which may even frighten off your attacker, and will also alert anyone in the vicinity that you are being attacked. These small devices are either gas or battery-operated and cost from around £5. Gas-operated alarms are louder but, if you buy one, make sure that when the top is depressed to sound the alarm, it will lock in position – that way, even if it is dropped, the alarm will continue to sound. Whichever type you buy, test it regularly to make sure that it is operating correctly, and when you are out and about make sure it is easily to hand – not buried at the bottom of your handbag!

Public transport

Try to avoid being alone on public transport. Avoid isolated bus stops and, if possible, unmanned, isolated railway stations. On the bus, sit on the lower deck near the driver, and on trains and tubes avoid empty compartments. If you can, sit in a part of the train near where you get off, and try to sit near other women whenever possible. Trust your instincts at all times. If you are sitting in a compartment with plenty of spare seats, and a man gets on and sits down next to you, making you feel uneasy, then move. Do not worry about offending him!

Men can play a part to help women feel safer. Think about how a woman may feel if, for instance you are walking quite close behind her in a secluded area. Simply by crossing the road and walking on the other side you can reassure her that she is safe. Similarly, do not sit too near a woman on her own in a railway carriage, unless there are plenty of people. Finally, help women friends and family members by offering them lifts, or agreeing to walk them home.

In the car

Make sure your car is in good running order at all times, and is regularly serviced. If it is playing up and you think you may break down, find an alternative means of transport, or take someone with you. Lessons in basic car maintenance

Trust your instincts when using public transport. If you feel threatened by someone's behaviour, report it to a guard, or other member of staff.

will at least give you the confidence to tackle smaller jobs, such as a puncture or broken fan belt.

Plan your route in advance and, where possible, try to keep to busy roads. Keep an up-to-date road atlas and local maps of your destination area with you so that you won't have to stop to ask directions. Always carry some change or a phone card with you so you can at least make a phone call if necessary, and make sure you have enough petrol for the journey.

It goes without saying that you should never pick up hitch-hikers. If somebody does flag you down, make sure that it is a genuine emergency before opening your door or winding down the window. If you are in any doubt, drive on to the nearest telephone, or police station and report the incident. Beware of other drivers trying to alert you to faults with your car. Drive on slowly until you reach a place where it is safe to stop, and then check your car.

When driving in towns, keep the doors locked and your handbag out of sight or on the floor. Do not leave

it on the passenger seat where it could easily be snatched. If you think someone is following you, avoid making eye contact. Slow down, lock your doors and shut your

windows. If he persists, drive on to a busy public place and flash your lights and sound your horn to summon help. When you park your car, pick a well-lit, populated spot. If you must use a multi-storey car park, try to park close to the exit on the ground level, and away from pillars. When you return, have your keys ready and check the inside of the car with a torch before you get in.

If you break down you will want to summon help as quickly as possible. It really does pay to join a motoring organization such as the AA or RAC, as they will give priority to lone women drivers. Even if you are not a member they will help you provided you are willing to join there and then. If you can afford it, a mobile phone will enable you to call for help quickly without having to even leave your car. If you break down on the motorway, pull on to the hard shoulder and follow the marker arrows to the nearest phone – try to get your car as near to one

At night check the inside of your car with a torch before you get in.

as possible. After you have called, wait on the embankment near your car or, if this is not possible, in the passenger seat of your car. This keeps you as far away as possible from passing traffic, and also gives the impression that you are waiting for someone to return.

'HELP – CALL POLICE' signs that are available from some motoring shops have been shown to be successful in summoning assistance. Placed in your rear window, the idea is that passing motorists will use their car phones to contact the police on your behalf, or stop at the nearest telephone to summon assistance. If a stranger does stop to offer assistance, get into your car, lock the door, open the window a fraction and ask them to obtain the help of the emergency services for you.

There are alarms available for the elderly which are designed to summon help in an emergency – like the Homelink from Scantronic.

WATCHPOINTS

OUT AND ABOUT

1 At night, arrange for transport to get you home safely.

2 Avoid walking through dimly-lit, deserted areas and alleyways.

3 Try to walk facing oncoming traffic and in the middle of the pavement.

4 Never hitch-hike, or pick up hitch-hikers.

5 Conceal expensive-looking jewellery.

6 Try to avoid being alone on public transport, and at bus stops and train stations.

7 Make sure your car is in good working order.

8 Join a motoring organization such as the AA or RAC.

9 Keep car doors locked in town, and your handbag hidden out of sight.

10 Park in well-lit, populated places – preferably near the ground floor exit in multi-storey car parks.

11 Consider buying a personal alarm.

Home alone

Even in your own home it doesn't pay to take chances. Security locks should be fitted to all doors and windows – and used! External doors should be kept locked even when you are indoors. Door locks should be changed when you move to a new home in case previous tenants still have keys that fit. Always draw your curtains after dark and, if you suspect there is a prowler outside, dial 999 immediately. Should you arrive home and suspect that your house has been broken into, do not enter. Run to a neighbour's house and call the police.

Do not advertise the fact that you live alone. Display only your surname and initials in telephone directories or by your doorbell so that a stranger will not know whether there is a male or female occupant. If you are selling your home, try to avoid situations where you have to show viewers around on your own. Either ask the estate agent to accompany the viewer, or arrange for someone to be at home with you.

WATCHPOINTS

HOME ALONE

1 Fit and use security locks on doors and windows – even when you are home.

2 Draw the curtains after dark.

3 Do not advertise the fact that you live alone.

4 Never give out your number on the telephone.

5 If you suspect there is a prowler or intruder at the house, phone the police immediately.

6 Do not admit strangers without checking their identity carefully.

Wrong number

When you answer the phone, never give out your number. If a stranger telephones, never admit that you are on your own. If calls are obscene or abusive, hang up without saying a word – the caller is after a response. If the calls continue, tell the police and the operator. Keep a record of the date, time and content of each call to help the authorities trace the caller.

The elderly

Most of these commonsense precautions apply to the elderly as well when out and about. But the elderly are also particularly vulnerable to doorstep tricksters (See Chapter 7). Elderly relatives should be discouraged from keeping large sums of money at home – this should always be deposited in a bank, building society or post office account.

There are alarms available designed specifically for the elderly and infirm which offer protection against burglary and will also summon help in an emergency. Systems may be linked to a central station where staff will notify the appropriate emergency service. Other systems operate as an emergency telephone system, automatically dialling several pre-programmed telephone numbers to alert neighbours, family or friends that an emergency has occurred. It continues to dial those numbers until the call is answered, and then relays a spoken emergency message. Some systems – like the Piper Lifeline from Tunstall Telecom, or the Emergency Autodialler from Smiths Industries – incorporate a radio transmitter which can be carried around by the user, or worn around the neck as a pendant. This means that the elderly person can summon help in the event of a fall, even if they are some distance from the phone.

If the worst happens

It's always wise to be prepared for the worst. Preparing yourself mentally could help you to think rationally should the situation occur, rather than just freezing with fear. Some women find that a self-defence class, targeted specifically for women, makes them feel more

If you are assaulted or raped, call the police straightaway. They are trained to deal with such situations.

confident when they are out and about. But, in terms of actually fighting off an attacker, shock and fear may make you forget what you have been taught, so the fact that you have attended classes should not lead you to take unnecessary risks. If you think someone is following you, cross the street. If he continues, run to the busiest place you can find. A description of the man will help the police track him down, but your priority should be to get away safely. Incidents such as these should be reported as soon as possible from a safe place. Do not use a phone box in the street as you could be trapped inside.

Should you be confronted by a flasher, try not to appear shocked. Simply walk away and report the incident to the police, with the most detailed description that you can manage. If you are threatened, or confronted by a stranger, shout or scream for help.

To protect yourself against an attack you are allowed to use reasonable force. You may use everyday items to fight off an attacker, such as keys, hairspray, an umbrella – anything which you would normally carry with you. The law does not permit carrying a knife, mace spray, or anything that can be described as an offensive weapon. If you are assaulted or raped, call the police straightaway. Do not wash until a doctor has seen you, and do not drink or clean your teeth as this could destroy vital evidence. Try to remember as much as possible about the attack – write it down if possible. The police are trained to deal with such situations, and to provide you with care and understanding. They can also put you in touch with counsellors who can offer valuable assistance to you and your family. Rape Crisis Centres or Victim Support Schemes can help you cope with an attack, and Social Services can help if you or your children need to get away from a violent person.

Keeping children safe

Children are naturally trusting and, unless they are warned, will quite happily talk to complete strangers. But it is not only strangers who are a danger; most child molesters know their victims – they may be relatives, family friends, neighbours, or someone else who the victim is often in contact with. That's why it is vital that children know that it is OK to say NO to anyone – stranger or friend – and that parents can recognize the danger signals.

'...It is vital that children know it is OK to say NO...'

Children should be taught never to go off with anyone without asking Mummy or Daddy first. But strangers are cunning. Unless a child is taught otherwise it is very easy for them to get in a car with

Unless they are warned, children will quite happily talk to complete strangers.

someone who claims that 'Mummy sent me because she isn't feeling well'. If you do ask someone else to collect your child it's a good idea to give them a password that the child recognizes so that they know the person is genuine.

Your child should also be taught that if a stranger asks for help (for instance to find a lost dog), or for directions, the child should still say NO, run away and tell you or another known adult or police officer about the incident immediately. They do not need to give the adult an explanation – NO is sufficient.

'...Police would rather have a false alarm than a potential tragedy...'

Make sure the child understands that nobody has the right to touch their bodies. If the child asks unusual questions about somebody, or shows fear when a particular person is coming round, do not ignore it – follow up on the questions. And if a child does tell you that someone has interfered with them, believe them – children rarely lie about such incidents. Often a molester will tell the child to keep the incident a secret. Make sure your children know the difference between good and bad secrets. Bad secrets are if someone has hurt them, or tried to take them away, or touched them where they shouldn't. Bad secrets should not be kept secret.

It's important that you know at all times where your child is, who they are with, and the time that they are expected home. Children should be taught to give you this information as a matter of course. Neither should they be allowed in anyone's house – even a friend's – without notifying

WATCH POINTS

KEEPING CHILDREN SAFE

1 Teach children that it is OK to say NO to anyone who tries to hurt them.

2 Make sure they know never to go off with anyone without telling you first.

3 Children must be taught that no-one has the right to touch their bodies.

4 Believe your child if they tell you someone has interfered with them.

5 Teach your child that there are some secrets that should never be kept.

6 Ensure you know where your child is, who they are with, and the time they are expected home.

7 Teach children not to answer the front door.

8 Teach them that it is OK to run, scream, shout, lie or kick to get away.

9 Make sure the child knows its address and phone number.

10 Don't send a child out with its name displayed on a badge or T-shirt. They may be confused if a stranger calls them by name.

11 Use someone you know well, or who has been well-recommended for babysitting.

12 Never hesitate to call the police if you are concerned about your child's whereabouts.

you first. If they are not home by the allocated time, then investigate immediately. The police would rather have a false alarm than a potential tragedy. Make sure that children know their own address and how to use a pay phone, and how to make reverse charge calls before they are allowed out without an adult. And when at home, they should be taught never to answer a call at the front door.

Finding a reliable, trustworthy babysitter can be fraught with

dangers. Where possible, ask a friend or member of your family, or ask friends if they can recommend someone they have used. Try to avoid using newspaper advertisements. Leave a number where you can be contacted, and ring home and ask to speak to your child if you are worried. Finally, be aware of the danger signs. Watch your child's reaction when he or she knows a babysitter is coming. If they react badly, don't take any chances. Far better to be safe than sorry.

CHAPTER 25

Have a break – not a break-in

Milk bottles collecting on the doorstep, and post sticking out of the letter box is an obvious indication that you are away.

Advance planning with a simple holiday checklist will help to ensure that you enjoy your break to the full, and return to a welcome homecoming – not a break in!

The main objective is to deter a burglar from approaching your home in the first place. To achieve this it is important to ensure that the house continues to look occupied all the time that you are away. Milk bottles collecting on the doorstep, post sticking out of the letter box, and a house in darkness every night provides an obvious indication that you are on holiday. Cancelling the milk and papers sounds an obvious precaution but a surprising number of people do forget – particularly if they are only going away for a weekend.

'...enlist the help of a friendly neighbour...'

Don't rely on a spoken agreement – make sure that the cancellation is written in the order book. To avoid a build-up of post by the front door you can, for a fee, arrange for the Post Office to hold this for you until you return. However, this does not prevent the delivery of leaflets and free sheets which are often not even pushed fully through the letter box.

Holiday preparations leave most people in a last-minute panic. Hunting around for passports, checking insurance details, remembering to pack all the necessary items – without the kitchen sink! Small wonder, then, that when you are on your way you have a nagging doubt that you forgot to lock the back door, or cancel the milk. It is signs such as these, however, that the opportunist thief is on the lookout for, particularly during the holiday season.

Good neighbours

For real peace of mind your best course of action is to enlist the help of a friendly neighbour. Leave them a key and they can collect your post for you, draw the curtains and switch the lights on, leave the dustbin out, and possibly even mow the grass. You can also invite them to park on your driveway to make the home look occupied. It may sound a lot to ask, but you can, of course, return the favour when they go away.

If you live in a Neighbourhood Watch area, your neighbours should be well aware of the importance of making sure neighbouring residences look occupied, and should be happy to help. It's a good idea to contact the local Neighbourhood Watch co-ordinator and leave them a key, as well as an address where you can be contacted. He or she can then keep an eye on your property, report anything suspicious to the police, and ensure that you can be contacted if anything untoward occurs. The local police should also be informed of your absence.

Homesitters

If you cannot or do not want to enlist the help of your friends or neighbours, there are agencies around that offer a home-minding service. Basically, for a fee, these agencies will send people round to live in and look after your house while you are away and, for an additional charge, look after pets as well. Usually you are also expected to pay the homesitter and provide expenses. The local Crime Prevention Officer may have information on agencies operating in your area, or try Yellow Pages or the Thomson Local Directory. Do be careful, though, as you may have no means of knowing how reputable

Leave keys with a friend or neighbour – never in a supposedly 'safe' place.

the people appointed to look after your home may be.

Prior to your holiday, take care not to inform too many people. Thieves can pick up casual conversations in pubs, restaurants and shops and use the information. Also take care when you label your luggage. Lookouts operate at coach and railway stations, ports and airports, noting return addresses on baggage labels and using the information, or selling it on to other thieves. Rather than putting your home address on your luggage, put the address of your office, or carry your home address inside your luggage.

If you have an answerphone, word the message you leave carefully so it is not possible to ascertain that you are on holiday.

Safe and secure

In addition to these common-sense precautions, it is up to you to ensure that your home security is up to scratch – and that you remember to use any security devices that have

been installed. Strong locks should have been fitted to all external doors and accessible windows, and they should be used. Remember also to lock, or padlock, the garage and shed. As well as containing items of monetary value, they probably have within them all the tools a burglar would need to break in to your home. Ladders should also be locked away in the garage, or secured to a wall with a padlock and chain.

> ## '...Take care not to inform too many people...'

If you have an intruder alarm system activate it as you leave the house, but do make sure that your visiting neighbour is fully aware of how it works and has a key to operate it. If your alarm is linked to a central station, do inform the operators that you are going away, and who the keyholder will be in your absence. Some Neighbourhood Watch schemes have raised funds to

Remember to close and securely lock all windows and doors.

Safekeeping

Objects of value, such as antiques, hi-fi equipment, televisions and videos should ideally be moved out of sight of prying eyes when you go away.

If you have installed a wall or floor safe, any small objects can be locked away securely. Alternatively you may wish to pay to deposit them at a bank for safekeeping. Any credit cards which you are not taking with you should also be locked away safely.

Holiday homes

Homes are particularly difficult to keep secure if they are only used for holiday purposes. Of course, if it is a chalet situated on a site, there may be staff present to keep an eye on it for you, or adequate site security to deter intruders. But a property situated on its own, or surrounded by other holiday properties, could be an easy target.

In such cases it is important to make it clear that there is nothing contained within the property worth stealing. Strip the property internally and leave

buy portable alarms which may be loaned to neighbours when they go away. These alarms are designed to protect a room or entrance hall, detecting a presence by sensing movement or heat change and, in response, activating an inbuilt siren.

Lighting-up time

Security lighting is invaluable when you are going away for any length of time. There are various devices available which will switch your lights on and off. More sophisticated ones work on a random principle and, installed in several rooms, can give the impression that an entire family is home. For holiday use, some timeswitches can be programmed to turn the lights on and off at random intervals over a seven day period – daylight operation is prevented by the incorporation of a sensor device. Time switches may also be used to control a variety of electrical appliances. By connecting one to a radio, for instance, you could use sound as a deterrent as well.

If you do leave lights or electrical appliances on in an empty house, do keep them away from curtains or inflammable materials, or a fire could result.

Exterior security lighting should also be fitted to ensure that an intruder risks being spotted by neighbours or passers-by.

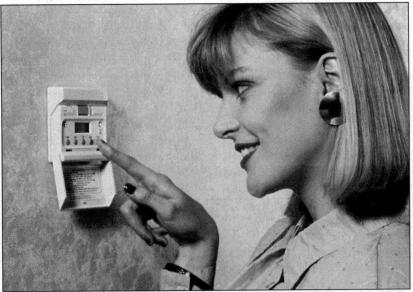

Use a programmable lightswitch to switch lights on and off while you are away. The Model 2304 from Superswitch operates lights at preset times over a seven-day period.

the curtains open so an intruder can see inside, and leave all the drawers and cupboards empty and open.

Again, security precautions must be taken. Locks should be fitted to all doors and windows, but if the property is in a remote location where it is unlikely that an intruder would be spotted and would have more time to break in, a higher level of security can be provided with the installation of grilles or shutters.

External security measures will also help, such as high, thick hedges around the sides or rear of the property (the front should be kept low so passers-by could see an intruder), and rose bushes or prickly shrubs in front of the lower windows to prevent an intruder climbing in. Again, automatic exterior lighting will help people to spot anything suspicious.

Try to ensure that all mail relating to the property is sent to your main address.

WATCHPOINTS

1 Don't leave the security of your home until the last minute.

2 Take steps to make sure the home looks occupied while you are away.

3 Cancel all deliveries and ensure this is noted in the order book.

4 Enlist the help of friends, family and neighbours.

5 Leave a key with a neighbour, and an address where you can be contacted.

6 Take care not to inform too many people of your forthcoming absence.

7 Make sure home security is up to scratch, and that devices are used.

Holiday checklist

Have you remembered to:

1 Cancel the milk? ☐

2 Cancel newspaper deliveries? ☐

3 Ensure that cancellations are written in the order book? ☐

4 Arrange for the Post Office and/or neighbours to keep your post for you? ☐

5 Ask neighbours to keep an eye on your home? ☐

6 Contact the local Neighbourhood Watch co-ordinator? ☐

7 Leave an address where you can be contacted? ☐

8 Inform local police of your absence? ☐

9 Lock all windows and doors? ☐

10 Lock the garage and shed? ☐

11 Lock away ladders? ☐

12 Set the intruder alarm? ☐

13 Instruct a neighbour or keyholder on how the intruder alarm operates? ☐

14 Activate security lighting devices – inside and out? ☐

15 Move valuable objects out of sight? ☐

16 Lock small valuable objects and credit cards away safely? ☐

CHAPTER 26

Are you travel-wise?

Sun, sea, sand, good food, good company – yet even the most idyllic holiday can be spoiled so easily. The loss of cash or credit cards, or the theft of clothing or valuables can all turn the perfect break into a nightmare if a few simple precautions aren't followed.

Goods in transit are naturally more vulnerable – from the time you leave home to the moment you return. Try to avoid taking items of real value with you. Any jewellery you take should be costume jewellery, and credit cards should be kept to a minimum. Before you set off, write out a list of what you are carrying in your luggage to assist you should you need to make an insurance claim. Keep a record of the numbers of all credit cards and your passport and driving licence, and carry a copy of this list with you, separate from your luggage, and leave another safely at home with someone you trust. Also carry telephone numbers with you to report credit card losses immediately.

Packed to go

Always keep valuable equipment, including money, documents, jewellery, cameras and electrical goods in your hand luggage so that it will remain with you at all times. Be prepared for your luggage to be lost in transit by carrying a few essentials in your hand luggage, such as a change of clothing and some toiletries. Keep your hand luggage zipped up, or fastened at all times, and your wallets in inside pockets to prevent both opportunists and professional thieves who often operate at airports, coach stations and ports.

'...Keep a record of the numbers of credit cards, passport and driving licence...'

Choose suitcases for strength, security and convenience rather than appearance. Soft-sided cases can be torn in transit, especially with air travel, whilst those with a stiffer construction can split if dropped. Check that locking devices operate securely. Padlock zipped cases, and use luggage straps to provide additional security, and to keep your possessions in place should the case

At your destination

Most hotels offer a safe deposit facility where you can leave cash, valuables and important documents. Items such as these should never be left in an empty hotel room, even if it is locked, unless the room itself is fitted with a safe. Many of the rules for personal safety at home apply in your hotel room. Keep the door locked at all times and, if there is a knock at the door, do not open it until you have ascertained the identity of the caller. If there is a door chain and door viewer fitted, then do remember to use them. If the caller claims to be carrying out repairs on behalf of the hotel, or to make a delivery, phone the front desk and check before admitting him. Keys should be left at the front desk whenever you are going out – not carried with you. Close and secure all accessible windows when you go out. Portable personal door locks are now available to provide additional protection. These can be used only when the room is occupied to increase personal safety, or to provide additional privacy for bathrooms. Portable locks are available in the UK from companies such as BodyGuard Security.

'...If you wake to find someone in your room...yell, scream...'

If you do return to your hotel room and think a burglar is inside, do not enter. Go down to the front desk and report it. If you awake to find someone in your room, do not pretend to be asleep. Yell, scream and call the front desk.

On the day of departure, do not leave packed luggage unattended in your room. Ask the hotel to keep it safely somewhere for you. Finally,

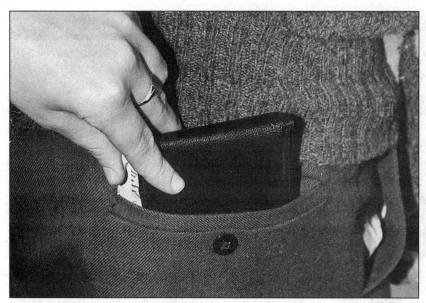

To deter pickpockets, do not keep wallets in a trouser back pocket.

burst open. Do not let your luggage out of your sight. Never ask a stranger to keep an eye on it for you while you slip off to use the phone, and never agree to look after someone else's luggage for them. Suppose it went missing whilst in your care or, even worse, was found to contain drugs or firearms!

Luggage must be labelled in case of loss, but avoid attaching your home address to the outside of the case. Criminals are on the lookout for such information – it is an obvious indication that your home is likely to be unoccupied for one or two weeks, and this information can be passed on to accomplices and used. Label your bags with your destination and put your home address inside the case, or put the address of your office on the label, so in the event of loss luggage can be returned to you safely.

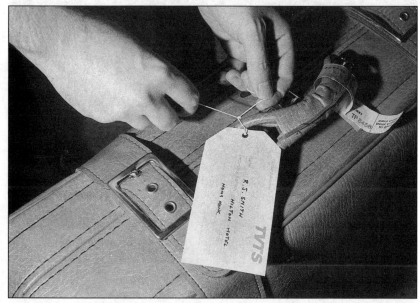

Luggage must be labelled, but avoid attaching your home address to the outside of your case.

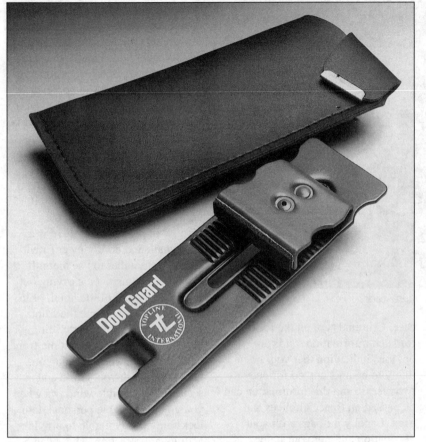

Portable personal door locks, like Doorguard can be used to increase personal safety.

Out and about

There are numerous common-sense precautions to bear in mind when travelling at home or abroad. Women travelling alone or with a few friends should follow the same safety procedures that they would at home (see Chapter 24). Carry bags close to your side, with the clasp towards you, and with your purse tucked right away out of reach. Never walk back to your hotel or apartment alone at night, and never hitch-hike, or accept lifts from strangers.

It's always a good idea to find out something about your chosen holiday destination before you make your booking. Ask the travel agent whether the area is regarded as safe, or contact the tour company. There are guide books available which are written specifically for women travelling alone, or with friends.

If you are taking your car abroad, remember that a GB sticker does mark you out as a possible target. To avoid attracting attention British

make sure you and your family are aware of fire procedure in the hotel and know which exits to use. NEVER use the lift in the event of a fire.

Campers and caravans should be locked up when you are inside at night, and should be properly secured when you leave them (see Chapter 23). Avoid leaving valuables in an unoccupied camper. If you are going on a camping holiday, avoid taking any items of value with you unless they are absolutely essential. Money and other valuables should be kept with you at all times. If you must take items of value, lock them away in the boot of your car and set the vehicle alarm.

Hold on to handbags. Do not tuck them away where you cannot see them.

tourists in Florida have been advised to personalize hire cars with stickers to prevent them looking too 'new'. It's important not to leave valuables in the car. If you get lost while driving, make your way to a safe place such as a garage or police station to ask for directions, rather than asking a passer-by. Do not study maps while driving. Luggage should be locked away out of sight and doors should be kept locked when driving and parked. If someone tries to 'nudge' your car or make you stop, drive on to a busy, well-lit area and call the police.

You can reduce the risk of being attacked by trying to 'blend in'. Dress down, don't wear valuable jewellery and keep cameras and video cameras hidden. Carry a map and make sure you know exactly where you are going so that you avoid dangerous neighbourhoods.

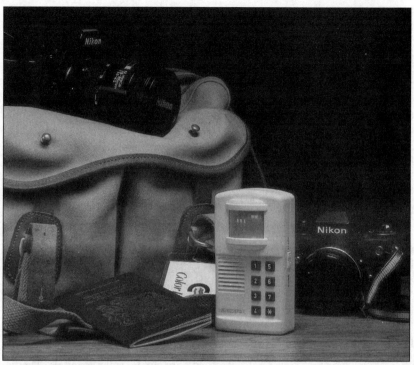

Superswitch's Model 6002 intruder alarm is so small and lightweight that it can be carried with you and used to protect valuable equipment on your travels.

Money matters

Most thieves will be after money. Avoid carrying a lot of cash – just enough for emergencies and casual expenditure. Ideally, use travellers' cheques and credit cards. Always follow the instructions issued with travellers' cheques and keep a record of the serial numbers – but not with the cheques. Cross each serial number off as you use the cheques so, in the event of loss or theft, you know which ones are missing.

Money, cheques and credit cards must be carried safely, out of reach of casual pickpockets. A money belt provides good security, worn around your waist under your clothes, or around your wrist or ankle for use on the beach. Make sure you understand the currency well enough to avoid pulling out huge wads of notes or travellers' cheques. If you can, avoid carrying all your money with you at one time. In a hotel it should be deposited in the

safe. Keep credit card receipts safely so that no-one can ascertain your number, and when you use your card, make sure that it is returned to you – not swapped for another. Try to carry travellers' cheques and credit cards separately, so if one is stolen you will still have access to some funds.

Business travellers

Those travelling on business are just as vulnerable as holiday makers. But business travel often involves carrying round expensive office-type equipment, such as laptop computers and mobile phones, as well as valuable demonstration equipment. Laptops are often carried in custom-made cases which do little to disguise what they are. Try to limit the amount you take with you to hand luggage only, so it can be carried with you at all times, and make sure that bags and cases are secured with strong locks.

Expensive equipment should be disguised or concealed in a bag or locked boot of a car, preferably with a vehicle alarm in operation. Make sure that vehicle insurance covers theft of personal and business property. Ask your hotel if they have a large safe where you could deposit demonstration equipment. Portable intruder alarms are also available which may be used in a hotel room to detect an intrusion, or a door alarm which, fixed to the door, will sense it opening and sound the alarm.

Insurance

When you are travelling in the UK you may find that your house contents insurance provides coverage for property lost or stolen outside the home, overcoming the need for separate holiday insurance. When travelling abroad, however, it's a good idea to take out separate holiday insurance which will cover your belongings for loss or damage

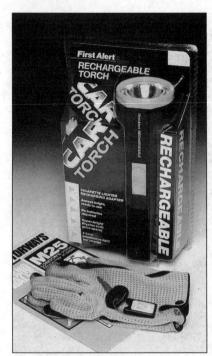

Travel wisely, be prepared to avoid dangerous neighbourhoods

while travelling, and for loss or theft during your holiday. The policy will also cover you for personal accident, medical expenses, travel delay, travel cancellation and personal liability. Carry the paper work with you while you are away.

When taking out holiday insurance, read the small print carefully – don't just accept the travel agent's word – make sure that the policy provides adequate cover, and that the maximum amount per any one item is sufficient. It does pay to shop around. You will need about £1,500 cover for personal belongings, enough cover for the money you are taking with you, £250,000 cover for medical expenses in Europe (or £1,000,000 in the USA and the rest of the world), cover for the full cost of your holiday and £1,000,000 personal liability cover in all countries except the USA where you will need at least £2,000,000.

You will probably be expected to pay an 'excess' if you make a claim – usually the first £25. Bear in mind

also that standard holiday insurance only provides indemnity cover, i.e., if you lose something the insurance company will only pay the second-hand replacement value. If your house contents provides new-for-old all-risks cover, you may be able to claim under this.

Britain has a reciprocal health care arrangement with other countries, but this is restricted. If you are visiting an EC country, complete an EIII form (available from the Dept of Health and Social Security, or main Post Offices). This form must accompany you when you travel and be presented if you require treatment. However, it's worth taking out separate medical insurance as it won't cover the cost of bringing someone back to the UK in the event of death or illness, and it only covers state hospitals. There are other restrictions in individual countries. If you claim medical

expenses be sure to keep all bills relating to treatment, medication and other expenses.

If you plan to take your car abroad, let your insurance company know. Some automatically provide comprehensive cover throughout the EC to people with fully comprehensive policies. Others will require a small additional payment to cover you. Ask your insurer for a Green Card – whilst this is no longer a legal requirement it can avoid problems in certain EC countries.

To avoid unnecessary delays, take out breakdown cover before you travel, available from most motoring organizations. Some insurance companies include European breakdown cover in their motor insurance policies. Emergency repairs abroad, plus the cost of hiring a replacement car can add up to a very expensive holiday.

WATCHPOINTS

1 Avoid taking items of real value with you.

2 Write out a list of what you are carrying.

3 Keep valuable equipment in your hand luggage, along with a few essentials.

4 Avoid attaching your home address to the outside of your luggage.

5 Make use of safe deposit facilities in hotels.

6 Never leave packed luggage unattended.

7 Find out as much as possible about your destination. Ask the travel agent or courier for areas to be avoided.

8 Try to 'blend in', and make sure you know your route in advance.

9 Always choose a busy, safe place to ask directions.

10 Carry travellers' cheques and credit cards, and limit cash to a minimum. Carry it in a money belt.

CHAPTER 27

Take cover

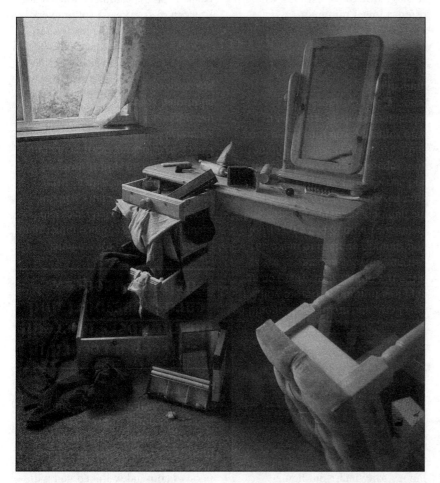

If the worst should happen and you are a victim of a burglary, the very least you'll want to be sure of is that you will receive adequate financial compensation for items lost. Yet figures from the Association of British Insurers (ABI) reveal that three million homeowners may incorrectly believe that they have bought adequate home contents insurance. There is no doubt that a very large number of households are under-insured and, in the event of a claim, would not receive nearly enough money to replace stolen or damaged goods.

Although home contents insurance is becoming increasingly expensive, it is a small price to pay for peace of mind. If you are not insured, it is vital that you get in touch with an insurance company or broker immediately. Most policies not only cover your home contents for theft, but also fire, lightning, escape of water from tanks or pipes, oil leaking from fixed heating systems, storm, flood, subsidence, falling trees or aerials, riot or malicious acts, explosion, earthquake, and impact by aircraft, vehicles or animals.

'...a very large number of households are under insured...'

The home contents policy will normally cover your furniture, furnishings, household goods, kitchen equipment and other appliances, food and drink, televisions, videos, computers and audio equipment, clothing, personal effects and valuables such as jewellery and personal money up to stated limits. It should include accidental breakage of mirrors, glass tops on furniture and fixed glass in furniture, and it may also include accidental damage to televisions, videos, home computers and audio equipment, with cover for accidental damage to all contents available as an extension to the standard contents cover. Most policies also offer extensions such as a contribution for alternative accommodation should your home be so badly damaged that it is not fit to live in, and for various legal liabilities.

Remember that a standard home contents insurance will not cover every eventuality or risk, and only limited cover applies to contents temporarily removed from the home, such as jewellery or cameras. Cover for such items is often available, as a special extension of home contents insurance, as 'All risks' insurance. To find out exactly what your policy offers, and whether the cover is adequate, make sure you read it thoroughly and, if in doubt, contact the insurance company who will be able to advise you.

Choosing a policy

It does pay to shop around for home contents insurance as rates can vary tremendously for similar cover. An increasing number of companies are now offering discounts to householders who have installed good locks to doors and windows, or who have a professionally-installed intruder alarm system. (Do bear in mind that in areas deemed high-risk, this may be a requirement before insurance is even granted and will not qualify for a discount). Also check your policy regarding the situation in the event of a claim; homeowners who receive a discount for security measures must use the locks or alarm. The policies may not pay out if the alarm is not activated, or windows left unlocked overnight or when the home is unoccupied. Other insurance companies offer discounts to members of Neighbourhood Watch schemes, or to householders over a certain age on the understanding that the home will be occupied most of the day; and some are now offering no-claims discounts or loyalty bonuses for those who remain with the same insurance company each year. You can also save money by offering to pay a voluntary excess, i.e., you

agree to pay the first part of any claim up to a pre-set limit. You may find that your policy imposes a compulsory excess of, say, £50, but you can sometimes offer to pay more to reduce the premium.

Also check the minimum sum each policy will insure for. You may find that you actually require less cover, so shop around for a policy which offers a lower minimum.

Basically, home contents insurance can be broken down into two main types, 'indemnity' and 'replacement-as-new'. If you insure on a 'replacement-as-new' basis, you will be paid the full cost of repairing damaged articles or the cost of replacing them with equivalent new articles if they are stolen or destroyed. With 'indemnity' insurance, you will be paid the cost of repairing damaged articles or replacing what has been stolen or destroyed, less an amount for wear and tear and depreciation. So, in the event of a claim, the money you get back from the insurance company will only be enough to buy second-hand furniture, or new furniture of inferior quality. You will normally find that items such as clothing and household linen can only be insured on an indemnity basis.

Sum insured

The sum insured is the amount of money for which your home contents are covered. In the event of a claim it is the most your insurers will pay, so it is vital that you calculate it accurately, but at the same time you do not want to pay for cover that you do not need. When you are assessing your sum insured it is easy to miss items. The most effective method is to study every room, including the loft, garage and shed, and estimate how much it would cost to replace each item at today's prices (visit the

shops if necessary to gain a comparison). You will also be responsible for rented items such as televisions and videos, so do not disregard them. Remember to deduct an amount for wear and tear and depreciation of clothing and linen. The ABI recommends that this is calculated on the following basis: A suit is estimated to have a lifespan of five years, so for every year, deduct ⅕th of the price of an equivalent new suit at today's prices. This is only a rough guide, and allowances will be made for the quality of the suit and its general condition.

For valuables and antiques an expert valuation may be required. There is usually a limit on the value of any one work of art, ornament or piece of jewellery, and often an overall limit on such articles. Keep valuations and receipts secure, as they may be required if you make a claim.

As you add up the total value for each room, write it down on the ABI checklist printed here. When it is complete, add up the figures you have entered in the boxes and write in the total. To ensure that the figure remains up-to-date, many policies are index-linked, i.e., your sum insured is automatically changed every month in line with the government's Retail Prices Index. If index-linking applies, the total is the sum insured you need. If your policy is not index-linked you will need to add a suitable allowance for inflation in the year to come.

It is very important that the sum insured is adequate, and you must remember to ask your insurer to increase your sum insured if you add to your possessions. Some policies state that if you are under-insured, claim payments will be reduced. Even if the policy is index-linked, the sum insured should be reviewed every few years.

CHECK LIST	Lounge	Dining room	Kitchen	Hall stairs	Landing and loft	Main bed-room	2nd bed-room	3rd bed-room	Bath-room/ toilet	Garage & out-buildings	TOTALS
Carpets, rugs and floor coverings											
Furniture: tables, chairs, stools, settees, cabinets, sideboards, bookcases. Bedroom, bathroom and kitchen furniture											
Soft furnishings, curtains and their fittings, cushions											
Televisions, videos and audio equipment											
Household appliances: cooker, fridge/freezer, washing machine, vacuum cleaner, electrical goods, heaters											
Cooking utensils, cutlery, china, glass, food, drink											
Valuables: gold & silver articles, jewellery, furs, pictures, clocks, watches, cameras, ornaments, collections											
Sports equipment, books, cycles, records, computers, tapes, toys, musical instruments											
Garden furniture, lawn-mower, ladders, tools, paint, fuel											
Household linen: table linen, towels, bedding											
Clothing											
Other items											

If your policy is not index-linked, add on a suitable allowance for inflation. You may, of course, have other rooms and possessions not listed here.

TOTAL £ _____

Allowance for inflation during year at ....% _____

Your contents should be insured for £ _____

Buildings insurance

As well as the structure itself, a buildings insurance policy will cover the permanent fixtures and fittings, such as sanitary ware and fitted kitchens, and interior decoration. Policies usually extend to cover out-buildings such as garages, greenhouses and sheds, and limited cover is provided for boundary walls, fences, gates, paths, drives and swimming pools.

Most policies cover damage to your home caused by a variety of risks, including fire, lightning, storm and flood, theft or attempted theft, subsidence or landslip (with an excess applying in almost all policies), explosion or earthquake, malicious damage or vandalism, riot, damage from leaking pipes, escape of oil, and impact by vehicle or animal. Among the usual extensions are the cost of alternative accommodation up to a certain limit; property owner's liability; accidental damage to underground service pipes and cables; and breakage of glass in doors, windows and skylights and sanitary ware.

The amount a building should be insured for is based on how much it would cost to rebuild it completely, and again the sum insured must be adequate as it is the most your insurer will pay under any circumstances. Most policies specify that the amount to be paid, even for less serious damage, can be reduced if there is under-insurance. Advice on how much to insure your home for is available in the 'Buildings Insurance for Home Owners' leaflet available from the Association of British Insurers. This gives details of the costs of rebuilding according to the type, size, age and location of the house.

Buildings insurance is normally offered by mortgage lenders when you buy your home, but it pays to shop around as this may not be the cheapest or most suitable policy available. However, if your home is at high risk from subsidence it's worth remaining with the same insurer as some won't pay if the damage was caused before you were insured by them. Ideally, policies should be index-linked so the cover is increased in line with the House Rebuilding Costs Index produced by the Royal Institute of Chartered Surveyors. Also you will need to increase the amount you are insured for should you carry out substantial home improvements.

Making a claim

Before you contact your insurance company, make sure that the type of damage you are claiming for is covered, and check whether you should claim under your buildings or contents policy. Then contact your insurance company, building society, broker, agent or adviser and request a claim form. This should be completed and returned as soon as possible, ideally with estimates for repairs or replacement.

If you are the victim of theft, malicious damage or vandalism inform the police immediately, and if cheque books, credit cards or cash cards have been stolen, notify the issuing company, bank or building society.

If temporary repairs need to be made to prevent further damage or intrusion, arrange for them to be carried out straight away. Keep the bills, as the cost may form part of your claim. Keep damaged items, as the insurance company may need to see them.

'...keep the bills...'

Once your insurance company receives the completed claim form they will request estimates for repair work or replacement if these have not already been submitted. They may then pay your claim; arrange for their claims inspector to call on you; or send a loss adjuster to handle the claim. The loss adjuster will advise you on any matter relating to your claim and inform you if the insurance company requires further information. They will also agree claim settlement figures with you. If you do not have purchase receipts and professional valuations for any item lost or stolen, ask the insurers what alternative evidence they will accept.

If you are unhappy with the way a claim is handled, write to the insurance company branch manager to say so. If you are still not satisfied, contact the head office. If the difficulty remains unresolved, contact the Association of British Insurers Consumer Information Department. Most companies subscribe to schemes which provide for an impartial body to consider complaints if you have been unable to reach an agreement with your own company.

WATCH POINTS

1 Shop around for discounts and adequate cover.

2 Read the policy carefully, paying particular attention to advice on claims and conditions.

3 Keep your property in good order. A policy does not cover the costs of maintaining your house or its contents.

4 You must take reasonable steps to prevent a loss occurring and, if it happens, do what you can to prevent further damage.

5 In the event of a claim, give full and accurate information, and inform the company immediately.

6 Make sure that you are adequately insured.

7 Remember that it is a crime to make a fraudulent claim.

CHAPTER 28

The future

A Secured by Design Award is presented by Essex police for homes at Seymour Gate on the 600 acre Chafford Hundred estate where burglar alarms are fitted as standard.

Look back a mere ten years and compare what you have read about in this book with what was available then. Not only were the most sophisticated measures – like alarm monitoring and automatic lighting – very new, but they were also well beyond the budget of most home-owners.

Those who were aware of Milton Keynes being built and the hi-tech homes that received so much publicity, may well wonder why we don't yet have those remarkable gadgets for controlling lighting and heating and conserving energy, as well as those which would lock all the doors and shutter the windows automatically at the press of a button.

There have been several 'live' experiments in the last ten years, and house-builders have shown considerable interest and support, particularly for systems which combine security with energy conservation. However, while we all enjoy buying gadgetry which entertains us, more down-to-earth devices, such as lighting and security are far more difficult for manufacturers and builders to sell, particularly where cost is a factor.

The automated home

Nevertheless, a number of large companies, such as Honeywell and Thorn EMI, are either selling 'automated' homes or have demonstration homes up and running.

There have been some false starts and, with the recent slump in the building of new homes, the last decade has not presented the right economic climate for home builders to think of enhancing their homes in what will undoubtedly be seen as a luxurious and expensive fashion. However, Honeywell has been selling its TotalHome concept in the United States. This integrated system is able to secure the home, warn of fire and smoke, control temperature, lighting and various appliances. It can be specially customized for each home-owner and operated using a touch-tone phone and an access code. In the USA TotalHome sells for $4,000, rather less than one may expect, and is professionally installed and monitored for 24 hours a day.

Here, the story is not so far advanced, with operational systems still to be decided upon and the promotion of the concept yet to begin. Nevertheless, the technology

is available, and with several development projects in progress, such as the EEC's Esprit Home Systems, it may not be long before you are hearing more about the automated home.

What we also see in our everyday lives is greater use of access control. In fact, every time we insert our credit card and punch a code into a cash machine outside the bank or building society we are using a form of security. Magnetic cards are increasingly used in door entry systems, and another version of these is the proximity or hands-free card where no contact is made with the reader at all. A code is programmed into the card and read using radio signals.

Other methods of identification are slowly coming on to the market, primarily for high risk commercial buildings. It is now possible to identify visitors and employees from their signature, the pattern of their fingers or hand, and even the structure of their eyes.

While average householders are unlikely to see these ideas in action in their homes for some years to come, builders are incorporating new ideas on security, and not only the obvious locks and alarms.

The design approach

Landscaping of new estates and built-in security, such as better lighting, grass mounds to create visible yet pleasant barriers and thorny bushes to deter intruders are all ideas being used to create a better and more pleasant environment. The Secured by Design scheme has the backing of over 200 developers and, working with police forces, they are designing homes with better layout, door and window design, locking, security lighting, intruder alarms and smoke detectors. Builders are now seeing these factors as giving a home sale value, and where they once left security until the end of a building project, when there was little left in the kitty, they are beginning to budget for such improvements. The National House Building Council also include security in the requirements which a builder has to comply with before being able to offer the NHBC ten-year warranty.

So security, whilst it is inevitably associated with crime, is being used to improve the homes we live in, create a better environment and ensure we can feel safer, happier and more secure wherever we are.

Part of Seymour Gate at Chafford Hundred in Essex, a Secured by Design development.

Glossary

Access control

Various methods of allowing entry. This could be with a digital lock, mechanical or electronic, a magnetic card, video or audio entry and the latest proximity and hands-free systems which use radio signals to confirm a code.

Biometric – Controlling access using personal characteristics (fingerprints, handprints, retina patterns etc.)

Fail safe – A locking device that unlocks the door if power fails, and requires continuous power to stay locked.

Fail secure – A locking device that locks the door if power fails and requires power to unlock the door.

Hands-free – Technology which allows a cardholder to gain access without having to actually present a card or enter a code.

Keypad – A non-QWERTY keyboard for inputting codes and information.

Magnetic stripe card – A card with a band of ferrous material that can be magnetically encoded.

PIN (Personal Identification Number) – A code assigned to a cardholder which is entered at the keypad.

Proximity – Technology using radio frequency or inductive principles to stimulate and read cards that transmit unique identification codes.

Stand-alone – An access control system, mains or battery operated, which does not require an additional controller.

Void – To delete a card or code.

(With acknowledgment to Cardkey)

Alarms

Anti hi-jack – On a vehicle security system this enables the car to be immobilized and the alarm sounded after the car has been driven a short distance.

Autodialler (or communicator) – Can be linked to an alarm system to send alert messages to a number of pre-programmed telephone numbers.

Bell box – Houses the external siren for an intruder alarm system. 'Dummy' bell boxes are available as a deterrent.

Central station – A remote location to which signals from the alarm are sent using a variety of methods (telephone line and radio networks, for example) to enable keyholders and emergency services to be contacted when necessary.

Control panel – The heart of the system, able to set, unset, turn zones on and off, process signals from the various devices connected to the system, including, in some panels, identifying faults.

Current sensor – Like the voltage drop sensor, this detects the opening of doors on a vehicle security system.

Detection pattern – Area of volumetric coverage of a detector.

Digital communicator – A device which allows the alarm system to 'pick up' a phone line and dial the central station to raise the alarm.

Exit/entry delay – A part of the alarm system which allows the user or engineer to set the amount of time allowed to enter and exit the premises before the alarm is triggered.

LCD – Liquid crystal display panel which provides a digital readout. Used in alarm and access control systems to display instructions to the user at the panel.

LED – Light emitting diode (often used to indicate alarm status).

Magnetic reed switches – Alarm system detection device fitted to doors and windows. If the door or window is opened the break in the circuit will trigger an alarm.

Microwave detector – A detector that uses microwaves (high frequency radio waves) to detect motion.

Motion detector – Passive infra-red, ultrasonic and microwave sensors.

Panic/Personal attack (PA) button – Alarm activation device which will trigger the alarm even when the control panel is switched off. Should be sited near the front door, or in the main bedroom.

Passive infra-red detector (PIR) – Sends out infra-red beams within its field of detection. Interruption of these beams will activate an alarm system or security lighting.

Personal alarm – A small battery or gas-operated alarm which can be carried in a pocket or handbag.

Pressure sensing devices – Activate an alarm by detecting a drop in air pressure.

Rechargeable self-contained siren module (RSCB) or Self-actuating bell (SAB) – ensures that an alarm siren will continue to sound even if the power is cut or interrupted.

Remote keypad – Where the control panel is hidden away, basic programming of a system is possible from one or more keypads.

Stand-alone alarm – A portable device that can be moved around to protect one room or specific area. Incorporates its own built-in siren and detection device.

Ultrasonic detection – Detects motion by transmitting a high frequency which reflects off objects in an area. If these 'reflections' are changed the detector triggers the alarm.

Vibration detection – A device sensitive to various frequencies (such as breaking glass or vibration).

Voltage drop sensor – Used in a vehicle security system, this detects when a door is opened, or other electrical load imposed.

Wire-free alarms – These utilize radio frequencies to communicate between detectors and control panel, overcoming the need for unsightly wiring.

General

All-risks cover – Insurance for items that are likely to be taken out of the home.

Anti-climb paint – A substance designed to remain sticky for a number of years which is painted on to drainpipes and other surfaces to prevent an intruder climbing to an upper storey.

Casement window – A window that is hinged vertically.

Ceramic markers – Permanently mark china and ceramics by depositing a metallic compound on the surface of the glaze.

Die-stamping – Method of property marking for large metal items using a special set of punches.

Etching – A permanent mark applied to hard surfaces with a hard-tipped engraver, acid or sandblasting technique.

Indemnity – For items insured on an indemnity basis you will be paid the full cost of repairing damaged articles or of replacing stolen or destroyed articles, less an amount for wear, tear and depreciation.

Louvre window – A window with glass fitted in narrow, horizontal slats which are easily removed.

Replacement-as-new – Insurance on this basis means you will be paid the full cost of repairing damaged articles, or the cost of replacing them with equivalent new articles if they are stolen or destroyed.

Security marking – A method of permanently marking property, normally with the postcode, to ensure its safe return.

Ultra-violet ink – 'Invisible' marking which can only be detected under ultra-violet light.

Locks

Automatic deadlatch – A rim lock with a main bolt which automatically locks or is deadlocked when the door is closed.

Bit – The part of the key which is specially shaped or notched to operate the mechanism of its own particular lock.

Blank – A partly made key, ready for cutting.

Cylinder lock – A lock which has its mechanism contained in a cylinder. Made up of pin or disc tumblers and springs.

Deadlock – A lock with only a square ended deadbolt.

Differs – An abbreviation of 'different combinations'.

Dummy ball – A device to protect the towball on caravans or trailers to prevent unauthorized towing.

Hitchlock – Prevents unauthorized towing of a caravan or trailer.

Jamb – The vertical member of a door or window frame.

Lever – A flat-shaped moveable detainer in a lock which provides security and differs.

Master-key – A key which will open any number of locks in a master-keyed system. Locks can be keyed at various levels to open certain doors and not others while one master-key will open them all.

Mortice – A hole cut into the thickness of one edge of a door to accommodate a mortice lock or latch.

Mortice lock – A lock mortised into the stile of a door or window, and key-operated.

Nightlatch – A rim or mortice latch with a bolt which can be withdrawn by key from the outside or by knob or lever handle from the inside. A snib will hold the bolt so the lock remains open and will deadlock the bolt when in the closed position.

Padbolt – Incorporates a bolt which shoots into the surrounding framework and is secured in place with a padlock.

Rim lock – A lock fitted by screwing it to the face of the inside of the door. It will have a rim cylinder on the outside.

Shackle – The shaped loop of a padlock.

Striker or striking plate – A shaped flat metal plate fixed to the door frame or jamb into which the bolts shoot. Used with all mortice locks and certain rim locks

Wheelclamp – A device fitted around a car or caravan wheel to prevent towing or driving away.

(With acknowledgement to Yale Security)

Video entry

The facility to see, using a camera and monitor, who is at the door, and often to open the door remotely.

Auto-iris – Automatic method of adjusting iris f stop number.

Camera – A unit containing an imaging device, requiring an optical lens and producing a video signal.

CCTV – Closed circuit television.

Coaxial cable – A specialist cable designed for use with wide bandwidth signals.

Lux – Light levels specified as daylight, lowlight, moonlight and starlight. Infra-red may be used to supplement ambient light.

Video monitor – The picture end of the system. The more lines per inch the better the picture.

British Standards you should know:

BS4737 – In numerous parts relating to various types of alarm, their components, planning and installation, maintenance, records and external alarms. All good installers should comply with this standard.

BS6799 – The standard for wire-free (radio-operated) alarm systems. Several grades are listed and their advantages and disadvantages are outlined.

BS3621 – The standard for thief resistant locks. Until recently the insurers' byword, but new guidelines have recently been introduced which extend the locks acceptable for insurance purposes.

BS5446 – Look for this standard if you are buying a battery-operated smoke alarm.

BS6707 – Specification for intruder alarm systems for consumer installation. Details components necessary for a kit.

BS5979 – Code of practice for remote monitoring stations.

BS6800 – Specification for home and personal security devices.

BS6803 Part I – The standard for alarm systems installed as original equipment by car manufacturers.

BS6803 Part II – Code of practice for installation of alarm systems in vehicles in the after-market.

BS7150 – Code of practice for intruder alarm systems with mains-wiring communication.

BS8220 Part 1 – Guide for the security of buildings against crime. Dwellings. Good general advice.

BS AU209 – Vehicle security standard in several parts covering locks, in-car entertainment, security marking of glazing, central locking and deadlocking systems.

Useful Addresses

Advanced Design Electronics
Dixon Road
Knowsley Industrial Park
North Merseyside
L33 7XR
Tel: 051 549 1550

Aritech UK Ltd
Essex Court
Ashton Road
Harold Hill
Romford
Essex RM3 8UF
Tel: 04023 81496

Secur + Systems
Artistic Ironworkers Supplies Ltd
Edwin Avenue
Hoo Farm Industrial Estate
Kidderminster, Worcs.
DY11 7RA
Tel: 0562 825252

A1 Security & Electrical Ltd
16 Brickfields
Huyton Trading Estate
Huyton
Merseyside L36 6HY
Tel: 051 480 4455

Arjan SPRi (Mister Security)
Ave la Toison d'Or 25
1060 Brussels
Belgium
Tel: 02 511 0506

Ashley Security Products
PO Box No. 106
Willenhall
West Midlands
WV12 5RQ
Tel: 0922 409533

Association of British Insurers
51 Gresham Street
London EC2V 7HQ
Tel: 071 600 3333

Audioline Ltd (Moss Security)
2 Enfield Industrial Estate
Redditch
Worcs BN4 6BH
Tel: 0527 584584

Autolok Security Products Ltd
Park Lane
Royton
Oldham
Lancs OL2 6PU
Tel: 061 624 8171

Automobile Inparts Ltd
7 Old Chapel Mews
Lake Street
Leighton Buzzard
Beds LU7 8RN
Tel: 0525 382713

Baddeley Rose Limited
Unit 9
Park Street Industrial Estate
Park Street
St Albans
Herts AL2 2DR
Tel: 0727 875301

Barrs Security
329 Fulham Palace Road
London
SW6 6TE
Tel: 071 736 7668

BC Technology, (Aiphone)
BC Tec House
Wallis Close
Park Farm South
Wellingborough
Northants NN8 6AG
Tel: 0933 405050

Benn Security
80 Wellingborough Road
Northampton
NN1 4DP
Tel: 0604 20707

Beta-Thief Security Products Ltd
Unit K4-K5, Cherrycourt Way
Stanbridge Road
Leighton Buzzard
Beds LU7 8UH
Tel: 0525 853888

BodyGuard Security Ltd
Unit 10
Vermont Place
Tongwell
Milton Keynes MK15 8JA
Tel: 0908 218400

Bonwyke Group of Companies
Bonwyke House
41-43 Redlands Lane
Fareham
Hampshire PO14 1HL
Tel: 0329 289621

BPT Security Systems (UK) Ltd
Unit 16, Sovereign Park
Cleveland Way
Hemel Hempstead
Herts HP2 7DA
Tel: 0442 230800

British Standards Institution
2 Park Street
London W1A 2BS
Tel: 071 629 9000

CeKa Abus
CeKa Works Ltd
Pwllheli
Gwynedd
North Wales LL53 5LH
Tel: 0758 701070

C & K Systems Ltd
Cunliffe Drive
Northfield Avenue
Kettering
Northamptonshire
NN16 8LF
Tel: 0536 412202

Checkmate Devices
6 St Andrews Industrial Estate
Bridport
Dorset
DT6 3EX
Tel: 0308 23871

Chubb Locks Ltd
PO Box 197
Wednesfield Road
Wolverhampton
WV10 0ET
Tel: 0902 455440

Chubb Safe Equipment Co
PO Box 61
Wednesfield Road
Wolverhampton
West Midlands
WV10 0EW
Tel: 0902 455111

Chubb Security Group
Chubb House
Staines Road West
Sunbury on Thames
Middlesex
TW16 7AR
Tel: 0932 785588

Churchill Safes & Sec. Products
Brymbo Road Industrial Estate
Holditch
Newcastle-under-Lyme
Staffs
ST5 9HZ
Tel: 0782 717400

Clifford Electronics Inc (UK)
Boundary Business Court
92/94 Church Road
Mitcham
Surrey CR4 3TD
Tel: 081 646 8440

Crime Concern
Level 8
David Murray John Bldg
Brunel Centre
Swindon
Wiltshire SN1 1LY
Tel: 0793 514596

Dicon UK Ltd
19 St George's Road
Cheltenham
Gloucestershire
GL50 3DT
Tel: 0242 222935

Dudley Safes
Unit 17
Deepdale Lane
Upper Gorral
Dudley
West Midlands DY3 2AF
Tel: 0384 239991

Electrical Contractors Association
ESCA House
34 Palace Court
Bayswater
London W2 4HY
Tel: 071 229 1266

Eliza Tinsley & Co Ltd
Reddal Hill Road
Cradley Heath
West Midlands
B64 5JF
Tel: 0384 66066

ERA Security Products
Straight Road
Short Heath
Willenhall
West Midlands WV12 5RA
Tel: 0922 710222

Euro Mul-T-Lock (UK) Ltd
Unit 4, Shieling Court
North Folds Road
Oakley Hay
Corby
Northamptonshire NN18 9QD
Tel: 0536 461111

Fire Protection Association
140 Aldersgate Street
London
EC1A 4HX
Tel:071 600 1695

First Alert
4 The Paddock
Hambridge Road
Newbury
Berks RG14 5TQ
Tel: 0635 528100

FM Electronics Ltd
Forest Vale Road
Cinderford
Gloucestershire
GL14 2PH
Tel: 0594 827070

Foxguard (Electronics) Ltd
Unit V, Wylds Road
Bridgwater
Somerset TA6 4BH
Tel: 0278 428473

Glass and Glazing Federation
44-48 Borough High Street
London
SE1 1XB
Tel: 071 403 7177

Guardall (see Chubb Security)

Hamber Safes
Radford Way
Billericay
Essex
CM12 0EG
Tel: 0277 624450

Homeguard Products
Unit 1
Hyle Farm
Sherborne
Dorset DT9 6EE
Tel: 0935 815576

Ingersoll (see Yale Security Products)

Jacksons Fine Fencing
337 Stowting Common
Nr Ashford
Kent TN25 6BN
Tel: 0233 750393

Laminated Glass Information Centre
299 Oxford Street
London
W1R 1LA
Tel: 071 499 1720

LCB Marketing
Greenacres International Group
Old Dartford Road
Farningham
Kent DA4 0EB
Tel: 0322 866313

Lionweld Kennedy Ltd
Marsh Road
Middlesbrough
Cleveland
TS1 5JS
Tel: 0642 245151

Locksecure Services Ltd
5 London Road
Sevenoaks
Kent
TN13 1AH
Tel: 0732 459908

Markitwise International
Homme Castle Farm
Shelsley Walsh
Worcestershire
WR6 6RR
Tel: 0886 812427

Master Locksmiths Association
Unit 4/5, Business Park
Great Central Way
Woodford Halse
Daventry,
Northamptonshire
NN11 6PZ
Tel: 0327 62255

Menvier Security Ltd
Hither Green
Clevedon
Avon
BS21 6XU
Tel: 0272 870078

Metro Products Ltd
98-102 Station Road East
Oxted
Surrey RH8 0AY
Tel: 0883 717644

Moat Doors
(Status Electronics Ltd)
Link House
42 Chigwell Lane
Loughton
Essex IG10 3NZ
Tel: 081 502 0136

Moorhouse Marketing
(Siemens Light)
Moorlynch
Bridgwater
Somerset TA7 9BT
Tel: 0458 210569

National Caravan Council
Catherine House
Victoria Road
Aldershot
Hants GU11 1SS
Tel: 0252 318251

National Approval Council for Security Systems (NACOSS)
Queensgate House
14 Cookham Road
Maidenhead
Berkshire SL6 8AJ
Tel: 0628 37512

National House Building Council (NHBC)
Buildmark House
Chiltern Avenue
Amersham
Bucks HP6 5AP
Tel: 0494 434477

Paxton Automation Ltd
Unit 1, Shepherd Industrial Estate
Brooks Road
Lewes
East Sussex
BN7 2BY
Tel: 0273 474509

Personal Watercraft Association (PWA)
Woodside House
Woodside Road
Eastleigh
Hampshire SO5 4ET
Tel: 0703 616888

Pilkington Glass Consultants
Prescot Road
St Helens
WA10 3TT
Tel: 0744 692000

Response Electronics PLC
Unit 1, First Quarter
Longmead Industrial Estate
Epsom
Surrey KT19 9QN
Tel: 0372 744330

Retainacar Limited
45 Tonsley Place
London SW18 1BH
Tel: 081 871 1333

The Royal Society for the Prevention of Accidents (RoSPA)
Cannon House
The Priory, Queensway
Birmingham B4 6BS
Tel: 021 200 2461

Safe & Secure Ltd
3 Swanscombe Road
Holland Park
London W11 4SU
Tel: 071 371 2242

Safeways Security Products Ltd
10 Grange Mount
Birkenhead
L43 4XW
Tel: 051 653 3414

Scantronic Ltd
Perivale Industrial Park
Greenford
Middlesex UB6 7RJ
Tel: 081 991 1133

Securikey Ltd
PO Box 18
Aldershot
Hants
GU12 4SL
Tel: 0252 311888

Security Services Association
70-71 Camden Street
North Shields
Tyne & Wear
NE30 1NH
Tel: 091 296 3242

Security Window Shutters
Unit 2, Middlegate White Lund
Industrial Estate
Morecambe
Lancs
LA3 3BN
Tel: 0524 33986

Selmar Alarms
The Causeway
Malden
Essex
CM9 7LW
Tel: 0621 854488

Sentry Safes
6 The Business Village
Pebble Close
Tamworth
Staffs B77 4RD
Tel: 0827 311888

Simba Security Systems
Security House
Occupation Road
London
SE17 3BE
Tel: 071 703 0485

Smiths Industries Environmental Controls Co Ltd
Apsley Way
London
NW2 7UR
Tel: 081 450 8944

Solartrack PLC
42 New Road
Dagenham
Essex
RM9 6YS
Tel: 081 595 1218

Sparkrite
Stadium Consumer Products Division
Stephen House
Brenda Road
Hartlepool
Cleveland TS25 2BQ
Tel: 0429 862616

Superswitch Electric Appliances Ltd
Houldsworth Street
Reddish
Stockport
Cheshire SK5 6BZ
Tel: 061 431 4885

TrakBak
Securicor Datatrak
Securicor Alarms
Auckland House
New Zealand Avenue
Walton-on-Thames
Surrey
KT12 1PL
Tel: 0932 252222

Tunstall Telecom Ltd
Whitley Lodge
Whitley Bridge
Yorkshire DN14 0HR
Tel: 0977 661234

UK ID Systems
Riverside Industrial Park
Catterall
Preston
PR3 0HP
Tel: 0995 606451

Viper Security Ltd
Lynch Lane
Weymouth
Dorset
DT4 9DG
Tel: 0305 783801

Yale Security Products
(& Ingersoll)
Wood Street
Willenhall
West Midlands
WV13 1LA
Tel: 0902 366911

Index

INDEX